D0025380

## DATE DUE

| | | | |
|---|---|---|---|
| 5-5-12 | | | |
| 9-5-12 | ILL93393500 | | |
| 5-6-21 | | | |
| | | | |
| | | | |
| | | | |
| | | | |
| | | | |
| | | | |
| | | | |
| | | | |

$1 per day late fee for DVDs, magazines, and ILLs

# EMOTIONAL EXORCISM

## Recent Titles in Contemporary Psychology

The Myth of Depression as Disease: Limitations and
Alternatives to Drug Treatment
*Allan M. Leventhal and Christopher R. Martell*

Preventing Teen Violence: A Guide for Parents and Professionals
*Sherri N. McCarthy and Claudio Simon Hutz*

Making Enemies Unwittingly: Humiliation and International Conflict
*Evelin Gerda Lindner*

Collateral Damage: The Psychological Consequences of
America's War on Terrorism
*Paul R. Kimmel and Chris E. Stout, editors*

Terror in the Promised Land: Inside the Anguish of the
Israeli-Palestinian Conflict
*Judy Kuriansky, editor*

Trauma Psychology, Volumes 1 and 2
*Elizabeth Carll, editor*

Beyond Bullets and Bombs: Grassroots Peace Building between
Israelis and Palestinians
*Judy Kuriansky, editor*

Who Benefits from Global Violence and War: Uncovering a Destructive System
*Marc Pilisuk with Jennifer Rountree*

Right Brain/Left Brain Leadership: Shifting Style for Maximum Impact
*Mary Lou Décosterd*

Creating Young Martyrs: Conditions That Make Dying in a Terrorist Attack
Seem Like a Good Idea
*Alice LoCicero and Samuel J. Sinclair*

Emotion and Conflict: How Human Rights Can Dignify Emotion and Help
Us Wage Good Conflict
*Evelin G. Lindner*

# EMOTIONAL EXORCISM

## Expelling the Four Psychological Demons That Make Us Backslide

*Holly A. Hunt, Ph.D.*

*Contemporary Psychology*

Chris E. Stout, Series Editor

**Praeger**

*An Imprint of ABC-CLIO, LLC*

Santa Barbara, California • Denver, Colorado • Oxford, England

**Library of Congress Cataloging-in-Publication Data**

Hunt, Holly A.
  Emotional exorcism : expelling the four psychological demons that make us backslide / Holly A. Hunt.
      p. cm. — (The Praeger series in contemporary psychology)
  Includes bibliographical references and index.
  ISBN 978-0-313-36021-3 (book : alk. paper) — ISBN 978-0-313-36022-0 (e-book : alk. paper) 1. Emotions. I. Title.
  BF511.H86 2009
  152.4—dc22                     2009021101

13  12  11  10  9    1  2  3  4  5

This book is also available on the World Wide Web as an eBook.
Visit www.abc-clio.com for details.

ABC-CLIO, LLC
130 Cremona Drive, P.O. Box 1911
Santa Barbara, California 93116-1911

This book is printed on acid-free paper. ∞

Manufactured in the United States of America

*To my clients, whose diligent efforts to exorcize their psychological demons brought this book to life.*

# CONTENTS

# ABOUT THE SERIES

## The Praeger Series in Contemporary Psychology

In this series, experts from various disciplines peer through the lens of psychology telling us answers they see for questions of human behavior. Their topics may range from humanity's psychological ills—addictions, abuse, suicide, murder, and terrorism among them—to works focused on positive subjects including intelligence, creativity, athleticism, and resilience. Regardless of the topic, the goal of this series remains constant—to offer innovative ideas, provocative considerations and useful beginnings to better understand human behavior.

### Series Editor

Chris E. Stout, Psy.D., MBA
*Northwestern University Medical School*
*Illinois Chief of Psychological Services*

### Advisory Board

Bruce E. Bonecutter, Ph.D.
*University of Illinois at Chicago*
*Director, Behavioral Services, Elgin Community Mental Health Center*

Joseph A. Flaherty, M.D.
*University of Illinois College of Medicine and College of Public Health*
*Chief of Psychiatry, University of Illinois Hospital*

Michael Horowitz, Ph.D.
*Chicago School of Professional Psychology*
*President, Chicago School of Professional Psychology*

Sheldon I. Miller, M.D.
*Northwestern University*
*Director, Stone Institute of Psychiatry, Northwestern Memorial Hospital*

Dennis P. Morrison, Ph.D.
*Chief Executive Officer, Center for Behavioral Health, Indiana*
*President, Board of Directors, Community Healthcare Foundation, Indiana*

William H. Reid, M.D.
*University of Texas Health Sciences Center*
*Chair, Scientific Advisory Board, Texas Depressive and Manic Depressive Association*

# PREFACE

The demon model described in *Emotional Exorcism* emerged from years of working with clients in private practice. As a result of their feedback, progress, and outcomes, I added, changed, and refined the various concepts and strategies that follow. Having also applied the demon model to my own life, I can personally attest to its power and usefulness. Ever since I began employing the tools daily, I can't imagine not using them. In addition to clients and mental health clinicians, this book is appropriate for anyone who wants to expel his or her psychological demons. If you continue to fall back in your efforts to conquer problems, beat yourself up, and feel like a failure, this book is written for you.

To every client who worked with me, thank you for trusting me and for sharing your life with me. I appreciate your willingness to learn this model and to apply its strategies in your daily experience. Without your efforts, *Emotional Exorcism* would not be filled with the rich array of genuine, vivid, and instructive illustrations. To preserve confidentiality, I've changed names as well as identifying information within the chapters.

Thanks to family and friends for your support, encouragement, and interest in this project: my parents, Faye and Dennis Hunt; sisters, Jennifer Skidmore, Polly Hunt, and Randee Allen; and colleague, Dr. Andrea Rosenbaum Vogel. Thank you artist Nikolay Koev, for providing a photograph of the stunning sculpture that you created with Boris Borisov and Chavdar Velchev, that became the cover for this book. Thank you Dr. Chris Stout and Debora Carvalko for your editorial expertise. Dr. Stout, I'm honored to have my book included within your Contemporary Psychology Series. Thank you for your steadfast support, positive feedback, and belief in this project from the very first day.

## CHAPTER 1

# OUTING THE DEMONS

Anita, Karen, and Jacqué meet for lunch at their favorite café once a month. They've been getting together since high school and look forward to these respites to share problems and receive support. Although their lives followed different paths after graduation, they remain friends. Anita married her high school sweetheart, has two children, works part-time as a teacher's aid, and cares for her elderly mother. She juggles many responsibilities and schedules and periodically gets very depressed. She soothes herself with food but then gains weight and feels ugly, fat, and disgusting. At lunch she resolves to avoid dessert this time, but she gives in and orders the chocolate cake.

Karen is recently divorced, has one child, and works full-time as an office administrator. She worries about everything—her divorce, what others think of her, finances, family, health, and dying. Every day she drinks wine to banish the worries, but they always return. At lunch she orders two glasses of white zinfandel. Jacqué is single with no children and works full-time in sales. She's hard-driving and often gets impatient and berates others when they make mistakes. Although she's become a top seller for her company, she feels dissatisfied with her performance. She orders the waiter to take back her fish, angrily informing him that it is overcooked.

As the three friends commiserate at lunch, their circumstances and problems appear to be very different. Their individual life paths have taken unique twists and turns. But their conversation and struggles sound eerily the same as they did each month and year before. They're all intelligent, articulate, and well versed in their issues. Each woman has taken steps to solve her problems. Anita began counseling, took antidepressant medication, and joined Weight Watchers. Karen attended Alcoholics Anonymous (AA) meetings, connected with a sponsor, and began the 12 steps. Jacqué enrolled in anger management and yoga classes.

As each woman engaged help, her problems diminished and she felt better. However, inexplicably, they all fell back from these positive efforts. Eventually, their problems returned and the cycles repeated. As each woman reengaged help, she resolved not to let anything derail her healthy approach. But again she fell back and her problems resumed. With each fall, she beat up on herself, feeling like a miserable failure. Why do these women continue to have to battle these troubles? Why—in spite of their knowledge, motivation, and progress—do they relapse and return to their negative habits?

## Why Our Problems Are So Relentless

Anita, Karen, and Jacqué are not alone. Millions of us are suffering every day with unwanted and debilitating afflictions such as depression, anxiety, and addictions.[1] Even more of us are beset with less severe but frustrating problems ranging from uncertainties to annoying habits that reduce the quality of our lives. We increasingly seek traditional mental health and alternative healing services to gain freedom from these troubles. Television and radio programs abound with popular hosts who dispense daily advice and resources to record-breaking audiences. Self-help sections of bookstores are packed with the latest offerings in response to our strong demand for assistance. In recent years, self-improvement products and services earned up to $11 billion annually and the market is forecast to grow by more than 6% each year.[2]

---

> More than ever, people are receiving help for their emotional suffering, but the level of their distress remains the same.

---

With more and more of us engaging help, you'd think that we'd be feeling better. We're not. Even though two-thirds more of us sought help for emotional suffering during the past decade, the pervasiveness of distress has not diminished.[3] Adults at every age have become more depressed in recent years compared to 10 or more years prior.[4] So many people have leapt to their deaths off the Golden Gate Bridge since it opened in 1937 that officials voted to install a suicide barrier.[5] In my nearly two decades of psychology practice, I'm struck by how many new clients I meet who are plagued with more debilitating problems and emotional pain compared to years ago. Why aren't we doing better—when we're engaging more resources and are more educated than ever before about the origin of our problems and the specific steps to solve them?

The answer lies beneath the surface as we listen to Anita, Karen, and Jacqué. Although each woman appears to have different problems, none realizes that the same underlying process is feeding her negative cycles. A unifying reason why they stay stuck in their difficulties is that they believe deep down that they are not good enough. They think of their problems as an integral part of themselves. Each woman learned through prior negative experiences to believe that she will never measure up because she is fundamentally defective. With that as the central assumption, the women face the relentlessly draining task of defeating themselves.

It's too much to ask.

> We can learn through early negative experiences to believe that we are fundamentally defective.

As a little girl, Anita watched her mother care for everyone's needs except her own. She tried everything to ease her mother's burden and make her happy, but nothing worked. She still secretly believes that it is her fault that her mother was so sad. She is now repeating the same unhealthy pattern that she tried so hard to fix for her mother.

Karen grew up with alcoholic parents. She learned to fear everything because she never knew what to expect at home. Her parents argued often, leaving little time to focus on Karen. Sometimes her father took off for days. Karen believes that her parents did not care for her because she was unlovable. When she was 10 years old, she began drinking vodka from the unlocked cabinet in the living room to numb her pain.

Jacqué learned very early that she must be perfect. Her family is well educated, financially successful, and highly regarded in the community. Jacqué did well in school and was a strong leader. However, when she brought home a report card with almost all As, her parents would point out the one B and tell her to try harder. She learned to never feel good enough, no matter how successful she became. She now views herself and others with a very negative eye.

## The Destructive Cycle of Self-Sabotage

Although each woman sought help and now knows some of the steps to change, her underlying negative self-concept steers her to disrupt the positive steps for gaining freedom from her problems. She may not always be aware of this destructive pattern because it is so ingrained through her earlier experiences. This process operates similarly for many of us. We learn to hate a part of who we are and to blame ourselves for the negative events in our lives.

> We can learn to blame ourselves automatically for aversive events that occur in our lives.

A survey of women across America asked, "What's missing in your life?" The top answer was not "a loving spouse or child," "more money," "a better job," or "health." The number one answer was "love for myself"; no other response came close. When Oprah Winfrey shared these findings on her popular television talk show, she added, "If you smoke, if you overeat, if you drink too much, if you overspend, if you work too much, these are all signs of self-hatred." Guest psychologist, Dr. Robin Smith, added, "It's the lie within you that says you're unworthy."[6]

Psychological theories, diagnostic categories of mental illness, and my own observations in practice reinforce the damaging consequences of perceived inner defectiveness.[7] It's extremely hard to attack and conquer the enemy when the enemy is us. However, it's very easy to flagellate ourselves again and again when we do not take the steps that we need to overcome our problems. Here is the inescapable irony: every self-criticism strengthens our core belief that we are defective, leading to another failure. And the cycle repeats.

Soon after starting in practice, I witnessed this vicious negative cycle again and again. It plagued men and women of different ethnicities, cultures, marital status, sexual orientation, age, income, or education, and the list goes on. Although each person presented a unique set of problems, he or she repeated a similar destructive cycle of self-sabotage, shame, and feeling like a failure. I became frustrated as clients came to sessions sharing how they fell back in their efforts, even though we had devised in detail the healthy steps that they planned to take. These people were motivated and well intentioned, and they often made strong initial progress.

> Every self-criticism fuels our core belief of deficiency, leading to self-sabotage and self-blame, and the cycle repeats.

It was as though they were possessed by demons that made them fail and then feel miserable and unworthy. I was the exorcist, but without the power to expel these evil entities. I saw this same negative cycle with everyone I knew: family, friends, colleagues, acquaintances, and myself.

Out of frustration, I started to share with clients how their struggles seemed as though they were battling formidable adversaries. I was surprised by how quickly people connected with this universal archetype of we/good versus them/evil. Over the years, I developed and expanded this demon model in working with clients to overcome their problems. I also use it to help with my own goals. Many features of this approach are similar to those in well-established therapies. People learn to identify destructive habits and tendencies in their thoughts, behaviors, and emotions. They practice steps to replace negative habits with positive ones. They learn problem-solving, solution-focused, and effectiveness skills.

## How the Demon Approach Is Different

In one crucial sense, however, the demon approach is different from its predecessors. Although other psychological theories and treatments recognize the damaging consequences of perceived personal defectiveness, they unwittingly deepen that perception by locating the source of the deficiency in the person. For example, various popular therapies point to a person's dysfunctional thoughts, beliefs, behaviors, and abilities as the cause of emotional distress and destructive behaviors.[8]

But directing people to look inward for the cause of negative patterns fuels self-criticism in people who already view themselves negatively. The more they put themselves down, the more they believe that they are a failure. The stronger their negative belief is, the more they think and act in accordance with this conviction of being defective. This critical self-focus makes it harder to stay strong and on track in order to reach desired goals.

I see this negative self-fulfilling cycle again and again in sessions with clients. Tim believes he is defective and does not deserve a relationship. He works the night shift and spends free time with his dog and his friends and working on his truck. When he does go out on the weekends, he avoids meeting new women. On his return home, he says to himself, "I knew it. No one is interested in me." Cynthia believes she is a failure at anything she tries. Although she's very creative, every time she begins to paint or write, she predicts that the project will never get done. True to her belief, at some point she stops, and then she beats herself up saying, "I'll never accomplish my goals. What's wrong with me?"

In contrast, instead of battling integral parts of ourselves, the demon model empowers us to view our problems as external entities to confront and dispatch. We learn how our troubles were created through early negative life experiences that were outside our control. We gain strategies to free ourselves from these outer foes without beating up on ourselves. This approach preserves and enhances our self-esteem and self-efficacy, helping us stay consistent in pursuing our goals.

---

> The demon model empowers us to battle our problems instead of ourselves.

---

The idea of demons afflicting us is quite ancient. Various forms of exorcisms, in which demons are identified and cast out from possessed people, have stood the test of centuries, persisting across religions, cultures, and countries. Central to this process is the belief that individuals who are possessed are not evil in themselves.

From its beginning, Christianity included the belief in external possession and exorcism. The Christian New Testament includes accounts of Jesus performing miracles by casting out demons. In Roman Catholicism, exorcisms are conducted by ordained priests, who invoke prayers, blessings, and invocations as part of their sacred rituals. In kabbalah and European Jewish folklore, a person may be possessed by a negative *dybbuk,* a spirit that is the dislocated soul of a dead person. Once it inhabits its host, a dybbuk creates similar chaos and problems

for the person that it experienced in its own lifetime. Rabbis lead ritual cere-
monies to exorcise dybbuks.

Hindu traditions describe methods for casting out demons in the holy book
Arthava Veda and texts Bhagavad Gita and Garuda Purana. Tools of exorcisms
include *mantras* (religious poems) and *yajnas* (rituals of prayer). From its start,
Islam warned of possession by evil spirits called *jinn,* and Islamic clergy conducted exorcisms to expel them. A Buddhist exorcism is performed by a temple's
chief priest reading from the scriptures of Buddhism and burning special incense.

Note that all of the major religions of the world address possession and exorcism from widely varied backgrounds and traditions, using diverse terms and
methods. However, they're all unified in the belief that the negative entities that
they describe are external to who we are as people: they are occupying forces that
come from another place than ourselves.[9]

Carmen came to therapy after suffering with panic attacks for years. After every
episode, she blamed herself and felt like a loser. During sessions, we identified
earlier traumas that were major factors in creating her panic attacks. She learned
how her mother's alcoholism and parents' fights had left Carmen feeling anxious
and out of control as a little girl. As an adult, she was rushed to the hospital with
a life-threatening ectopic pregnancy. When she awoke from emergency surgery,
she couldn't breathe and suffered her first panic attack. As we pieced together
these pivotal events, Carmen felt relief as she realized that she didn't create her
panic attacks. She began to practice self-calming tools, without the added burden
of the automatic self-blame that she was so used to heaping on herself.

## The Crucial Role of Personal Responsibility

Although we're not responsible for creating these afflictions, we are responsible for expelling them. You may know people who will insist that they remain
victims of their demons and are not responsible for what they do. They argue,
"The devil made me do it," so it's not my fault. Just the opposite is true. By
learning how the demons operate, not only do we acquire the strength and
power to starve them out, we assume the responsibility to do so. It's up to us to
challenge them, to prevent them from generating misery and unhappiness in
our lives. The most powerful people who can banish our demons are us. If we
don't fight them, we're collaborators and we are responsible for allowing our
demons to thrive.

> It is our responsibility to expel our psychological demons.

For example, Sherry sought help with poor parenting habits. We processed her
memories and feelings in order to heal from old psychological wounds. Sherry
was able to identify and stop faulting herself for the reasons that she yelled at her

children so much. However, she continued to view herself as a helpless victim, helpless to change the negative habits she'd learned. She didn't practice the tools she received in therapy to change these habits. She didn't ask for help from her church, family, or friends. After a few sessions, she dropped out. As a result, her demons continued to thrive.

## The Master Demon Metaphor

The demon model reveals how our negative core belief is formed from earlier negative life experiences and is fundamentally separate from our true self. This core belief of unworthiness is represented by an easily identifiable metaphor, the Master Demon. I began to use this metaphor after working with client after client, who, like Anita, Karen, and Jacqué, deep down felt unworthy, defective, and fundamentally flawed. To help them identify and begin to separate from this negative core belief, I called it the Master Demon. This image conveyed exactly what I had confronted in weekly sessions, a formidable foe that thrived on human misery. It was relentless, and, it was often not easy to spot because it was typically created well before clients sought help. Anita, Karen, and Jacqué were all plagued with the Master Demon of unworthiness from the time they were little girls.

> Our Master Demon is the core belief that we are unworthy.

### How Our Master Demon Forms

Negative life experiences create our Master Demon in many different ways. However, a unifying aspect of this process is that we attribute the source and the reason for the negative experience to ourselves.

> Our Master Demon of unworthiness forms when we blame ourselves for our negative life experiences.

*Direct Experience* The Master Demon usually forms in childhood. One way that it generates is when we're direct targets of others' inappropriate negative words and actions. These others are most often our caregivers or other important people in our lives. What they say or do to us ranges from minor to major, but each negative incident hurts us in some way. They occasionally criticize us, or they may frequently express their disapproval of us. They fire degrading messages at us and call us names. Theresa's mother barked over and over at her, "You are so selfish. No one will ever love you."

Our basic needs, such as adequate food, clothing, shelter, or safety, may also be neglected. When Melissa was small, her father often lost track of her when she was under his care. In one recurring situation, he would become engrossed in watching a game on television. On more than one occasion, her mother arrived home to find Melissa wandering outside in the front yard.

In less obvious ways, our elders ignore our emotional needs. They don't spend time with us or show an interest in our lives. They don't praise our accomplishments or attend our important activities. Even when they do, we sense that they're going through the motions and not genuinely caring for us. David was an excellent student and a star athlete. He worked hard and received many honors for his accomplishments. However, the one thing he really wanted he didn't get. His father never came to his football games or track meets. He missed the annual dinner awarding David for his academic success. Although his dad always said that he wished he could attend these events, deep down David did not believe him.

Occasionally, our caregivers can hurt us physically by slamming doors or throwing objects at us. Or they push, shove, slap, kick, punch, beat, sexually abuse, and even torture us. When Sara's mother became angry, she would take off her flip-flops and hit Sara in the head with them. Maria's mother punished her by making her kneel on coffee beans for hours outside in the hot sun. Anne's father sexually abused her, from the age of 5 until she was 12.

> Our Master Demon is created through directly experiencing others' destructive words and actions.

Aversive incidents such as these cause us much pain and distress. Research confirms the strong relationship between experiencing negative life events and suffering emotionally.[10] Sometimes we may be told that we're the cause of the negative experience. Regardless, every time we blame ourselves, our Master Demon of feeling unworthy grows larger and more powerful. As this process becomes automatic with repetition, we begin to blame ourselves for other harmful incidents that happen around us, even when we do not directly experience them.

As I read information to prepare for this book, I was not surprised to see how rampant self-blame is. In a five-year study, researchers found that negative events early in childhood can produce negative attributional styles—assigning oneself the blame for all misfortunes—which leave children vulnerable to developing depression in the future when more negative events occur in their lives. Another study confirms the powerful effect of parents' negative attitudes and parenting styles with their children. Adult children whose mothers had negative attitudes and fathers who were not emotionally accepting of them were more likely to view themselves in negative ways. Children whose parents blamed them for the stressful events in the children's lives were more likely to develop depression during the next two and one-half years.[11]

> Our Master Demon of defectiveness grows every time that we blame ourselves for stressful events that occur in our lives.

As adults, additional stressors enter our lives and cause us emotional pain. We suffer from illness, the inability to afford medical care, and other financial problems. We lose our jobs, go through relationship breakups, experience marital conflict, lose loved ones, feel lack of support, acquire multiple responsibilities, and experience many other hardships. In a national survey, people reported more of these types of troubles compared to the previous decade. More than 90% of the respondents said that they had experienced at least one significant negative life event.[12]

For me, the mental health problem is not so much that these stressful events occur but that people internalize (blame themselves for) them and see their occurrence as evidence that they are defective people. Women internalize problems more often than men. Thus, most women, whether they seek help or not, are vulnerable to feeding a Master Demon when they experience these adversities. Although their numbers may be fewer, many men internalize problems too and are similarly beset with a Master Demon.[13]

*Observational Learning*   Our Master Demon of not feeling good enough also forms when we learn to blame and criticize ourselves by watching our caregivers perform these self-destructive habits. Imitating models in our lives is powerful. We don't have to experience events directly in order to learn. We can learn just as much by observing what happens to someone else in these situations.[14] Especially as children, we soak up information like sponges as we observe what others do around us. If we often see our mother blaming herself for things that happen outside her control, we're likely to learn and repeat this negative habit. If we watch our father berate himself for falling short of his expectation, we pick up this self-critical habit and our Master Demon thrives.

Michelle grew up watching her father criticize himself whenever he tried something new. The vision of her father saying "yeah, but" became etched in her mind. When Michelle thought about taking a photography class, her father's negative mantra popped up instantly. She said to herself, "yeah, but it will cost too much; it won't be worth it; my photos will be a disaster." More often than not, Michelle abandoned her projects before she got started.

> Our Master Demon forms when we learn to blame ourselves by watching others engage in this destructive habit.

*Reinforcement*   Our Master Demon of low self-worth also grows when others reward us for blaming or otherwise criticizing ourselves. Reinforcement has a strong effect on us.[15] The more we're reinforced for putting ourselves down, the more we learn this habit of self-criticism. Positive rewards often involve special attention or sympathy. Favorite foods are prepared for us. We receive a new pair of shoes or get to go on a special outing.

Linda grew up in a chaotic household. Both her parents were troubled. They fought often, and Linda felt alone much of the time. Her two brothers were much older and stayed away from home as often as they could. Linda discovered that she had a gift of telling amusing stories. When she shared tales from her day, making fun of herself, her parents listened and laughed at her. Linda learned to receive attention by creatively putting herself down. She continues this self-deprecating style to this day.

We're also rewarded for self-criticism by negative reinforcement—the removal of an aversive event. Every time that Linda told a funny story, her parents stopped fighting, much to her relief. We may confess to things that we did not do to end a bad situation. Or we interrupt our mother with an exaggerated emotional crisis to stop her from talking on the phone with her girlfriend. Our reward comes when she stops ignoring us.

Self-criticisms can also release us from responsibilities that we don't want to assume. We may profess that we're too nervous or sad or we're not capable. As a consequence, we escape chores, homework, music or sports practice, or school tasks that we don't want to do. We may not start out believing our damaging statements. But every time we put ourselves down, we're more likely to accept as true the negative things we say. As novelist Kurt Vonnegut states at the outset of his acclaimed novel *Mother Night,* "We are what we pretend to be, so we must be careful about what we pretend to be."

Allan hated eighth grade. His family had moved to the area two years prior and he was starting his second year at this junior high school. He was an only child and his mother and father were much older than his peers' parents. He didn't have friends and was picked on at school for being bad at sports. When Allan told his mother that he felt sick to his stomach and didn't want to go to school, she didn't question him and let him stay home. When he didn't want to go to dances, sports events, or any other activities, his parents believed his claims of extreme social anxiety. Over time, Allan began to believe his proclamations of debilitating social fears. The more he sat home, the more anxious he felt. He became certain that he wasn't capable of making friends, having a girlfriend, or doing much of anything beyond solitary activities.

---

> Reinforcement and punishment mold our Master Demon of low self-worth.

---

*Punishment*    Punishment also feeds our feelings of defectiveness. If our caregivers chastise or hit us for being ourselves, we learn to quash our inner selves. When Patty was a little girl, she loved to sing and dance. This didn't last long. Every time she started a song, her mother criticized her for wasting time on frivolous activities that served no purpose. Patty stopped singing and dancing and told herself that her desire to do so meant she was lazy and no good.

Gina never knew when her mother would get angry and scream at her. When it happened, her mother swore at her and called her names. Many times she hit Gina too. Gina learned to be very quiet and tiptoe around the house. Instead of playing and being a child, she focused her energy on avoiding her mother as much as possible. She believed that she must be a very bad girl for her mother to get so angry at her in so many unpredictable situations.

Through these learning experiences, our caregivers install the Master Demon program into us, just as a technician installs software onto a computer's hard drive. With each new hurtful incident and self-blame, the Master Demon grows and is strengthened by our negative emotional energy. Since it forms so early, through childhood experiences, we don't realize that it is separate from us. We go through life believing that we're defective and unworthy. In reality, the Master Demon is just an ingrained program that was installed without our awareness or approval.

---

> We go through life not knowing that our belief of unworthiness is our Master Demon program that has been installed without our awareness or approval.

---

## The Soldier Demon Metaphor

Negative life experiences also produce self-destructive thoughts and behaviors. These negative patterns are represented by a similarly recognizable metaphor, the Soldier Demon. Soldier Demons are programmed to protect and serve the Master Demon in order to keep the negative core belief intact. They generate emotional negativity in their hosts, which provides a power supply, an energy source for the demons. Negative emotions include fear, anxiety, sadness, depression, despair, anger, hate, self-loathing, guilt, jealousy, etc.

The Soldier Demons feed on this emotional negativity and grow bigger and stronger and work harder to produce more emotional negativity in their unknowing hosts. With each growth spurt, they become a more formidable guardian of the Master Demon. They also feed the Master Demon of low self-worth with negative emotional energy so that it grows more powerful and resilient.

**Table 1.1**

Soldier Demons are
- Self-destructive thoughts and behaviors produced by aversive life experiences.
- Programmed to protect and serve our Master Demon.
- Designed to generate negative emotional energy in us that feeds them, and they in turn feed our Master Demon.

### The Four Soldier Demons

I've identified four different Soldier Demons. Each one operates with a unique directive in a variety of situations and settings.

The Blocker Demon stops us from doing something positive for ourselves. Anita cares for everyone but herself and becomes very depressed. Alyson is 50 pounds overweight. She makes plans to exercise at the gym after work, but something always comes up and she doesn't go. She feels sluggish and unhappy and beats herself up for not going.

The Negator Demon steers us to focus on negative things about ourselves and our lives. Karen worries constantly, jumping from one topic to the next. Lisa ruminates, mostly about finances or health. Gene is always second-guessing himself. Before he completes any project, he convinces himself that there was a better way to approach it. As a consequence, he's never satisfied with his work.

The Rouster Demon makes us criticize and attack others. Jacqué gets irritated and disparages people when they make mistakes. Tanya gets annoyed easily and yells at bad drivers on the freeway. Will sees red when he thinks other men are flirting with his girlfriend; he was kicked out of the neighborhood bar after losing control and punching a perceived rival.

The Tempter Demon lures us to do something destructive to ourselves. Anita overeats and feels fat and ugly. Karen drinks too much and suffers terrible hangovers. Olivia shops too much; she maxes out her credit cards and ruins her credit rating.

In every scenario, the Solider Demons orient us toward negative thoughts and actions, which create the negative emotional energy that feeds them and, in turn,

**Table 1.2**

The Four Soldier Demons

| Name | Directive |
|------|-----------|
| 1. Blocker Demon | Stops us from doing positive things for ourselves. |
| 2. Negator Demon | Orients us to focus on the negative aspects of ourselves. |
| 3. Rouster Demon | Steers us to criticize and attack others. |
| 4. Tempter Demon | Lures us to do destructive things to ourselves. |

feeds the Master Demon. Each time the Soldier Demons feed the Master Demon, we feel more like a failure, unworthy and defective, and the cycle continues.

If you don't like using the word *demon*, you can substitute another name to describe your Master and Soldiers. Although most of my clients prefer demon, on occasion somebody will express an aversion to this descriptor. Some alternate names they've chosen are Bully, Gremlin, Monster, and Parasite. If you prefer something else, select a name that conveys the intense, harmful, and relentless qualities of these external foes. If you'd rather not use a descriptor, you can simply call them the Master, Blocker, Negator, Rouster, and Tempter.

The next four chapters describe each Soldier Demon and the common situations and settings in which it operates. You'll read the common warning signs and triggers to watch for that leave you vulnerable to demon attacks. They sometimes assail you in obvious ways, but more often they are stealthy in their operations. Specific strategies are described to catch the demons in the act and to replace the negative programs with counter thoughts, actions, and feelings.

One crucial tool is the Reprogramming Record (RR), a daily self-confirming journal that replaces self-defeating tapes that have been acquired earlier. Equally essential is the Demon Disrupting Diary (DDD), which helps you detect and refuse your demons. This positive reprogramming starves both the Soldier Demons and the Master Demon, which require negative emotional energy to survive.

As positive habits become the new norm, the demons weaken and fade away, eventually expelled for good. However, they do not recede easily: they hover in the background until a situation triggers them to strike. You'll learn to watch for and refuse a particularly virulent type of assault called the Sniper. All four Soldier Demons activate in this way, especially when things are going well and you're feeling good.

Soldier Demons can attack in pairs, threesomes, and sometimes all four. Common alliances are profiled in Chapter 6, along with steps to recognize and protect yourself from these potent group demon assaults. Chapter 7 offers tips to maximize your success in using the strategies that you learned from earlier chapters to exorcize your demons.

## Four Steps to Exorcize Your Demons

As you read detailed strategies in the chapters that follow, use this brief outline to help remind you of the four crucial steps to exorcize your Master and Soldier Demons. In sum, first beware: always remain alert to the possibility of a demon attack. Second, name: know the description of each demon and how to spot them when they assault you. Third, refuse: learn ways to deny the demons the negative emotional energy that they require. Fourth, triumph: find out how to celebrate your victories.

**Table 1.3**

Exorcize Your Demons
1. Beware
2. Name
3. Refuse
4. Triumph

## Genetic Vulnerability

One factor that makes us susceptible to the demons is our genetic predisposition. Do you have blood relatives who are depressed, anxious, or alcoholic? If so, you're more prone to developing these afflictions, especially when you experience stressful life events.[16] By learning your family history, you'll identify your specific weaknesses. This knowledge allows you to take proactive steps to protect yourself from attacks and to deny the demons the negative emotional energy that they require.

Elise came to therapy feeling very depressed. She had struggled off and on with this affliction her entire life. When I asked about her family history, she shared that her mother, sister, and brother also suffered from depression. Tragically, a year ago her brother hanged himself. As the anniversary date of his death neared, her depression was worsening.

I cautioned Elise about her high risk of severe, chronic depression because of her genetic susceptibility. She agreed to see a psychiatrist to explore antidepressant medication options. She made an appointment right away, started medication, and continued weekly psychotherapy. By the date of her brother's prior suicide, Elise was not so depressed. She was able to grieve for him without having thoughts of ending her own life.

## Anger Toward Our Caregivers

When people identify the experiences that created their demons, they often become very angry at their caregivers. They ask, "How could they have done this to me?" As reality becomes clear, they alternate between feeling enraged and sad. Sadness progresses to grieving for the loss of the loving and nurturing times that never were. As we shine the light on our demons, it's understandable to feel this way.

Our caregivers are beset with their own demons.

However, if we blame our parents, we fall into the trap of feeding our Master Demon of unworthiness. Finding fault with them is faulting ourselves, because genetically we are our parents. Our caregivers are not the enemy. They're plagued by their own demons, which remain powerful because our loved ones are unaware that they are hosts—feeding the demons with emotional negativity. These destructive patterns are passed from generation to generation. Fortunately, this cycle can be stopped by identifying and starving our demons.

CHAPTER 2

# THE BLOCKER DEMON

Beverly examined her hair in the mirror and liked what she saw. For the first time in months, she'd gone to the salon and gotten a cut, color, and style. As a result of our weekly sessions together, she was beginning to take care of herself in ways she never did before. Because of her long work hours, home chores, and caring for her husband and children, she rarely made time for herself until now. It sure felt good. "It's about time I do something for me," she said to herself. Next on her list was a manicure/pedicure, planned for the following week after work. After that, her first body massage, something she had always wanted but until then never thought she deserved.

The shrill ring of the phone startled Beverly out of her reflections. She automatically cowered upon hearing her father's booming voice. He announced that he was coming to live with her and her husband. He was tired of living alone since her mother divorced him two years ago. Beverly froze on the phone. She didn't want her father to move in. In that vulnerable instant, her Blocker Demon activated. It stopped Beverly from even considering that she could say no. Her sister Joyce, a homemaker, lived nearby in a larger house with a guest room. It didn't occur to Beverly to suggest this option. Instead, familiar feelings of helplessness and hopelessness washed over her.

> Our Blocker Demon stops us from doing positive things that would increase our self-worth.

Beverly quickly agreed and asked when he planned to arrive. She cleaned the entire house for her father. She cleared the spare room, arranged furniture, and moved the good TV so that it was next to his bed. She shopped for his favorite foods and planned special meals for him. Once he arrived, she continually attended to his needs, canceling her nail appointment and massage. Her new self-care approach had vanished, but Beverly was so busy, tired, and depressed that she didn't even notice. Instead, she beat herself up for not having enough energy and time to take care of everything.

Beverly is beset by a Blocker Demon (BD). One of four Soldier Demons, its directive is to stop its host from doing positive things that would counter feelings of unworthiness. Beverly didn't recognize her BD when it attacked. It stopped her from saying no to her father and from taking care of herself. When she became exhausted and unhappy from ignoring her needs, it feasted on her misery and fed her Master Demon (MD) of worthlessness. When Beverly berated herself for not being able to handle everything, she unknowingly nourished her demons with additional emotional negativity.

## Detect Your Blocker Demon

Blocker Demons can be difficult to spot. They thrive in the dark, operating optimally below our awareness. Like Beverly, you may not realize that you're feeding one. BD attacks run the gamut from small roadblocks to those that shut you down in every area of your life. Signs that you have a Blocker Demon include the following:

- You take care of others' needs first and always put yourself last.
- Your health is poor, but you haven't found time to go to the doctor.
- If you seek help from professionals or loved ones, you keep falling back away from following their suggestions.
- You're unfulfilled and stuck in old patterns at work, home, or school, which makes you tired and depressed.
- You feel so defeated you don't even try to figure out how to make something better in your life.
- When you do set goals, self-critical thoughts, images, and beliefs stop you from taking steps to reach them.

Although each of our lives is unique, every BD operates to fulfill the same directive that is designed to prevent the positive activities that bolster self-worth. If you're not doing positive things to nurture your self-esteem and you feel bad as a result, you're probably afflicted with one. Fortunately, there are key strategies to recognize and ways to deny your BD the destructive emotional energy that it craves.

These specific strategies are detailed in the following pages. In sum, as a general rule, always beware for potential attacks. Identify places, situations, and people that make you vulnerable to these assaults. When it strikes, expose your Blocker Demon by name to gain control and to separate yourself from it. The sooner you catch it, the sooner you can deny it its power. Your BD often activates through undermining thoughts, images, and feelings. Refuse it by countering it with heartening thoughts, images, and feelings. Follow through with your constructive actions and celebrate your triumph with a self-enhancing reward. Consider, for example, the experiences of another client of mine who did triumph over his BD.

Derek hit a wrong chord and paused in the middle of his new song. He rested his hands on the keyboard and sighed. As he sat alone in his apartment, it was quiet except for the sputtering of his ailing refrigerator. In that brief moment, a barrage of deflating thoughts flooded his mind: "There's no point in even playing because you're no good. You're not focused enough when you play. You're just wasting your time."

As a result of the therapy work we'd done over the previous few weeks, Derek immediately recognized his blocking force. He understood that it activated whenever he pursued a goal, even a small one such as practicing a new song. Its directive was always the same: to stop him and to make him feel miserable. Derek pulled out the journal that I urged him to keep near his keyboard. He added his Blocker Demon's debilitating messages to his list. Next to each critical BD statement, he wrote down his own encouraging ones: *Anytime I play I get better. I'm not wasting my time. This is not me; it's my Blocker Demon trying to prevent me from pursuing my goals and doing something I enjoy.*

As he'd agreed in therapy, Derek read his affirming messages out loud. He put his journal down, turned back to his keyboard, and played his song to the end. He smiled to himself. He'd refused his BD and triumphed by playing. Plus, it didn't sound that bad, he thought. After playing his song once, it was easier for Derek to play again. After he had finished practicing, he rewarded himself by going out that night to hear his favorite local band.

To recap, Derek caught his Blocker Demon right away, when it attacked through destructive thoughts. He instantly gained power by shining a light on his BD and recognizing that he was separate from it. He refused its blocking attempt by countering its negative messages with positive ones. His final triumph came when he followed through with his productive plans and rewarded himself for doing so. If Derek hadn't busted his Blocker, he would've missed the chance to engage his passion of playing music on his keyboard. He wouldn't have gained the satisfaction that came from successfully practicing his new song.

**Table 2.1**

Steps to Defy Your Blocker Demon:
1. Stay alert to potential BD attacks.
2. Identify your BD when it strikes.
3. Refuse your BD by engaging your positive thoughts and actions.
4. Celebrate your triumph with a self-enhancing reward.

## How the Blocker Demon Forms

Like all of the Soldier Demons, our Blocker Demon is created through various adverse life events. One way that it forms is through direct experience. This happens when others don't do supportive things for us and we repeat the same pattern that we directly experienced.

Beverly's BD formed through direct experience. When she was a child, her father mostly ignored her. She faced this inevitable fact every evening. Her mother worked nights and he stayed home with her and her three siblings. Beverly doesn't remember being happy with her father. What she does recall is how he doted on her younger sister, taking her on special outings. From these earliest experiences with her father, Beverly felt rejected and unloved. Without realizing it, her Blocker Demon formed as Beverly learned to ignore herself, just as her father had ignored her. When she was around the men in her life, her self-neglect was the most severe.

Our BD is also created through reward and punishment. If we're rewarded for not doing constructive actions, we learn not to do them. Likewise, when we're punished for doing beneficial activities, we learn to stop doing them.

Derek's Blocker Demon formed through punishment. From his earliest days, he loved music. When he was very young, he got from his uncle just what he wanted for Christmas, a portable keyboard. Immediately he was hooked. He played it constantly, in the living room, kitchen, bedroom, family room, and garage. When he started to play, his mother often exclaimed, "Stop that noise. You're hurting my ears. Why can't you go outside and play sports like your brother does?" Derek's blocking program was installed. He was stung by his mother's criticisms and felt like a failure whenever he played. His playing slowed to a stop as he learned to avoid his mother's verbal punishment.

A final way that the Blocker Demon forms is through modeling or observational learning. This occurs when we watch others not taking self-enhancing steps and then we repeat what we observed. Celeste's BD formed through modeling. As a child, she watched her mother stay home from work for days at a time. We can observe how Celeste learned to refuse her blocking force when it directed her to repeat what she'd witnessed.

Celeste jolted awake as the Monday morning news blared from her alarm radio. As she rolled over and pushed the pause button, her husband was already

**Table 2.2**

Our Blocker Demons Are Created by the Following:
1. Direct experience: when others do not do things that support us.
2. Reward: being rewarded for not doing self-promotive activities.
3. Punishment: being punished for taking self-enhancing actions.
4. Observation: watching others not take beneficial steps for themselves.

on his long commute to work. In eight short minutes, she'd have to start her weekly routine. She reviewed her tasks: wake up the kids, make breakfast, get them ready for school, feed the dog, get ready for work, drop the kids off at school, and go to work. As her responsibilities piled up in her mind, her BD attacked by saying "You're tired, you have no energy, you're depressed. Stay here, don't get out of bed, don't go to work today."

As Celeste luxuriated in these thoughts, a flash of familiarity dawned on her. She sat up wide-eyed. From our therapy sessions, she recognized that this was her Blocker Demon. It had attacked this way many times before. All too often she'd stayed in bed. When she did, her BD continued its assault of negative thoughts and she became lonely and depressed. Inevitably, she would call her sister to help with the kids. Every day that Celeste stayed home, she missed talking with her friends at work and fell behind in her reports. The following morning, instead of feeling rested, Celeste always struggled harder to get out of bed.

As she reviewed her past reactions, Celeste realized that it wasn't worth it to give in to her blocking agent. She said, *"I know this is what my Blocker Demon wants but, it's not me. If I stay home today, what will I do, be sad and cry? I will not feed my BD with my misery. I'm going to work today and see my friends. Once I get going on Mondays, I always feel better."* She turned off her alarm and started her routine. As she predicted, she began her tasks and focused on what she was doing. After arriving at work, she enjoyed seeing her friends and forgot all about her blocking program. If instead Celeste had succumbed, she'd have missed the chance to prove her blocking demon wrong and feel good about herself.

---

> The demon model empowers us to beat up on our demons instead of ourselves.

---

Crucial to Celeste's success was that she had identified and detached from her BD. She didn't blame herself for her BD attack or view herself as defective. Freed from battling herself, she fully focused her energy on confronting and dispatching her Blocker. This approach differs from other psychological theories and treatments, which locate the source of negative thoughts, behaviors, and beliefs inside the person. Instead of criticizing ourselves for the cause of problems, the demon model empowers us to use our resources to gain freedom from external foes. When we're not burdened with beating up on ourselves, we're able to stay strong and consistent in pursuing our goals.

## Identify Your Specific Vulnerabilities

Once the Blocker Demon forms, usually in our childhood, it can attack at any age. As with every Soldier Demon, we each have unique negative experiences that created our BD. When we encounter situations, people, and places that are similar to those that formed our BD, we're especially prone to its attacks. By identifying your specific vulnerabilities, you can prepare for potential BD assaults and deny the BD the negative emotions that it craves.

Celeste was susceptible to her Blocker before she got out of bed in the morning, the same situation in which it had formed as she watched her mother stay in bed. Derek's BD activated every time he began playing a new song. Just as his mother had done, his BD criticized him to stop him from playing, and so he felt miserable. Beverly's BD struck when she encountered her father, the same person who was instrumental in creating her blocking program.

---

Identify specific situations, people, and places that make you vulnerable to your Blocker Demon.

---

As you identify the hurtful experiences that created your BD and make you vulnerable to it, be careful not to get stuck repeatedly replaying these unpleasant memories. Doing this will generate old, upsetting feelings again and again. Your Blocker (and Master Demon of self-loathing) will feed on your continual supply of negative emotions. The worse you feel, the stronger they grow—and the more trapped in the old programming you'll be. The energy and time you could be using to separate from and deny your demons is instead lost to serving them. Many of my clients are caught in this trap when I meet them. To break free, we talk about the role they've unwittingly played in feeding their demons. I redirect them to use the knowledge that they acquire from reviewing past hurts to prepare for and resist actively any future demon strikes.

### Overload

We also fall prey to our blocking force during situations that we all experience. By recognizing these situations, you can protect yourself from assaults during these times. In working with clients in my practice I've identified two such situations: when we're overloaded and when we're depleted. Overload occurs when we acquire too many responsibilities at work, home, school, or any other place. As we become consumed with commitments, our blocking force steers us to forgo doing good things for ourselves.

My client Angela found herself in this trap. She's a newly divorced parent of two and works full-time. Although she likes her job at a financial institution, her workdays are filled with meetings, phone consultations, and direct customer service. More tasks wait at home: driving her daughters to after-school activities, preparing dinner, helping her children with their homework, and getting ready for the next day.

As Angela was consumed with these tasks, her BD stopped her from going to the gym, something she had enjoyed regularly before her divorce. It said, "You've been busy all day. You deserve to give yourself a break and stay home." In her weakened state of overload, Angela listened to it, forgetting that her workouts were energizing and made her happy. She thought she was nurturing herself by skipping exercise, but instead she felt tired and sluggish. In the time she used to spend on the treadmill and lifting weights, she sat home, watched TV, ate junk food, and gained 10 pounds.

As Angela grew, so did her Blocker, feeding on her sadness and exhaustion. When she became upset and criticized herself for gaining weight, she nourished her BD. Like my other clients who were compromised by their BDs, Angela missed out on taking the steps to identify her BD, separate herself from it, and triumph over it by following through with self-enhancing activities.

---

> When we're overloaded or depleted, we're at risk for blocking demon attacks.

---

### Physical Depletion

Another common condition that leaves us prone to BD attacks is when we're physically depleted. The top forms of depletion that I see in practice are sleep deprivation, fatigue, illness, injury, hormonal deficiency, and poor nutrition. These deficit states may be brief or chronic. No matter, our blocking program can activate in an instant and shut us down from taking helpful actions. Here's how another of my clients prepares for and thwarts her Blocker when she becomes depleted.

Carol walked into my office wearing her usual professional attire—tailored slacks, blouse, and jacket. When she sat down, I immediately noticed a glaring mismatch. Her right shoulder and arm were encased in a bulky sling. A shoulder problem had worsened to the point that she had finally scheduled the surgery that her orthopedist recommended. In two weeks, she would go under the knife and then begin her recovery, lying in bed. She was very nervous about becoming physically depleted. She had good reason to worry.

Carol had begun therapy with me three months prior. She was depressed after enduring a painful divorce and financial mess. During these hardships, her blocking program—telling her that she was helpless—repeatedly activated and stopped her from taking care of herself. She became sad and withdrawn, and she blamed herself for not functioning the way she used to. By identifying her demons and how they operated, we devised steps to stop feeding them.

One way her that BD struck was through helpless feelings in the pit of her stomach. Carol learned to recognize these feelings as a signal that her BD was attacking. She used her feelings "alert" as a cue to take care of herself and to refuse her BD. Instead of isolating herself at home, she made herself go out. She ran errands, set up dinner with friends, visited her children and grandchildren, and browsed the bookstore for a good novel. If she had no prior plans, she walked at the mall.

Carol was getting good at following these steps and was feeling much better. Her antidepressant medication, prescribed by her psychiatrist, boosted her efforts. Now she faced a hardship that required her to stay home. As Carol envisioned herself lying helpless in bed and vulnerable to her BD, she became understandably upset.

One thing in our favor was advance notice; we knew her blocking demon would strike as she recovered from surgery. Her most vulnerable time would be when she was at home in bed. Her two biggest challenges were to stay active and focused on self-care. By planning ahead and sticking to her plan Carol protected herself from her BD's attempts to stop her vitalizing activity.

One essential but difficult step was to ask for help. Because Carol liked phone conversations, we made a list of supportive family and friends that she could talk with during recovery. She told everyone about her surgery and asked them to call while she convalesced. When she needed to talk, she also picked up the phone to call them. She prioritized tasks and asked her children to do what she couldn't while she was restricted to bed.

Carol also arranged for ways to pamper herself. During recovery, she read new books, watched videos she'd long wanted to see, listened to music, and solved crossword puzzles. She nurtured her self-esteem by writing self-affirming entries in her journal. She practiced positive visualization and meditation exercises. When her Blocker attempted to stop her, signaled through helpless feelings in her stomach, instead of blaming herself, Carol realized this was her BD attacking. Freed from her old habit of beating up on herself, she focused her energy on separating from her blocking force and resuming one of the many positive activities that she'd prepared in advance. By the time she was up and walking around, her demons were weaker and she was much stronger.

As Carol experienced, our BDs can attack through negative feelings or thoughts. Fortunately, we don't have to change everything at once to deny them successfully. We can start by changing just one thing—our images, thoughts, or actions.

Carol chose actions. When she did good things, the rewards that she experienced as a consequence made her feel better naturally. As her mood lifted, it was easier for Carol to think about herself in favorable ways. Research findings support the therapeutic value of Carol's action approach in reducing symptoms of depression. Well-known psychotherapies incorporate behavioral approaches in their treatment.[1]

Once you start taking action to refuse your BD, the more positive things you do, the more protection you create. If your blocking demon stops you from doing one thing, it won't defeat you—because you'll be protected by the layers of other actions that you're taking. As your situation and vulnerabilities change, modify your action steps as needed.

**Table 2.3**

| Blocker Trigger | Ways to Defeat Your *Depleting* Blocker |
|---|---|
| When you're physically depleted. | 1. Use helpless feelings as a cue to engage self-nurturing steps. |
| | 2. Plan for vulnerable times in order to stay actively focused on self-care. |
| | 3. Prioritize tasks and ask for help; employ self-enhancing actions, thoughts, and/or images to block your Blocker. |
| | 4. Build layers of self-positive steps to protect against repeated Blocker assaults; modify them as your needs change. |

## Start a Reprogramming Record

One of Carol's crucial action steps was to write daily self-bolstering entries in her journal. I began routinely recommending this activity when I witnessed the enormous power it has to starve demons. When clients work it, it works for them. It's simple, time-effective, and virtually cost-free. All you need is a journal and a pen.

When I discuss journal writing with new clients, many tell me they already do this activity. However, their journals are predominantly filled with what's wrong in their lives. They write about the terrible things that happen to them and how awful they feel. They describe in detail their fears, insecurities, and self-criticisms. Noticeably absent are words of support, praise, or encouragement to themselves. This negative focus keeps people stuck in destructive programming, continually generating debilitating feelings that feed their Soldier and Master Demons. Clients forgo the chance to break free from and starve their demons.

In contrast, when we focus on the beneficial aspects of our lives, we engage the power of a mood/memory connection to work in our favor. Every self-confirming journal entry provides a daily boost to our mood. When we're in a good mood, we're more likely to remember pleasant events from our past. We interpret these memories and current experiences more favorably. We're also more receptive to favorable cues in our environment, such as supportive feedback from others.[2] In sum, the more often we write self-affirming entries, the better we feel. The better we feel, the more we remember and view ourselves in a constructive light.

Here's how I introduced this tool to Carol: "One thing I'd like you to start is a daily positive journal. By habitually writing good things about you and your life, you learn to think, feel, and believe positively about yourself. This self-confirming programming eventually records over the old self-negating tapes that you

**Table 2.4**

For each Reprogramming Record entry include:
• Date: One positive thing related to you
• <u>An underlined description of what the favorable item means about you</u>


acquired earlier. Your Soldier Demons and Master Demon of defectiveness shrivel as you no longer feed them aversive feelings.

Because this activity involves reprogramming, I call the journal the Reprogramming Record (RR). Use a separate blank journal for your RR. Select one with a color and style you like, one that makes you feel good when you look at it. Choose a size suitable for home and travel. Many people keep the RR on the night stand as a reminder to write before going to bed or as soon as they wake up. Others prefer to carry it in a purse or a briefcase. They like the convenience and flexibility of writing entries at different times during the day. If you prefer high-tech options, type entries on your computer or other electronic organizer. Save each entry to the same file, named Reprogramming Record. If your device has limited memory, print your entries and keep them together in a binder.

Title your journal Reprogramming Record. Date each entry and write one thing that's favorable and related to you. It could be a compliment you received from someone, a quality you like about yourself, a personal accomplishment from that day or the day before, a fun activity or trip you've scheduled, and so on. Include a description of what the favorable item means about you and underline it. Each entry can be many pages long or as short as a few words. Your writing doesn't have to be neat, spelled perfectly, or grammatically correct. However, it does need to be positive, real, and directly connected to you. If you can't think of anything that day, you can rewrite an earlier entry. If you write more than one item each day, that's great. However, one daily entry is sufficient. The most important thing is to build a habit of writing positive things about yourself." I asked Carol to bring her RR to each session so that we could review it.

After Carol started her Reprogramming Record, I could tell right away which weeks she'd written about, even before she told me. Her demeanor was calm and light as she entered the therapy room. Her face lit up and she smiled as she began sessions, relaying good things about herself and her life. Later, when she read her RR, many entries were the same things she'd shared earlier. Here are some examples of Carol's entries:

*Sunday 2/20:* I took myself out to breakfast today and enjoyed talking with my waiter. <u>I'm able to go out and socialize easily.</u>

*Monday 2/21:* I went through some boxes of old files at work. I'm cleaning and getting organized each time I go through a box. <u>I'm willing to do unpleasant tasks that need to be done.</u>

*Tuesday 2/22:* I went to dinner and a movie with my friend Janis and we had a great time. <u>Janis and I enjoy each other.</u>

*Wednesday 2/23:* My neighbor Darla said I looked pretty in my stylish, colorful outfit. <u>I have a good sense of fashion.</u>

*Thursday 2/24:* I'm looking forward to my trip to Nevada to visit my grandchildren. <u>I am a caring grandmother.</u>

*Friday 2/25:* I went to the office party and had fun once I got there. <u>People enjoy my company.</u>

*Saturday 2/26:* I made dinner for my son and granddaughter. We had a very nice time. <u>I'm a caring mother and grandmother . . . and a good cook.</u>

When Carol read her daily list out loud in session, she frequently paused and spontaneously added more self-affirmations she just remembered.

For simplicity, the year is not listed in these and other RR entries throughout the book. However, when dating your entries, do include the year. This allows you to track and reflect on your progress from year to year when reviewing your RR. If you'd rather not list the year in every entry, write the year on the cover or whenever the year changes.

Because this tool works so well, I've also seen how forcefully our Blocker Demon operates to prevent us from building this daily habit. Like most people, Carol struggled in the beginning. When I asked about her RR, she said she forgot, she didn't feel like doing it, she was sick, she didn't have time, etc. Every excuse had BD smell all over it. Each week in which she forgot, I alerted her to BD attacks. I became relentless because I wanted her to become as relentless as her blocking program was. Over time, Carol got better at defying her BD by writing. The more she wrote, the better she felt and the better she viewed herself. This natural reinforcement provided the boost Carol needed to continue her writing routine.

As you consider starting your own Reprogramming Record, you may think, "I don't like to write. I especially don't want to write something down every day." This is very likely your Blocker Demon attacking to stop you. Some people who do not want to write can just say a positive truth to themselves each day instead.

However, when my clients choose not to write, their results are weaker. It's possible they're not saying daily positives, even though they tell me they do. However, they usually share their positive statements in sessions, suggesting that they have done the exercise during the week. What's different about these people compared to those who write is that they refer to themselves and their world more negatively. They also come to sessions more restless and irritable, similar to how Carol and other clients appear when they haven't written in their RR.

Perhaps these clients are more depressed to begin with compared to those who write. If so, these sadder clients are especially in need of the reinforcement that

**Table 2.5**

Review Your Reprogramming Record Entries to:
1. Boost your positive reprogramming.
2. Recover from a Blocker Demon attack.
3. Prepare for a future Blocker Demon assault.

comes from writing a tangible record of self-positives. Research reveals that we're more likely to believe the things that we write down.[3] By writing in our RR, we employ this process to help us separate from and starve our BD (and MD of inadequacy).

Whatever your emotional state, after you start writing, flip back through the pages and read your entries as often as possible. Every time you review your RR, you strengthen your positive reprogramming. To amplify results, read your entries out loud to yourself or to a supportive partner, family member, or friend. For couples living together, a popular time to do this is in bed at night before going to sleep. Clients tell me how reinforcing it is to have their loved ones listen and validate their self-enhancing reports. By sharing your RR with someone else, you're more likely to act in ways that are consistent with the constructive things you say.[4]

Another good reason to read your RR is to help recover from a demon attack, especially when you feel upset and bad about yourself. Also review it to help protect yourself when you anticipate a demon attack. Focusing on self-positives before you face a threat to your self-esteem will help prevent you from reacting negatively after you've been threatened.[5]

My client John read through his Reprogramming Record between every major work project. He had learned from past experience that he was especially vulnerable to his Blocker Demon before beginning a new job. It always barraged him with defeating thoughts such as "Sure, your customer liked your last project, but it doesn't mean that you'll do a good job with this one. You don't know what you're doing on this one. Don't even try; you'll just fail." John was so blocked by these negatives that he struggled for days before getting anything done.

After he began writing and reading his RR, the positive evidence from his entries helped safeguard John against Blocker attacks. He was able to start jobs faster and complete more projects within the same time frame. His earnings rose, giving him more good things to write. If John hadn't written and reviewed his RR entries between work projects, he wouldn't have enjoyed the benefits of improved productivity and compensation.

If you doubt whether the RR will benefit you, experiment by writing a positive entry every day for 30 days. Beware of any BD attempts to stop or sabotage you. Signs of sabotage include writing things that aren't true or affirming,[6] skipping weeks and then filling in entries all at once, or always writing the same item

> Entries from John's Reprogramming Record:
>
> *Monday, May 7:* A prospective client called me today, referred by a previous client. <u>I have a strong reputation: people trust me with their projects.</u>
>
> *Tuesday, May 8:* After talking with the potential customer, he decided to hire me. <u>I describe and sell my services effectively.</u>
>
> *Wednesday, May 9:* I began a new project today when I didn't feel like starting. <u>I am able to take action regardless of how I feel. I follow through on my commitments.</u>

every day. See how you feel after you finish each entry. Examine your thoughts: are they more positive or negative? After a couple of weeks, check your general orientation. Do you go through your days looking for favorable things to write about yourself? Near the end of the month, ask someone you are close to whether he/she notices any difference in you. Often our loved ones observe changes before we do. They can give us valuable feedback that we might otherwise not see.

## Shield Yourself with Support

Fortunately, we don't have to battle our Blocker Demon alone. We can add a thick layer of protection from our demons by requesting assistance and supportive evidence of our worth from others. Social support provides numerous physical and mental health benefits. It also buffers us from the negative effects of the stressful events that we encounter.[7] Carol asked her family and friends to be there for her after her surgery. With the help of their phone calls and visits, she was able to recover without the extra burden of feeling lonely or isolated.

> Social support enhances our health and buffers us from stress.

I was reminded of the power of support when I worked with Anna. She sought help because, at 32 years old, she was tired of being unhappy. She immediately impressed me as a kind, smart, responsible person. She'd worked as an office manager at the same company for years. Unfortunately, she was beset with a huge Blocker Demon. It stopped her from doing almost everything except essential tasks. Her typical weekly routine was to go to work and come home. On weekends she ran errands.

Her blocking program replayed a litany of defeating thoughts to Anna day and night. She was so used to listening to it that she rarely tried new things. She wanted to be married and have children, but in reality she was single and living at home. Other than her parents and siblings, she had little contact outside work. Her Blocker and Master Demon of feeling unworthy had formed when she was a child. Her parents were very critical of Anna and they overprotected her. Although they'd mellowed with age, they continued to engage her in these confidence-depleting ways.

Anna began her Reprogramming Record right away. She also agreed to add one new activity each week. I encouraged her to choose something she would enjoy and that would involve contact with others. I suggested a social activity because one reason Anna's BD had grown strong was that she was isolated from outside supports. During early sessions, we focused on social, assertiveness, and relaxation skills. We covered the basics of exercise, healthy eating, and getting enough sleep. We role-played setting limits with others and asking for what she wanted. Anna followed these steps, more or less, and reported feeling a little better.

Anna's fourth session was dramatically different. She beamed as she glided into my office and she wasted no time telling me why. She'd chosen a church group for singles as her new activity that week. Although her blocking agent had tried to stop her by assuring her that she wouldn't enjoy it, she made herself go to the group gathering. She had a wonderful time. She talked with some nice women whom she liked and, more important, who liked her. As she shared her most significant news, she broke out in a big smile. A man in the group introduced himself to her and they hit it off. He asked her out and she had a date planned with him that weekend.

Anna's action step of seeking support diminished her demons in one night. Her Blocker Demon was proven wrong and, therefore, busted when she ignored it and went to the church group. Her Master Demon shrank as she received nurturing and positive feedback from supportive others. It shriveled further when a man she liked asked her for a date. She had achieved in less than three hours what could have taken her months or even years of effort by herself—by defying her demons and giving the group a try.

I've seen the power of many supportive groups in helping clients do positive things to counter feeling unworthy. In addition to Anna's church group, here are some others: professional networking clubs for business promotion, toastmasters groups for public speaking, authors groups for writing, volunteers groups for helping others, walking clubs for exercise, art classes for creativity, hobby groups for special interests, singles clubs for dating, and caregivers groups for support.

When my client Carol was recovering from her divorce, she defied her isolating BD, which tried to convince her that she was too depressed to function. Her triumph came through volunteering for the office holiday party committee. The group meetings got her out of the house and active. The planning activities took her mind off her personal and financial hardships. She enjoyed being a part of the group and collaborating with her co-workers. They liked her too and praised her for her organizational and management skills.

As Carol felt a valued and successful member of the party committee, her Master Demon of unworthiness weakened. If Carol had instead listened to her isolating Blocker, she would've missed out on the enjoyment and self-esteem enhancement that came from participating in the group.

> Elise's depression worsened after her brother hanged himself. Although her family and friends offered support, she didn't return their calls. When co-workers invited her to socialize, she turned them down. Some mornings she woke up so depressed that she missed work. Elise's BD thrived as she shut down and suffered in isolation. If instead Elise had accepted support, she wouldn't have missed the comfort that she so desperately needed. With others' help, she could've felt better and taken steps sooner to stop feeding her Blocker Demon.

If you or your loved ones struggle with a resistant BD, additional supportive help is available through individual, family, or group psychotherapy. Angela called me after her close friend Lisa confided that individual therapy had benefited her. Lisa sought help when she became depressed and shut down after separating from her husband. Unfortunately, her marriage ended. But fortunately, her therapy continued. She told Angela that her therapist's support and intervention were crucial in helping her cope with and recover from her painful loss.

## Begin a Demon Disrupting Diary

The sooner we catch our demons, the sooner we can detach from and stop feeding them. Another tool to help us do this is the Demon Disrupting Diary (DDD). I developed the DDD after noticing that clients often came to sessions reporting the same setbacks. Although we had repeatedly reviewed therapy goals and specific strategies to reach them, clients continued to be stymied in their efforts by subsequent demon assaults.

**Table 2.6**

| Blocker Trigger | Ways to Defeat Your *Isolating* Blocker |
|---|---|
| When you're feeling lonely and isolated. | 1. To buffer yourself from the negative effects of stressful events, ask for assistance and support from others. |
| | 2. To counter feeling lonely and unworthy, join groups; you'll quickly boost goals and skills and receive positive feedback from others. |
| | 3. To thwart a resistant, isolating BD, add support through individual, family, and/or group psychotherapy. |

Because the demon programs activated quickly, I suspected that an extra tool was crucial to detect and interrupt them. I began asking clients to write down details of each attack, including the demon's name, its method of assault, and how the client reacted. As diary entries accumulated, we identified patterns of places, people, situations, and times when attacks occurred.

With this information, we devised and reinforced strategies to prepare for and refuse the demons when they activated. Derek, mentioned earlier, had discovered through writing in his DDD that his Blocker Demon attacked when he practiced new songs. He placed his DDD near his keyboard every time he played. As soon as he spotted an attack, he pulled out his DDD and wrote a new entry to help separate from and deny his BD.

To begin your Demon Disrupting Diary, use a different journal from your Reprogramming Record. Select a journal with a style and cover that reinforces your determination and power in catching your demons. Choose a size suitable to carry with you wherever you go. Because your demons can attack at any time, having your DDD available allows you to write as soon as you catch them, to interrupt them quickly. As with the RR, if you prefer high-tech options, use an electronic organizer or portable computer. Save each entry to the same file named Demon Disrupting Diary. If your device has limited memory, print your entries and keep them together in a binder.

For each entry, write the date (include the year), the demon's name, when and how it attacked, and how you responded. If the demon prevails, add what you learned in order to refuse it the next time. This may seem like a lot to write, but once you get started, you'll see patterns emerge from your entries. Each time you rewrite details from a recurring pattern, your writing becomes easier and faster. With every entry, you strengthen your awareness of factors that make you vulnerable to demon attacks. You also reinforce steps to separate from and deny your demons the negative emotional energy they require.

Within the first week of starting her DDD, Celeste realized that she was plagued by her BD. As you read earlier, her attacks often occurred in the morning while she was still in bed. Here is one of her DDD entries:

*March 12:* I'm at home in bed by myself on Monday morning. I just woke up and my Blocker Demon attacked. It said, "You're depressed, don't get up; if you do, you'll feel worse. Stay in bed, don't go to work today." I knew right away this was my BD and not me. I said, "I see what you're up to. Get

**Table 2.7**

| For each Demon Disrupting Diary entry include: | | |
|---|---|---|
| • Date: | • Demon name | • When and how it attacked |
| • How you responded | • What you learned | |

away from me. I know I will feel better once I get going. I'm getting up now to get ready for work."

If you don't catch your BD right away, write in your DDD whenever you become aware of attacks, even if it's days later. You might prefer not to remind yourself of these painful experiences. However, we often learn the most from reviewing our biggest slips. The more you uncover how your Blocker operates, the more you can externalize its negative programming.

Other therapeutic approaches direct us to look inward for the source of damaging thoughts, actions, and views. Instead of battling integral parts of ourselves, the demon model orients our attention away from ourselves to recognize and catch our demons, the destructive patterns that we learned through early aversive life experiences outside our control. Instead of depleting ourselves by feeding our Blocker Demon with self-blame and self-criticism, writing in our DDD roots it out, starves it, and keeps us on track to reach our goals.

Rachel called to request a phone appointment versus an in-person appointment. She explained that, rushing to get chores done, she fell down the stairs. The worst part was that, at eight months pregnant, she'd lost her mucous plug. Fortunately, she didn't land on her stomach and the baby was fine. However, her doctor had placed her on bed rest until the birth.

I asked Rachel to write about her trauma in her DDD and read it to me in our phone session. Although she hadn't been writing entries regularly, being confined to bed presented an opportune time to develop her habit. Rachel wrote:

*September 5:* I was at home Wednesday night trying to get everything done and feeling overwhelmed. As I hurried down the stairs with my laundry basket, I fell. Earlier that afternoon, I had planned to rest while Hanna took her nap. Just as I got her down, my neighbor Jill called. She was upset with her husband, which wasn't unusual. They've been having marital problems for the past year. As soon as Jill started in, my Blocker Demon attacked. It said, "Jill is upset; don't rest, her problems are more important; if you don't talk with her now, she won't like you anymore." I listened to my BD and did not take care of myself or my baby.

As we reviewed her DDD entry during her phone session, Rachel recognized how much Blocker attacks such as this one had contributed to her overload. Whenever her neighbors, friends, co-workers, or extended family asked her to do something, she almost never said no. She didn't want to let anyone down. Rachel's blocking program had been created and had grown in childhood, when she repeatedly saw her mother put others' needs first. Just as her mother had done, Rachel learned to put herself last. Even as her pregnancy advanced, she kept the same pace at work, caring for Hanna and her husband Lloyd, volunteering at Hanna's school, and doing most chores at home.

If Rachel had been less burdened with these responsibilities, she still may have fallen. Accidents happen. But we knew for certain that her BD stopped her from doing necessary things for herself. Instead, it steered her to do too much for others at her own expense. Her constant state of overload was unhealthy, and it left her vulnerable to harmful situations.

I encouraged Rachel to focus on what she could control: reducing her overload, asking for help, and caring for herself and her baby. Fortunately, she was already resting in bed. She called her employer to begin early maternity leave, and she asked Lloyd for help. He took time off work to care for her and Hanna. He also called Hanna's school to share Rachel's condition and inability to volunteer. She asked friends and family to assist with home and child care chores.

As we reviewed her BD attack, Rachel realized that, counter to her BD's prediction; her friend Jill would probably understand her need to rest. Regardless, Rachel deserved to prioritize her needs. If Jill did become upset, that's not the kind of friend she wanted anyway. If Jill called again when Rachel felt overloaded, she planned to override her blocking program and say, "I've been very overwhelmed with things to do and my doctor tells me I need to rest. Can I call you another time when I have more time and energy?"

---

An Entry from Pat's Demon Disrupting Diary

*October 11:* I was stuck in traffic on my way home from work when my Blocker Demon struck: "By the time you get home, it'll be too dark to walk. You'll have to miss your exercise today." As I felt helpless and upset, I realized this was my BD trying to stop me. I saw an exit sign for a familiar, safe neighborhood. I took the exit, stopped on a side street, changed shoes, and walked while it was still light. I rewarded myself on my traffic-free drive home with a low-fat frozen yogurt.

---

## Post Reprogramming Reminders

Because our demons typically form in childhood, by the time that we spot them, they've spent years wreaking havoc in our lives. We've responded to their directives repeatedly and generated a steady supply of negative emotional energy to feed them. As we begin steps to exorcize them, our demons will not go easily. It takes much repetition to replace entrenched harmful habits with new beneficial ones. Reminders provide a simple, easy way to keep us on track.

The most prevalent reminder that my clients use is Sticky Notes. They're readily available, inexpensive, and small enough to fit most spaces. With little effort, you can jot down reprogramming reminders and post them where you'll frequently see them. By surrounding yourself with affirming reminders, you'll keep the spotlight on your demons and boost your efforts to separate yourself from them. The top places that my clients choose are the bathroom and bedroom mirror, car console and steering wheel, office at home and work, computer, and personal organizer. You can write the same or different messages on each note. As your needs change, discard old notes and replace them with new reminders.

Derek put Sticky Notes where he was most likely to see them: on his bathroom mirror, refrigerator, keyboard, steering wheel, and computer. His reminder messages included the following: *"I'm focused on my music goals," "I'm disciplined in practicing my music," "I'm creative in writing my songs," "I refuse my Blocker Demon. It's not me."* Every time that he glanced at his notes, he reinforced productive steps to weaken his BD. If he hadn't posted his reminders, Derek would've gone without the supportive boost that they provided throughout his day.

---

Jot down reprogramming reminders, such as the following:
I finish my homework for class.
I'm a compassionate person.
I write Reprogramming Record entries every day.
I'm making changes to be a positive model for Hanna.

---

Reminders can also be stickers, postcards, posters, photographs, objects, etc. You can choose anything, as long as it serves as a reminder to you. Celeste placed a simple green dot sticker on her computer at work. She liked having a private reminder that only she understood. The color was soothing to her and reminded her to do short relaxation exercises during her breaks throughout her workday.

Rachel hung a purple "soap on a rope" from her showerhead. Purple was her favorite color. She loved the delicate design carved in the soap. Every morning when she took her shower, she saw her soap but never used it. It reminded her to review her RR entry that she had written the day before in her purple journal.

John put his DDD on his night stand next to his bed. He saw it every night as he got ready for bed and every morning as he prepared for work. He rarely opened the book at those times. Just glancing at it reminded him to use the strategies that he'd identified earlier to block his Blocker Demon.

Also, post reminders of your talents and accomplishments. Surround yourself with your diplomas, certificates, plaques, art work, ribbons, medals, trophies, etc. Place them where you'll see them often. Periodically move your reminders to different places so they remain conspicuous in your environment. Every time you see and rearrange them, you'll reinforce your worth.

I was surprised to learn early in practice that many of my clients had stuffed these items in drawers and boxes, never to be seen again. Tangible evidence of hard work, personal excellence, and appreciation from others was relegated to

**Table 2.8**

| Blocker Trigger | Ways to Defeat Your *Entrenched* Blocker |
|---|---|
| When you forget to follow your reprogramming steps. | 1. To help replace old negative habits with positive ones, post reprogramming reminders where you'll frequently see them. |
| | 2. As your needs change, discard old notes and replace them with new reprogramming reminders. |
| | 3. Boost your self-worth by displaying evidence of your hard work, talents, and accomplishments; periodically rearrange your self-enhancing reminders to keep them noticeable. |

the dark recesses of homes, offices, and storage sheds. I asked clients to find these items and bring them to sessions. We discussed what each one revealed about their favorable qualities. They agreed to post those that made them feel good about themselves.

Gina came to my office with a beautiful poem she wrote in fifth grade. As a child, she had endured both physical and emotional abuse from her parents. Her Blocker and Master Demons had thrived, as she grew depressed and believed that she was unworthy. In spite of these hardships, Gina and her poem had survived. She agreed to frame her poem, place it on her bedroom wall, and read it often. With every reading, Gina's demons shrank—as she embraced her inner child, who was creative, worthy, and deserving of love.

David posts reminders of his achievements on a corkboard above his office desk. He regularly rearranges these items so that he'll continue to notice them. They include letters of thanks from his supervisors, testimonials from clients, and postcards from earned vacations. David reports that by rearranging them—sometimes chronologically, sometimes by topic, sometimes by source—he experiences his successes anew in ways that he wouldn't by just seeing them each day.

## Pace Yourself

As you acquire strategies to starve your BD, beware of pushing to do too much at once. Pace yourself by setting realistic goals that fit your life situation. In working with clients and observing myself, I've noticed that we're most vulnerable to our blocking forces before we start a beneficial activity. For protection, begin with a small doable task and then schedule a break early on. This jump start will often bust your BD. Once you initiate an activity the first time, it becomes easier to get started the second and subsequent times. Check your progress frequently and adjust steps accordingly. There's a fine line between staying on track and veering off by doing too much. Our Blocker hovers over the steering wheel, waiting to veer us off course if we go too fast and lose control.

---

An Entry from Ray's Reprogramming Record:
*April 4:* I began a new lesson plan today. My students asked many questions and showed interest in the topic. <u>I teach at a good pace with confidence and enthusiasm.</u>

---

My client Mike worked up to 50 hours a week as a mid-level manager. Between scheduled meetings and unexpected management problems, he rarely completed his paperwork. To remedy this problem, he decided to take reports home to finish on the weekend. He figured that extra work hours would pay off as his superiors observed the evidence of his productivity. However, during the weekend, when he could've worked, he didn't. This scenario repeated and his unfinished reports grew. As he dragged his stack of work back to the office each Monday, he felt like a failure.

As we looked closely at his dilemma, we spotted Mike's BD. When he thought about doing his tasks on the weekend, his BD repeatedly said things such as "You've worked hard all week. Don't do the reports now. You have plenty of time to finish them." Mike listened and did no work. On Sunday night, reality hit hard as Mike realized that it was too late. As he beat himself up for not working, his Blocker (and Master) Demon fed off his frustration and self-criticism, growing stronger in the process.

Once we identified his blocking agent and how it operated, we planned how to disengage from it. Like most of us, Mike was very susceptible to his BD before he began working. To get started, he agreed to pace himself by breaking his work down into manageable chunks. His first goal was to spend 15 minutes working on a report Saturday morning. If he needed a break after that, he could take one.

To Mike's surprise, he found that once he got started, he didn't need to take a break. He finished the report and then another one in the same sitting. Feeling very good about himself, he treated himself to a movie later that day. The next week, he increased his objective to two reports. Breaking the ice the first week had made it easier for him to begin working again. Once he got started, he kept going until both reports were done.

Mike agreed to follow the same approach at work, with a target of finishing one report by the weekend. To discourage distractions, he closed his office door and set his phone to voice mail before getting started. Just like at home, after 15 minutes, he didn't need a break and completed two reports. He increased his goal. Subsequent weeks were mixed. Sometimes he was successful and other times new

**Table 2.9**

| Blocker Trigger | Ways to Defeat Your *Overloading* Blocker |
| --- | --- |
| When you're pushing to do too much at once. | 1. Pace yourself by setting realistic goals and chunking work into small, doable tasks.<br>2. Jump-start your efforts by scheduling a break early on.<br>3. Reduce distractions by privatizing your work environment.<br>4. Write and review DDD entries to discover additional specific strategies in order to refuse your BD in the future. |

management problems arose that required his attention. As a consequence, unfinished reports piled up.

However, now when he got behind, Mike was no longer his own worst enemy. Instead, he transformed his frustration into determination to defeat his blocking program. To learn from BD assaults, he described them in his DDD. We reviewed these entries and his previous triumphs in order to reinforce how to resist the attacks. The key to defying his Blocker Demon was the 15-minute break that Mike promised himself, if needed, before he began working. It provided the jump-start that he needed to overcome his inertia.

## Care for Yourself

To facilitate your goals, program self-care habits into your day and week. By building in exercise, enjoyable activities, and other forms of self-nurturing, you'll feel physically revitalized, mentally strong, and emotionally satisfied. You'll stop supplying the destructive emotions that your BD depends on to exist. By regularly attending to your needs, you'll become more efficient at work, home, and other areas in your life. Anytime your BD attacks, you can engage these self-care tools to resist its influence.

> To shrink your Blocker Demon, build in exercise, enjoyable activities, and self-nurturing.

### Get Physical

If you're not sure what to do for yourself first, choose physical exercise. This is the single most beneficial habit that you can create to shrink your Blocker. More than 100 research studies confirm that exercise reduces depression and improves physical health. Vigorous exercise provides a quick, sizeable mood booster. Even a short 10-minute walk creates two hours of enhanced well-being. Occasional exercise lowers the risk of death by close to one-third compared to no exercise. Daily conditioning workouts cut the death risk by nearly one-half. [8]

Fortunately, you have many exercise options to consider. Choose one that appeals to you and fits into your schedule. Beware of BD attempts to stop you. Counter its attacks by problem solving to make your exercise routine doable. Like my client Rachel, you may opt for something traditional, such as going to a gym. Working out away from home around motivated people is very appealing to her. Having a variety of equipment to use is a plus.

However, as soon as Rachel got excited about joining a gym, her blocking program activated by telling her, "You can't go; you have no one to watch the children." She immediately felt deflated and dejected. Although she didn't catch her BD, fortunately she shared her distress with her husband that night. He offered to watch their children on days that he didn't have to work late. He suggested she contact some gyms to see if they offered child care as a back up when he couldn't be home. Rachel had been so defeated by her Blocker she hadn't considered these possibilities. With renewed resolve, she found a nearby gym with quality child care. She also thought of another child care option: asking her friends with children to arrange reciprocal play dates.

---

An Entry from Rachel's Reprogramming Record:
*June 3:* I worked out at the gym today: 20 minutes on the elliptical machine and 30 minutes lifting weights. I take good care of myself by exercising. I do not let my Blocker Demon stop me.

---

Rachel alternates between weight training, riding the elliptical machine, and running on the treadmill. Her goal is to go to the gym three times a week, but she usually makes it there once or twice. When I ask her in sessions what happens, she's getting better at identifying the BD attacks that stop her. We read her Demon Disrupting Diary entries to learn ways to defy her BD. In one example, it attacked when Rachel had arrived home from work. Her plan was to change clothes and drive to the gym. Her Blocker said, "You're tired; don't go to the gym. You can go later when you're rested." Rachel listened. The more time that passed, the less she felt like getting out and driving to the gym. As she got ready for bed, Rachel criticized herself for being lazy and skipping her workout. Her Blocker (and Master Demon of defectiveness) thrived on her disappointment and self-blame.

To thwart her BD, I suggested that she pack her gym clothes in her car the night before workout days. Then she could drive directly to the gym from work, bypassing her dangerous stop home. This strategy works pretty well, but her Blocker finds other vulnerable times to attack. To fill in for missed gym workouts because of BD assaults, Rachel walks outside with her neighbor once a week. Her commitment to her walking buddy helps her get up for their morning walks. Once she starts, she enjoys the benefits from exercise and catching up with her good friend. Every time she triumphs by walking or working out at the gym, Rachel becomes healthier and happier and her BD and MD of inferiority gets weaker.

Perhaps your workout preference is different, like my client Derek's. He rides his bicycle around his neighborhood and jogs along the nearby beach. His budget is tight, so it's important that his choices are low cost. His schedule varies, and he prefers the convenience of exercising by himself whenever he chooses. When he feels creatively stuck writing a song or practicing music, he cycles or runs, to release tension and clear his head.

As you consider options, stay alert for your BD. It may say, "You don't have enough money to begin an exercise program." Like Derek, you can resist your BD by choosing something low cost, such as walking, running, or bicycling. Rachel denied hers by arranging for child care during her workouts. Here are some other common Blocker attacks and how my clients successfully responded:

BD: "Don't exercise, you'll miss out on what little time you have to spend with your partner." Beverly's solution: *Exercise with him/her.* She bowls with her husband every week in a bowling league. They walk together on weekends at their local mall.

BD: "You don't have enough time to exercise." Amy's answer: *Do short workouts at various times in the day.* She jumps rope for a minute or two while her children are taking naps, watching DVDs, or playing.

BD: "Exercise is boring and painful." Kendra's response: *Choose enjoyable physical activities.* She takes salsa dance lessons twice a week. She bought tap shoes, a dancing board, and a tap dancing workout DVD. She dances to her DVD at home whenever she wants.

BD: "You look fat and ugly. You can't exercise around other men (women); they'll laugh at you." Celeste's reply: *Join a same sex gym.* She joined a popular women's gym with locations near her work and home.

## Enjoy Yourself

Of course, there are many ways besides exercise to take care of ourselves. It's important to recognize that an essential part of doing so is having fun. With work tasks, home chores, appointments, and errands competing for our time, it's easy to succumb to our BDs and neglect this important self-care step. By routinely scheduling pleasurable activities, you'll defy your BD and satisfy your need for enjoyment. You won't miss out on having fun. Anytime you feel negatively, you can lift your mood by giving yourself a shot of self-nurturing.

Choose things that you truly like to do, even if no one you know has similar interests. Options range from hobbies to entertainment to pampering your body. Carmen enjoys going to weekend yard sales to look for salt and pepper shakers to add to her collection. John likes to plan for and participate in Renaissance fairs with his wife. Other clients nurture themselves by growing an herb garden, watching Seinfeld reruns, listening to classic comedy radio shows, square dancing, and painting ceramic figurines.

> To thwart your blocking demon and lift your mood, schedule pleasant activities that you enjoy.

You may favor popular choices, such as watching television, renting movies, surfing the Internet, listening to music, reading magazines or books, going to a movie, eating out, shopping, attending a sports event, or seeing a play. With every activity, you'll enhance your mood and protect yourself from your blocking program. Beverly and her husband rejuvenate after work by singing at a karaoke bar. Carol defies her isolating BD on weekends by going out to the movies with her friends and grandchildren. Derek feels energized by checking out different clubs with live music.

The number one body-pampering choice among my female clients is a manicure/pedicure. Other top contenders are a nap, massage, haircut and color, facial and bubble bath. All of these options appealed to Beverly. However, when she began therapy, she hadn't been to the hairdresser in months. She couldn't remember the last time she had had a manicure or bubble bath. She'd never experienced a pedicure or a facial. Popular body-nurturing picks for male clients are naps, physical intimacy, and massages.

> An Entry from Lea's Reprogramming Record:
> *June 9:* I sat outside on the back patio today and read my new novel.
> I am good at nurturing myself to block my Blocker.

When I ask new clients to describe the enjoyable things they regularly do, I often hear the same answer. Besides watching TV, many don't do anything. If this sounds familiar, discover your preferences by remembering what you liked doing in the past. Reflect on what you've wanted to do but haven't. Browse local publications and the Internet for ideas. Consult loved ones for their suggestions. To start with a manageable goal, select a pleasant activity to do once during the week. Choose something new that you're not currently doing.

Don't wait to become motivated before getting started. This is a common trigger that activates your BD. The longer you wait, the worse you feel and the less you do. To block your Blocker, take action, regardless of how you feel. The natural reinforcement you'll receive from enjoying yourself will motivate you to do it again. The more you do, the better you'll feel and the more you'll want to do. Established psychotherapies incorporate this action-first approach into their protocols.[9]

> Don't wait to feel motivated to begin a pleasant activity. The rein-
> forcement you'll receive from doing something enjoyable will boost
> your mood and starve your Blocker.

Darrell couldn't think of anything special that he routinely did for himself. His work in law enforcement takes its toll on him physically and emotionally. Since his divorce, he's maintained half-time custody of his two children. When he started therapy, he was spending almost all of his time meeting responsibilities at work, caring for his children, and being at home. Other than working out at the gym, he did nothing for himself weekly. When I asked him to think of one special thing to do, he immediately replied, "Watch a football game on TV on Sunday." To ensure success, he agreed to arrange his day to prioritize the game. If his mother or brother called to ask for his help, something they often did, he resolved to set limits so that he would not miss the game.

Once you develop a weekly self-care habit, add more ways to enjoy yourself. Your choices don't need to take much time, money, or planning. For example, you can listen to a song, take a coffee break, pet your cat, or call a friend. After Darrell met his goal of watching his first football game, I asked what else interested him. He reflected that from childhood he was always intrigued by architecture. When shopping at the grocery store, he often glanced at architectural magazines but never stopped to get one. For his next self-care activity, he agreed to buy one and give himself time to read it.

On nice days, Beverly eats lunch outside on the back patio at work. This requires no extra time and she comes back to her desk energized from the fresh air and sunlight. Mike cares for himself by reading the sports section of his newspaper in the morning. Carol looks forward to solving the Sunday newspaper crossword puzzle. Karen takes pleasure in knitting. She brings her needles and yarn with her to frequent medical appointments. She used to get very impatient and frustrated during her inevitable waits. Now she lifts her mood by knitting some rows.

As you build pleasant events into your week, ideally you'll eventually be doing something for yourself daily. Rachel created a habit of asking herself every morning in the shower, *"What positive thing am I going to do for myself today"*? When she looked at her purple soap on a rope, it reminded her not only to review her Reprogramming Record entry but also to ask this question and plan something for herself that day. She placed a purple smile sticker on her day planner cover as another visual reminder to follow through with her self-care activity.

If you enjoy social activities, include these in your weekly choices. You read earlier that Anna chose a singles church group. Mike plays poker with friends from work. If you're in a relationship, set aside time to spend time together without distractions. Katie and her boyfriend go out to dinner every weekend. Rachel and her husband add dates to their calendars when they review schedules for the upcoming month. If you're a parent, do a family activity. Kendra pops popcorn and watches movies at home with her two children on Friday nights. If doing something every week sounds daunting, start with every other week or less often. Raquel joined a monthly book club. Olivia goes to neighborhood card parties every other month.

---

Celeste, her husband, and children go to church together on Sunday. Later that day, they do another family activity. Their preferences vary from riding bikes, going to the park, having a barbecue, or going to a movie.

---

To deplete your BD fully, plan special events to do throughout the year. David likes going to local minor league baseball games. Anita, Karen, and Jacqué treat themselves to lunch together every month. Gene and his wife enjoy attending concerts. Rachel and her college friends look forward to spending a weekend together in a different city every year.

**Table 2.10**

| Blocker Trigger | Ways to Defeat Your *Neglecting* Blocker |
| --- | --- |
| When you put your self-care needs last. | 1. To optimize your mood and physical health, choose an appealing exercise option that fits within your schedule. |
| | 2. For exercise success, plan ahead, problem-solve, and get help. |
| | 3. For fun, schedule routinely some activities that you find pleasurable; for the best options, review past and future choices. |
| | 4. Exercise and initiate activities regardless of how you feel. Doing something will make you feel better and motivated to do more. |

## Beware the Sniper

The more you incorporate these beneficial steps into your life, the better you'll feel. You'll stop supplying your Blocker Demon (and Master Demon of inadequacy) with destructive emotions. As you become happier and more confident, beware of surprise attacks from your Blocker. It'll be ravenous because you're not feeding it. To survive, it will amass its remaining strength to shut you down. When successful, it gets you to slip, feel defeated, and blame yourself for messing up. It feeds on your negative emotions and restores its power. It triumphs when your self-criticism stops you from resuming positive steps.

This type of assault happens so often to my clients, to me, and to everyone else I know that I named it Sniper. All four Soldier Demons operate with this Sniper function. They strike out of the blue when you don't expect it. To protect yourself, consistently follow your demon-depleting strategies. Stay alert for Sniper assaults, especially when things are going well and you're feeling good. Remember that you're human and bound to fall prey to Sniper hits at times.

When blindsided, the quickest way to stop supplying your demons with destructive emotions is to be your best friend and to forgive yourself. Write about Sniper attacks in your Demon Disrupting Diary. Review when and how you were hit, the situations you were in, how you responded, and what you learned. Use what you uncover to become stronger in defying future assaults. Tell yourself, *"It's okay, I slipped. I forgive myself. I'll learn from this Sniper attack, reset, and move on. I'll use what I discover to resist my Blocker Demon in the future."*

Carol suffered a Sniper attack one weekend. Until then, she was having a wonderful time. On Friday, she had nurtured herself after work by changing into comfortable clothes and preparing a good meal. She lounged on the sofa and read a novel by one of her favorite authors. On Saturday, she enjoyed spending time with her family. However, on Sunday morning, Carol's Blocker Demon struck in classic Sniper fashion. She woke up feeling down; as she lay in bed, she didn't feel like doing anything. The longer she stayed inactive, the worse she felt.

Although she was miserable, Carol remembered from our therapy sessions to be kind and forgive herself for her slip. She pulled out her Demon Disrupting Diary and wrote in it, which allowed her to identify and learn from her BD Sniper attack. As she paused to review what happened, she realized that, as soon

**Table 2.11**

After a *Sniper* Blocker Demon Hits:
1. Write about it in your Demon Disrupting Diary.
2. Forgive yourself, reset, and move on.
3. Use what you learn to defy future BD assaults.

as she had woken up, her BD had said, "You don't have enough money. You can't do the things you want to do. Don't balance your checkbook; you'll feel worse."

From our discussions, Carol knew what she had to do: say no to her Blocker and balance her checkbook. She did it that day. Her money was tight, but not as bad as her BD had said. She reviewed her priorities and revised her budget. She decided to cut back on expensive restaurant dinners to save for her most desired activity, trips to visit family and friends. Contrary to her BD's prediction, Carol felt much better. She'd successfully stopped feeding it: by forgiving herself, uncovering its Sniper attack, and taking action to refuse it.

**Table 2.12**

| The Blocker Demon | |
| --- | --- |
| Directive | • It stops you from doing positive things that would increase your self-worth. (pp. 17–18) |
| Ways to Identify (p. 18) | • You always put your needs last.<br>• You keep falling back away from following helpful suggestions.<br>• You're stuck in old patterns that make you tired and depressed.<br>• You feel defeated before you even try to figure out how to make something better in your life.<br>• When you set goals, self-critical thoughts, images, and beliefs stop you from taking steps to reach them. |
| Ways to Defeat | • Detect your blocking demon and how it formed (pp. 18–21).<br>• Reveal your specific and common vulnerabilities to your BD (pp. 21–25).<br>• Stay alert to identify your blocking force when it strikes.<br>• Refuse your Blocker Demon with your positive thoughts and actions.<br>  • Start a Reprogramming Record (pp. 25–29).<br>  • Shield yourself with support (pp. 29–31).<br>  • Begin a Demon Disrupting Diary (pp. 31–34).<br>  • Post reprogramming reminders (pp. 34–36).<br>  • Pace yourself (pp. 36–38).<br>  • Care for yourself (pp. 38–43).<br>    • Get physical (pp. 38–40).<br>    • Enjoy yourself (pp. 40–43).<br>• Celebrate each triumph with a self-enhancing reward.<br>• Beware of the Sniper (pp. 44–45). |

## CHAPTER 3

# THE NEGATOR DEMON

Gloria ordered the chicken enchilada and burrito combo, her favorite dinner special. When she looked around the table at her friends talking and smiling, her uneasiness grew. Undercutting thoughts popped into her mind: "You don't know what to say, you're boring, you'll make a fool of yourself." As she surveyed other diners joking and eating, the criticisms continued: "People don't even notice you, you look ugly, no guy here wants to date you." Gloria wanted to melt into the floor. Instead, she put a smile on her face and tried to act interested in what her companions were saying.

Although she nodded in agreement, Gloria remained too preoccupied by the deflating thoughts to listen to what her friends were saying. She stayed through the entire meal, managing to keep secret how uncomfortable she really felt. Although the food was excellent, she didn't enjoy it because her stomach was queasy. When she said good-bye to everyone and drove home, she felt like a failure. She beat herself up for worrying, feeling self-conscious, and not having a good time.

When she shared her nerve-racking experience with me in her next appointment, Gloria was noticeably anxious and confused. The group dinner was the largest social activity she'd undertaken so far after a stressful breakup with her boyfriend Troy. She'd worked hard in our initial therapy sessions to catch and stop feeding her Blocker Demon, which had grown strong from her sadness and withdrawal after Troy had moved out. Her blocking program was much weaker now that she was refusing it by exercising and resuming the activities that she enjoyed. One thing she had always loved was to meet her good friends for dinner. Once she got to the restaurant and triumphed over her BD, sharing a delicious meal with her friends was supposed to be a well-deserved reward. What went wrong? Why was she now plagued with self-critical thoughts and uneasy feelings?

> Our Negator Demon orients us to focus on the negative aspects of ourselves and our lives.

Gloria's experience was all too familiar; I'd witnessed this pattern again and again. As we reviewed her upsetting dinner, covert demon maneuvers became clear. While her attention was focused on triumphing over her Blocker by going out socially, her Negator Demon (ND) attacked. The second of the four Soldier Demons, its directive is to orient us to focus on negative aspects of ourselves.

Gloria's ND struck in classic Sniper fashion, when she least expected it. She assumed that she would enjoy her victory, after arriving at the restaurant to see her friends. Instead, her negating program spoiled her outing by steering her to worry about her social skills, her appearance, and what others thought of her. This is one way that the Negator operates, making us miserable even when we successfully deny our Blocker and engage in beneficial activities. Gloria's ND fed off her anxiety, self-consciousness, and self-blame, in turn nourishing her Master Demon of defectiveness.

## Name Your Negator

Telltale signs that you have a Negator Demon include the following:

- You worry often about one or more areas of your life.
- It's difficult to relax and enjoy activities because you frequently feel anxious and afraid that you'll do something wrong.
- You're habitually nervous and self-conscious when you're with other people because you worry that you might make a social blunder.
- When you're successful, you don't praise or reward yourself very much.
- Making decisions takes a long time because you're constantly second-guessing yourself.
- It's easy to find fault with yourself.
- It's hard to forgive yourself.

A unifying clue to spot your ND is any time that you're focused on negatives about yourself and your life and you feel anxious and fearful as a result. Beware that your negating agent may operate beneath your radar. Research reveals that negative self-thinking can become a mental habit; occurring often, unintentionally, and automatically.[1] To reveal an otherwise undetectable Negator, ask your family and friends for feedback. Do they see you continually complain about yourself? Are they noticing that you talk mostly about your mistakes? Do they become frustrated after they point out your positive qualities and hear you counter with "yes but"? Are they drained by your constant need for reassurance?

Discovering that you have a Negator may be unpleasant. Gloria was frustrated to learn of her negating force, especially after she'd worked so hard to starve her blocking agent. However, once we identified it, we could uncover its tactics and devise a plan to refuse it. Fortunately, she could apply the same four steps to defy her Negator Demon that she was already using effectively to shrink her Blocker Demon. These steps, first presented in Chapter 1, are essential to starving all four Soldier Demons: 1) stay alert to potential ND attacks, 2) identify your ND when it strikes, 3) refuse your ND with your positive thoughts and actions, and 4) celebrate your triumph with a self-enhancing reward.

Upon review of her attack, it was clear that Gloria was vulnerable to her ND in social situations. Her confidence was shaky because she hadn't been out with others very much while in her relationship with Troy. By repeatedly declining her friends' invitations, she was out of practice when it came to socializing.

## Strengthen Skills to Disarm Your Negator

A key way to disarm your Negator is to strengthen the abilities that you feel anxious about and that are important to you. As your skills improve, your confidence grows and you'll be protected from your ND's criticisms in those areas. To Gloria, social skills mattered a lot. To improve these skills, rebuild her social assurance, and thwart future Negator attacks, we role-played during therapy, as if she were out talking with her friends. Research confirms the effectiveness of role-playing and rehearsing social interactions in improving social skills and reducing anxiety.[2]

As Gloria did, you can role-play with a confidant. For ideas about things to say, browse your newspaper or Internet for information about current events, movies, sports, etc. Review your experiences and select one or two to mention, perhaps something unexpected, unusual, or amusing. Assess what you know about who you'll be seeing and tailor questions to ask them. You'll easily facilitate conversations this way because others will appreciate your interest and enjoy sharing information about their lives. To prepare for outings, write down and review your questions. For additional practice before going out, talk with someone on the phone. The act of preparing and rehearsing also reduces the worry of your mind going blank.

During our role-play, Gloria shared her thoughts about a movie she recently saw and her initial steps to train for her first marathon. Because a friend she was planning to see had recently returned from a trip to Europe, Gloria practiced asking questions about her travels. She agreed to phone two friends, to gain additional experience and confidence socially before going out again. She used to love talking on the phone, but she had stopped calling her friends when she was living with Troy. For additional preparation, she wrote down her questions to review. As expected, Gloria's ND struck the next time she went out: "You don't know what to say, you're boring." However, this time it was easier for her to dismiss its criticisms because she'd prepared questions, personal experiences, and an interesting news story to discuss.

### Examine Negator Criticisms for Veracity

To tailor a plan to starve your ND, examine its derogatory messages. At times, they'll contain some truth, such as the put-downs of Gloria's social abilities. If so, remember to pause and ask yourself, *"Is this skill (quality) important to me"?* In my experience, Negators usually target areas that matter a great deal to us, which is why their barbs are so effective. In these cases, like Gloria, deny your Negator by improving changeable attributes. If, on the other hand, the skill or quality is not significant to you, take steps to disregard your Negator: name it, separate yourself from it, and shift your focus to another activity or thought. For example, you can tell it, *"I see what you're up to Negator. You are not me. Your judgment doesn't hurt because it's not important to me. I'm not feeding you with anxiety; I'm busy having dinner with my friends."*

### Enlist Your Reprogramming Record

Often, your Negator's critiques will be unfounded. Because it can seem convincing, it may be hard to know what's true or not. When in doubt, ask family, friends, or others you trust whether they see evidence to support the criticisms. Sometimes no one will be available or you're not convinced the person will be honest or objective. Whatever the case, your Reprogramming Record is an invaluable ally. By habitually writing entries, you'll amass evidence you can review to ensure that your negating force doesn't get away with unfounded disparaging attacks. If you don't have examples pertaining to what your Negator says, focus on that area in future RR entries.

Although Gloria was already writing in her RR when her Negator attacked, her positive entries were mostly about refusing her Blocker. When her negating program said, "People don't even notice you, you look ugly, no guy here wants to date you," she was hit hard. Her attractiveness to others, especially men, mattered a lot to her, and she feared these denigrations were true. There was no countering evidence in her RR and she didn't trust her family or friends to give unbiased feedback. To discover whether the negating messages had any merit, I asked Gloria to add an entry whenever she received favorable feedback about her attractiveness, such as verbal compliments, smiles, hellos, or looks from men. Examples could be current or recent ones. She also agreed to record when she engaged in efforts to enhance her appeal.

Research reveals that when people are first presented with positive information and then given both positive and negative information, their bias toward attending to the negative information is lessened or eliminated.[3] By directing Gloria to record self-affirming incidents, we engaged this corrective phenomenon daily to help strengthen her focus on self-enhancing evidence and away from her negating force. To her surprise, once she started monitoring for evidence of her desirability, she found examples to write in her RR. The more entries that Gloria

**Table 3.1**

| Negator Trigger | Ways to Exorcize Your *Skill-Focused* Negator |
|---|---|
| When you feel anxious about a particular ability. | 1. Examine your ND's specific criticisms for veracity.<br>2. For invalid critiques and valid but insignificant critiques, name and separate from your negating program and shift your focus to something else.<br>3. For put-downs with merit, strengthen the criticized skills that you deem important and feel anxious about.<br>4. Write and review Reprogramming Record entries specifically tailored to deflate your Negator. |

accumulated and reviewed, the more easily she could refuse her negating agent when it told her she was unattractive:

*Thursday, 9/6:* When I was at the market today, a cute guy smiled at me. I nodded and smiled back. <u>I am desirable and responsive to interesting men.</u>

*Friday, 9/7:* When I was at a club with Troy last summer, someone I didn't know asked me to dance when Troy left our table. <u>Different men find me appealing.</u>

*Saturday, 9/8:* Today, during my running group, my new friend Tamika said I looked great and asked if I had lost weight. <u>By training for the marathon, I'm improving my health, shedding extra pounds, and getting my figure back.</u>

### Refuse the Negator's Shifting Tactics

*Within the Same Domain*   As you get better at denying your Negator's put-downs in one aspect of your life, it grows hungry—because you're not feeding it with anxiety or fear. To generate more "food," it swings around and attacks you from behind—by criticizing something else personal. Every time your mind shifts to a different negative focus, you have to reengage efforts to refuse your ND. Left unchecked, these Sniper assaults keep you constantly bombarded by undercutting messages, focusing your attention away from the positive things you're doing. Every time you respond with worry and anxiety, you're nourishing your Negator and your Master Demon of inadequacy. You miss the chance to review your progress, give yourself credit, and celebrate your triumphs.

I observe these attacks all the time in my office. Jim came to his session with good news. He'd followed the steps we talked about and asserted his needs with his ex-wife Debbie. He asked her to stop calling him multiple times to check on things on the days he cared for their seven-year-old son Scott. He told her the calls disrupted the limited (20%) time he had with Scott and requested that she call only if there was a schedule change or true emergency.

Although Debbie was initially upset, they negotiated a compromise: Scott would call her once every night after dinner. This was a major triumph for Jim. Throughout his marriage and divorce, he had had difficulty voicing his concerns; instead, he would let things go to avoid a confrontation. As I congratulated him on his success, he looked away, sighed, and said, "If only I could speak up to my supervisor like that." Without pause, he described times when he had remained silent as his manager, Craig, took advantage of his productivity by giving him more responsibilities but no increase in pay or support staff.

Jim looked up in surprise when I informed him that his Negator had just attacked. It operated in one of two common ways, shifting his focus from a success to a failure experience in the same domain. In Jim's case, the domain was assertiveness. He'd barely acknowledged speaking up to his ex-wife when his negating program steered him to think about times when he wasn't assertive with his supervisor. By quickly shifting from his achievement to another failure to assert himself, he lost the opportunity to feel proud and enjoy his pivotal accomplishment.

I assured Jim that expressing his concerns with Craig was important and we would focus on that goal. However, to record evidence of his progress, I first asked him to write in his RR about his assertiveness with Debbie. Like many clients I see, he'd forgotten to add this major triumph to his daily entries. To help resist his Negator in the future, he also agreed to document this attack in his DDD. I asked him to bring both journals to the next session so that we could review them. Plus, he deserved to celebrate his victory with something special that week just for him. He decided on a vanilla latte, a pleasure he'd been passing up since tightening his monthly budget.

Jim's Reprogramming Record:

*Saturday, 8/11:* I asked Debbie to stop calling so much on days I have Scott. We agreed to a compromise that Scott will call her once a day after dinner. I'm able to assert my needs and negotiate important issues for me and my son.

Jim's Demon Disrupting Diary:

*August 13:* During therapy, I'd just brought up how assertive I was with Debbie when my Negator Demon attacked. It turned my attention away from my success to times when I didn't stand up for myself with Craig. I got caught up in my failure at work and didn't realize it until afterward. Next time I reach a goal, I'll stay alert in case my ND strikes. If it does, I'll refuse it and stay focused on my success.

**Table 3.2**

Our Negator commonly attacks by these means:

1. Shifting our focus from a success to a failure experience in the same domain.
2. Shifting our focus from a triumph in one domain to a defeat in a completely different domain.

*Between Different Domains*    The second common way the Negator Demon operates is to shift your focus from a triumph in one realm to a defeat in a completely different area. This happened to my client Diane, as we reviewed letters attesting to her success as a teacher and administrator. As a reprogramming assignment to shrink her negating force, which had habitually belittled her about her career in education, I asked her to bring this evidence, which she'd saved over the years. I was immediately impressed as I flipped through the many glowing evaluations and thank-you letters from principals, teachers, and parents. As I read various praises out loud, Diane smiled and nodded, adding details about her experiences with each person. She even brought a photograph of herself, the teachers, and the students from a special assembly honoring her as the outstanding administrator that year.

Before I could hand the letters back to Diane her face changed from a smile to a frown. She began describing her strained relationship with her adult son, Kevin, and how distressed she felt about it. She reviewed her failings as a parent when Kevin was small, elaborating on her troubled marriage and prescription drug abuse. In the blink of an eye, Diane's Negator Demon had shifted her attention from her career success to her parenting failure.

Assaults such as these can be formidable, even when the failures that they orient us to are years past or no longer true. In Diane's case, we'd talked often about her parenting mistakes and regrets. Many years ago, she'd ended her unhappy marriage and her substance abuse. Her efforts in recent years to engage Kevin and make up for past emotional neglect were already having a positive effect. Diane saw none of this. She was too blindsided by her ND to notice this contradicting evidence.

## Tune Out Your Negator

The fastest way to recover from these attacks is to catch your negating demon in the act and restore your original focus. Any time that your attention abruptly shifts from success to failure experiences, recognize this as a signal that you're under assault. Ask trusted others to do the same, to marshal a unified front to expel your ND. After returning to your original positive self-focus, on your time frame and not your Negator's, address the self-negative experiences if you wish. You'll be in a strong position to examine and learn from your mistakes because you'll be fortified from reinforcing your triumphs. Research shows that by focusing on self-positives before you face a threat to your self-esteem, you won't react so negatively after you're threatened.[4]

---

> Whenever your focus quickly shifts from success to failure experiences, use this as a signal that your Negator is attacking.

---

Our negating programs do not yield easily. Once interrupted, they quickly resume their undercutting messages. My clients often report this happening, especially when they're beginning to spot and disrupt their NDs. If you're feeling so anxious that it's hard to refocus on affirming reflections, listen to calming music. By tuning into soothing sounds, you'll ignore the critical chatter. As your body relaxes, your mind will too, and it'll be easier to steer it back to favorable thoughts again.

Numerous research studies support the anxiety-reducing benefits of music, especially if the music is self-selected or classical.[5] Prepare for times you need it by arranging restful music to be readily available wherever you are. Select songs in advance that you find relaxing, even if other people do not. Keep your music selection at home and in portable players so that you can listen anytime and anyplace. Preset car and home radio stations so you can hear peaceful music at the touch of a button.

Sometimes you'll find yourself in places or situations with no music available. If you're alone or won't disturb others, generate your own by singing or humming. If you've identified specific criticisms that your negating program repeats, fashion songs that counter its destructive messages.

My client Renee discovered through her Demon Disruptive Diary entries that her negating demon beat her up every morning while she was taking her shower to prepare for work. It primarily targeted her abilities at the office, which included coordinating and administering group projects. For example, it told her, "You're not organized, you're not prepared for today, you'll make a fool of yourself, something will go wrong and you won't know what to do, no one will want to help you."

Renee could've turned on the radio to her favorite restful station, but she didn't want to wake up her husband, who slept an hour later than her. Instead, to ignore her negating bully, she created her own soothing songs to replace the work criticisms and sang them softly in the shower. She improvised lyrics from her reprogramming record entries and affirmations that she jotted down in our sessions. She used melodies from pleasant songs she knew by heart, for instance, *"I'm calm, I'm really calm, today is a great day. I'm organized and ready; when things go wrong, I remain steady. I solve problems with ease; I ask for help whenever I need. People come to my aid; I've got it made. I'm calm, I'm really calm, today is a great day."*

To keep her mind actively engaged and focused away from her Negator, Renee frequently changed the words and tunes. Some mornings, she forgot to sing and

**Table 3.3**

| Negator Trigger | Ways to Exorcize Your *Recurring* Negator |
| --- | --- |
| Your Negator quickly resumes after you've interrupted it. | 1. Shift your focus back to self-affirming thoughts.<br>2. If your ND persists, listen to calming music and then resume step 1. Make this music available wherever you go.<br>3. When music isn't accessible, sing or hum; replace your ND's criticisms with self-enhancing lyrics.<br>4. Beware and refuse it if your negating agent steers you to select anxiety-provoking songs. |

she noticed that her negating demon was more active that day. To reclaim her power, I encouraged her to recognize and use its criticisms as a cue to start singing. When she felt too tired to sing, she hummed instead, reviewing her lyrics silently or just focusing on her calming tones.

As you're preparing to tune out your Negator Demon, beware—it can still prevail by steering you to select anxiety-provoking songs. This happened to my client Elizabeth, who thought she was nurturing herself by preparing a soothing bubble bath with soft music and scented candles. She didn't notice when her ND influenced her to select an upsetting CD. On its face, the songs appeared soothing. Without knowing, Elizabeth became a sitting duck when she sank into the warm water and closed her eyes.

Only later, after the water turned cold and the candles burned down, did she realize how frozen and tensed up she'd become. Her boyfriend Ron had given her that CD, the boyfriend she'd finally left after years of verbal abuse. Listening to those songs brought back memories of her stressful relationship and Ron's constant criticisms, turning her relaxing bath into a distressing immersion.

### Build a Repertoire of Negator Disrupters

There are many ways in addition to music to interrupt your Negator Demon and give your mind the freedom and peace it deserves. What works for you may be completely different from what someone else prefers. For best results, choose activities that strongly focus your attention; this derails your ND's destructive, disparaging blather. Popular choices for my clients include meditation, visualization, self-hypnosis, and breathing exercises. These practices are well documented as useful anxiety reducers.[6]

> For optimal results, choose ND disrupters that intensely focus your attention.

Many favor options combining physical movement such as gardening, golf, yoga, knitting, etc. Use disrupters simply to gain reprieve from your Negator or to seize control by actively replacing its criticisms with your affirming messages. Here again, your Reprogramming Record provides you with a rich source of self-enhancing statements to use. If you have a hard time generating RR entries, ask a supportive confidant to help you come up with daily positive examples to write about yourself. Seek assistance also when writing in your DDD at times when you can't figure out what to say or do to resist your Negator and other Soldier Demons. Your demons thrive by dividing (isolating you from resources) and conquering. By engaging help when you're stuck, you instantly puncture and step out of their sphere of control.

---

If you have difficulty generating RR and DDD entries, ask a confidant for help.

---

Katie's Reprogramming Record Entries:

*Monday, 9/24:* I got up at 5:15 and finished the laundry. I changed the sheets and had breakfast before work. <u>I am organized and take good care of myself.</u>

*Tuesday, 9/25:* I woke up early to reflect and plan. <u>I make time for myself.</u>

*Wednesday, 9/26:* I set up and delivered training manuals to staff in building 255. I got a loading permit so I could park close to unload the boxes. My years of experience make it easy to plan ahead for tasks. <u>I am organized and efficient.</u>

*Thursday, 9/27:* I made a healthy lunch to bring to work. <u>I take care of my body.</u>

*Friday, 9/28:* I sent out emails for price quotes for new equipment. <u>I get tasks done in a timely manner. I do not procrastinate.</u>

If you're beset with a Blocker Demon, beware of its attempts to stop you from implementing these strategies. To defeat it, go back to the steps we discussed in Chapter 2. Know that your Blocker's directive is always to keep you from doing positive things for yourself. It will seize any opportunity to shut you down.

---

Block your Blocker

---

Greg's negating force activated often when he was home, at his studio, meeting with friends, running errands, relaxing on the weekends, etc. It said things such as "You're no good at this (whatever he was doing)," "What's wrong with you?"

"You'll never remember this," "You shouldn't have said that," "Why couldn't you do this right the first time?" "Your work isn't any good," "You're too short," "You're a failure," and so on.

Upon reviewing his background, it was clear that Greg's father had primarily installed his ND by alternating between criticizing and ignoring him when he was growing up. Greg had identified and addressed these hurtful experiences previously, but he was still plagued by worries and anxiety and his Master Demon belief that he was defective. When we talked, he understood intellectually that the constant disapproval he experienced was not about him—it came from his father's programming that was passed on to him. However, Greg's Negator Demon was deeply entrenched after operating for decades, generating the same negative emotions he felt as a child.

Because Greg's ND activated at many times, places, and situations, we created disrupters he could use anywhere quickly, plus others for when he had privacy and time to employ them fully. After experimenting with different options, he used the ones that were most helpful as often as possible. You can do the same by trying Greg's strategies and/or letting them stimulate you to create your own.

*Short Disrupters*   Greg's first step was to identify his Negator as soon as possible when it belittled him. Then, for rapid relief, he practiced saying "stop" out loud or to himself while picturing a red stop sign in his mind. To punctuate his command, when he had privacy, he pushed his right hand straight out in front of him, signaling stop with his open palm. When in public, he clenched one or both hands and then released them.

For another quick fix, Greg took one deep breath while imagining a beach in Hawaii he remembered from his favorite calming vacation. When at his home or studio, where he'd displayed photos of that beach, he didn't have to imagine this scene. If time permitted, he continued slow deep breaths, counting each inhale and exhale as one, up to five or more. He either focused on the Hawaii beach scene or turned his attention inward to his breath.

When Greg had more time, his favorite deactivator was his mental shooting gallery, modeled after the game you play in amusement parks. Each Negator criticism that surfaced became his target, and he visualized shooting them down one by one. He had to be fast on the draw because the denigrations often popped up rapidly one after the other.

With any option, for additional reinforcement, he sometimes said out loud or silently statements such as *"Get away from me Negator Demon, get out of here right now, I am separate from you, you're losing, you're history."* When time permitted, he replaced the ND's injurious messages with a vitalizing affirmation or two, saying them vocally or to himself; for example, he told himself, *"I'm willing to try new methods to achieve success," "It's okay to make mistakes," "I forgive myself and use what I learn in the future," "I'm dedicated and hard working," "I stay in good shape," "I'm living up to my potential because I'm doing my best."*

*Longer Disrupters*   Greg also wrote in his RR and DDD. Because he had a habit of misplacing things, he chose to combine both journals in one. To keep them separate, he had found a spiral bound notebook that was partitioned in two by a central cardboard divider. He carried his RR/DDD with him so that he could write entries at his discretion at various times and places. Because his Negator Demon attacked the most, much of his writing focused on replacing its put-downs and examining its attacks to learn and reinforce ways to expel it. Many psychotherapies include writing as an integral component of their treatment protocols. Both researchers and clinicians acknowledge the therapeutic benefits that writing provides.[7]

---

Use your RR and DDD to deflate your Negator.

---

Greg's Reprogramming Record:

*Wednesday, 6/27:* Although I was upset on Monday, I was able to recover my inner strength. <u>I can take control of my life. The more self work I do, the more I am able to deal with my problems.</u>

*Thursday, 6/28:* I worked in my studio today for approximately eight hours. <u>Spending this kind of time on photography shows my dedication to my goals.</u>

*Friday, 6/29:* I took Friday off from working in the studio, to give myself a break and charge up for the rest of my time off. <u>I can take breaks when I need them. My interests extend beyond working by myself.</u>

*Saturday, 6/30:* I stopped by to have lunch with my Mom. <u>I am thoughtful and interested in others. Relationships are important to me.</u>

*Sunday, 7/1:* I took a bike ride to alleviate stress. <u>I honor my health when I exercise.</u>

Greg's Demon Disrupting Diary:

*Monday, 7/2:* One of my old instructors stopped by this morning to pick up some equipment for a photo shoot he is working on. As we talked, my Negator Demon struck: "You're unintelligent." I felt very foolish, thinking I was unable to hold a conversation with him. After he left, I realized my ND had attacked. I know I wasn't thinking clearly, because it was early in the morning and I wasn't fully awake yet. By the end of our conversation, I was more able to speak than in the beginning. I am intelligent and articulate.

When Greg had five minutes or longer, he disrupted his Negator with meditation. He closed his eyes, slowed his breathing, and focused on each inhale and exhale. Every time his ND tried to distract him, he directed his attention back to his breath. When possible, he meditated for 15 minutes in the morning and again before bed.

For a mental and physical ND buster, Greg scheduled monthly massages. The salon he went to allowed him to play his own music during his sessions. Listening to the relaxing sounds while feeling his muscles kneaded gave him a pleasurable break from his negating program. Later, when he played this music in other situations, he received the additional benefit of having those sounds associated with pleasurable massage.

During times of extreme stress, Greg increased massages to every week. When time and weather permitted, he golfed at a course within easy driving distance from his home. The intense concentration he achieved with each stroke warded off his ND. He found the sun, fresh air, and rolling greens to be both restful and energizing.

Some weeks, Greg incorporated many of these disrupters; other times, he performed just one or two of them. He suffered some bad periods when his Blocker Demon shut him down. However, his Negator disrupters always remained available, and Greg found it easier to reengage them every time he recovered. He also gained experience in forgiving himself, reviewing his slips, and applying what he learned in the future.

## Experiment with Disrupters

Greg's choices are just a few of the many ways to interrupt your Negator. What works for you is limited only by your ingenuity. Experiment to find the best ways to zone out your negating demon and get the peace of mind you deserve. More options that my clients use are labyrinth walking, surfing, needlepoint, crossword puzzles, watercolor painting, throwing pottery, watching sports, listening to meditation CDs, woodworking, scrapbooking, beading, etc.

Raquel swims year-round at her indoor community pool. She goes during adult lap swim hours because it's less crowded then and most of the pool is roped off for swim lanes. As a result of her advance planning, she almost always gets a lane all to herself. For her, swimming is the best way to meditate. Her rhythmic strokes drown out her Negator and the smooth water is soothing to her body as she glides through it. With each lap, more of her ND's criticisms are washed away.

When Raquel emerges, she feels physically fortified and cleansed of emotional toxins. Her ideal is to swim twice a week, but she often falls short of her goal because of many factors, including her blocking program. However, when she does go, Raquel experiences the benefits that remind and reinforce her to keep coming back. For a substitute meditation until returning to the pool, she mentally transports herself there by closing her eyes and replaying her swim. She remembers the clear blue water, its smooth texture on her skin, and the peaceful sound of the waves lapping against her as she propels through the water.

*Group Disrupters*   If you like being with others, schedule group Negator disrupters. Many clients tell me they like practicing calming strategies with like-minded people. They find it easier to follow through when they know that someone else is there doing the same thing. Just as when you are battling your Blocker, the social support you'll receive will empower you to refuse your Negator.[8]

To learn what's available in your area, ask family, friends, and colleagues. Peruse offerings in local newspapers and community-based Web sites. Do an Internet Google search by typing in the name of an activity that you're interested in and your city or neighborhood name.

Many of my clients prefer taking classes in yoga, meditation, craft, music, and dance. Some join informal walking, prayer, golf, or music groups. A few sign up for weekend meditation retreats and group health spa bus trips. Diane drives 50 miles to her monthly Saturday group meditation class. She looks forward to these breaks from her routine, where she has time to herself on the road. On her way back, she feels relaxed and peaceful after the lecture and shared meditation. For her, these benefits are well worth the long drive.

> For social connection and support, join live and/or virtual group ND busters.

If you like connecting with others but don't want to travel, consider virtual groups. All you need is Internet access. To find a group, use a search engine (e.g., Google) and type in your interest(s). You might be surprised at what develops. My client Marcia joined an online anxiety support group. She worried and felt anxious often because of her Negator Demon. Whenever she drove to a group social event, her Negator jabbed at her with critical commentary: "You're a terrible driver," "You'll get lost," "You won't make it on time," "You'll have nothing in common with the people there," "You look tired," "You're not wearing the right clothes," "Your hair looks awful," and so on.

Commiserating with others from the comfort of her bedroom was a welcome relief from Marcia's ND, especially when her Internet companions were similarly beset with negating agents. Every day, she looked forward to turning on her computer to chat with her new friends. To her surprise, she learned that two of the women lived nearby. They all got along so well that they decided to meet in person. One group outing led to another, and eventually they were meeting in different places every couple of weeks. What had started as a virtual connection turned into a neighborhood group. The best thing was that Marcia and her friends' NDs shrank as they replaced criticisms with mutual encouragement and support while exploring their surroundings together.

**Table 3.4**

Build a Repertoire of Negator Disrupters
1. For optimal results, choose disrupters that strongly engage your focus.
2. Use disrupters simply to gain reprieve from your ND or to facilitate replacing its criticisms with your self-affirming messages.
3. Test various Negator disrupters (i.e., mental, physical, short, long, group) to create your personal collection.

### Stop Debilitating Negator Comparisons

Especially when participating in groups, watch out for a specific Negator maneuver: directing you to compare yourself negatively to fellow members. You'll know your ND is operating if you frequently worry and feel anxious that you are less worthy than others in the group. Fortunately, Marcia didn't experience this very much when she was with her neighborhood friends.

However, my other client Lea did. She chose yoga as one of her Negator disrupters and found a nearby studio that offered introductory classes at times she could go. As soon as she arrived, her negating bully started in: "Look at the other women here: you're so much older and fatter and uglier than them." As class proceeded, the instructor advised, "Go at your own pace. Yoga is not a competitive sport. Do not watch your neighbor; focus instead on a spot on the wall or the floor." No matter, Lea's ND steered her to look at every woman as the class moved through the poses, saying, "See how flexible they are? You can't even touch your toes. They're so graceful; you look like a fool. The instructor isn't coming over to help you. She thinks you're a failure too."

If you experience this kind of Negator attack, as always, the sooner you spot it, the quicker you can refuse it. Refocus on what you're doing and, for added effect, substitute affirming statements. Identify and implement actions that prove your ND wrong. For outside support and encouragement, share what happened with someone who is caring and nurturing.

Lea knew she enjoyed yoga from taking classes years ago. Her body was never very flexible, but she remembered how good she felt after each class. She also recalled how the poses became easier the more she practiced them. Because of our work together, Lea was well aware of her Master and Soldier Demons when she showed up at the new yoga studio. Soon after her Negator had activated, she spotted its derogatory barbs. To face her fear and call its bluff, she went up to her instructor after class to introduce herself. Contrary to what her ND would have her believe, her instructor was complimentary and encouraging. Lea had effectively punctured her negating program. She felt an immediate reward of a great weight lifting, as she put her shoes back on and walked out of the studio.

As Lea shared her triumph in my office, we discussed what else she could do to deactivate her negating agent. To thwart its effort to pit her competitively against her classmates, she set a goal to smile and say something to at least one person in every class. She resolved to buy attractive yoga outfits to enhance her appearance and confidence in class. To relearn poses at a comfortable pace, she decided to stay with beginner classes for awhile. She opted to skip the back bends to protect her vulnerable spine. To maximize yoga's calming benefits, she committed to keep going back. As Lea took each self-enhancing step, she threw off her negating demon. It had no choice but to shrink, because she refused to take it seriously.

Sometimes a disrupter will backfire and make you more vulnerable to your ND because you really dislike performing it. If so, switch to something else you like to do. Before replacing disrupters, make sure the original activity is actually a poor fit for you and not just that your negating and blocking agents are behind your decision. If you keep changing disrupters and you're still not satisfied, your demons are likely at work. In this case, stop and spotlight the demons. Write what happened in your DDD, and use what you learn to tailor steps to shrink your Negator and/or Blocker Demon.

---

Marissa's DDD Entry:
*July 11:* I arrived at the time-share and felt like I didn't belong and I was not good enough to be there. The accommodations were very luxurious. I started to cry as I felt overwhelmed by how nice the place was. My Negator Demon was at work making me feel like I did not belong or I was not good enough to be staying at this place and my time-share neighbors would soon see this. I cried and then reevaluated the fact that I paid for this time-share and, due to my planning and vision, I was able to have this time-share and be the owner. *No one* gave it to me for free. I had to work hard to buy this for me and my family.

---

**Foil Disrupting Negators**

As Lea experienced, even when engaging calming disrupters that you enjoy, your ND can spoil your peaceful activity by catching you off guard and surreptitiously focusing your mind on worries and self-doubts. Although Lea didn't do it, I'd advise you to use your Demon Disrupting Diary to identify details and tailor strategies to resist these ND assaults in the future. Here's an example from my client Diane's DDD:

*10/3:* As I began meditating and quieting my mind this evening, my demons, especially Mr. Negator, intruded. He said, "You are so unattractive that no one will ever want you." I immediately said, "Get out of my meditation. I'm not putting up with your message. It isn't true." I stopped the meditation and put Mr. Negator in his place- this DD. Diary. Now that he's been relegated to silence, I'm closing this book on him and going back to do a peaceful meditation. He receives no attention in my R Record.

Like my other client Heather, you may not catch your Negator right away. She relished her time in the garden, alone and free from responsibilities to her husband, children, and co-workers. She found the repetitive movements of planting, watering, and weeding to be calming and meditative. The sun, breeze, and earth felt good on her skin. One day, after losing track of the time, she looked up from weeding to survey her garden. In that instant, her Negator Demon attacked, "You think you're making progress on the garden, but now you see how much there really is to do. See, you've indulged yourself in the garden too much and now you don't have time to make a healthy dinner for the kids."

Heather felt overwhelmed and anxious about the garden work that remained as she rushed inside to attend to dinner. Although her children and husband were happy to have pizza delivered, Heather beat herself up for not preparing a home-cooked meal. She felt like a failure as a gardener and mother, feeding her Negator and her Master Demon of defectiveness.

Later that night, as Heather ruminated about what had happened, she realized that her Negator had spoiled her peaceful gardening experience. She remembered from our sessions how negating programs can activate at any time, even when we think we're successfully disrupting them. She pulled out her DDD and wrote in it. By examining what her ND had said, she was able to separate herself from it, challenge it, and stop feeding it. Heather reasoned that, although it takes a while to weed the whole garden, she can get a little bit done each time, relax, and give herself credit for her progress. At the end of her DDD entry, she summarized what she had learned about refusing her ND in the future: *"Stop. I'm human. Step by step, enjoy what you've done, and enjoy relaxation."*

## Table 3.5

| Negator Trigger | Ways to Exorcize Your *Comparing* Negator |
|---|---|
| When you worry and feel anxious about being less worthy than others. | 1. Stay alert, to catch your ND quickly and to refocus on what you're doing; for added effect, substitute affirming statements.<br>2. Identify and take actions that prove your ND wrong.<br>3. To invalidate your ND further, garner additional support by sharing what happened with someone who is caring.<br>4. Spot and thwart demon attempts to switch and ruin your disrupters; enlist your DDD to aid in your efforts. |

## Three Common Negator Triggers

In working with clients, I've identified three common situations that render us highly vulnerable to our Negator: 1) interacting with those who installed our negating programs, 2) receiving negative feedback, and 3) facing new uncertain experiences. Everyone I know, myself included, encounters these circumstances. Sometimes two or all three occur at the same time.

### Interacting with Negator Installers

The most challenging trigger that I have discovered in my practice happens when clients have contact with their Negator installers. This often occurs around holidays when visiting their families. Typically, their primary ND installers are one or both caregivers, whose demons are still thriving. Sometimes siblings or other relatives are additional ND programmers. The families spend concentrated time together, and old critical interactions resume, which activate clients' negating programs. Even when they've worked hard, made significant progress, and are well aware of the high risk, clients fall prey to their NDs when reactivated in this way.

The more you prepare for this trigger, the easier it will be to resist it or minimize its damage. First, remember how difficult this situation is. Always practice kindness and self-forgiveness when your ND gets the best of you. Identify self-protective strategies to implement during family visits. Ask for help and support from trusted others. If possible, identify one person who plans to be there whom you can confide in and receive validation from during your stay.

Amy's Negator activated before every family visit back east. As soon as she started planning her trip, it began replaying her mother's criticisms from long ago, some of which she hadn't thought of in years. As the memories repeated, Amy's anxiety grew, fueling her negating demon. Although her father had passed away years ago, her mother still lived in the home where Amy grew up. Amy was the only one who'd left; her brother, sister, and their families lived nearby. Even many of her high school friends had stayed in the area.

Whenever Amy went back to the old house, her anxiety surged, as she vividly recalled her parents' arguments and her mother's critiques. Her brother and sister were much older, leaving Amy, as the only child at home, to experience this during her formative years. Her father was powerful, but Amy's ND was created primarily from her mother's disapproval. She'd aged over the years and become less forceful, but her mother still scrutinized Amy in every visit. Amy's Negator thrived on her anxiety and self-consciousness, as she reacted to the current and past judgmental remarks. When her brother and sister arrived, they became critical too, until eventually everyone was relating in old negative ways.

Before her trips, Amy hoped things would be different. Although she hated the put-downs, she still loved her family and yearned for their approval. She always resolved to remain calm, confident, and positive. By the end, she felt strung-out, self-conscious, and worthless. On flights home, her Negator and Master Demon flourished, as she beat herself up again for feeling so anxious and diminished by her family's critical ways.

I'd been meeting with Amy for a while when she shared anxiety about her upcoming family visit for the Christmas holiday. By now, she knew that spending time at home with her mother and siblings was a major Negator trigger. She wasn't very close to her brother or sister, so she didn't feel comfortable confiding in them. Years ago, she tried more than once to talk with her mother about the hurtful experiences. Her mother disagreed that she was critical and told Amy that she became upset too easily over little things.

Because her mother was not likely to change, Amy's best approach was to protect herself as much as possible during her stay. Although Amy's husband and children would be there too, their presence alone was not enough of a shield. After discussing various strategies, here's what she did.

A primary factor that made Amy vulnerable to her Negator was spending constant time with her mother in the house. To reduce this hazard, she shortened the trip from seven to five days. For breaks, whenever needed, she rented a car. Although her mother's car was accessible and the rental was not cheap, knowing that she could easily drive away at any time was worth it to Amy. For privacy in the house, she and her husband stayed in a room to which they could retreat and lock the door. In bed before sleep, she wrote in her Reprogramming Record and Demon Disrupting Diary, safe from her mother walking in unannounced. Although she slipped up and didn't write every night, the entries that she completed reinforced and complemented her new approaches.

For scheduled breaks, Amy called two high school friends before her trip in order to set up a visit and then drove to meet them as prearranged. She planned an outing with her husband and children and invited the extended family to come. Although her mother went too, being out of the house and focused on the new activity helped diffuse her mother's negativity, which had been fueling Amy's Negator.

During this excursion and at other times that Amy spent with her mother, she visualized a violet bubble that surrounded and protected her from her mother's hurtful comments. She practiced responding with humor to deflect the criticisms further. Amy and her husband agreed in advance to take daily walks outside for exercise, fresh air, and sun. She used this time to vent her frustration about her mother's and siblings' negative comments. Her husband, who witnessed these interactions, validated her feelings and offered his support. They were not used to the cold weather but always felt better after taking these outside breaks.

When Amy came back to my office after her trip, she was pleased to report that she'd followed her plan. On her return, she felt better emotionally and resumed healthy routines sooner compared to previous visits. However, she was

**Table 3.6**

| Negator Trigger | Ways to Exorcize Your *"Blast to the Past"* Negator |
|---|---|
| Interacting with Negator installers. | 1. Identify self-protective strategies to implement during visits.<br>2. Ask for help and support; identify one witness and confidant with whom you can vent and receive validation.<br>3. Remember how hard this is; practice self-forgiveness when your negating program gets the best of you. |

disappointed that she still felt somewhat anxious around her mother. I reminded her how young she was when her Negator had formed and how long it had been operating on her. Being in the same environment with her primary installer was bound to trigger it.

Amy also encountered a second trigger during her visit: her mother's continued negative feedback to her. I encouraged Amy to recognize that feeling calmer and recovering faster, compared to earlier trips, represented a major success. Repeating these protective steps in future visits will continue to weaken her ND and strengthen her peace and self-confidence. However, spending time with her mother remains her oldest and most formidable trigger. She deserves to be kind and self-forgiving whenever her Negator gets to her, especially when she's most vulnerable, visiting her mother.

### Receiving Negative Feedback

The second major Negator trigger occurs when we receive criticism. Sometimes, as Amy experienced, the put-downs come directly from our ND installers. However, as adults, we typically spend most of our time with others: spouses, children, supervisors, co-workers, employees, friends, and neighbors. When my clients receive negative feedback, it typically comes from these individuals with whom they interact frequently. The critiques are often mixed together with positive feedback. However, my clients' Negators steer them to focus exclusively on the negative, making them feel anxious and believe they are failures.

To prepare in advance for this trigger, periodically peruse and change your reprogramming reminders: awards, certificates, complimentary notes, thank-you letters, etc. Review your Reprogramming Record entries regularly. These habits strengthen your ability to focus on self-enhancing information. The more powerful your negating bully is, the more of this preparation you'll need. Then, when encountering this trigger, you'll more easily deflate your negating agent by giving equal attention to both the affirming and unfavorable comments you receive. This balanced attention interrupts your automatic response of exclusively fixating on and beating yourself up for the criticisms. As you review the feedback, remind yourself: *"Everyone has strengths and weaknesses. It's okay to make mistakes. The more I put myself out there, the more errors I'll make. My core self-worth is constant; it doesn't depend on how well I do."*

Then pause to consider whether the person has valid critiques. If you're concerned that your Negator will cloud your judgment, ask others you trust who are knowledgeable to give you their objective assessment regarding the unfavorable feedback. If the points are well founded, use this information to your advantage—for instance, to correct mistakes, to target skill(s) you'd like to enhance, or to help make beneficial changes in your life.

Rita walked into my office with an anxious look on her face. She sat on the edge of her chair and divulged what had happened the previous day at work. She was sitting at her desk and reading public comments posted on her company's Web site, something she did routinely. As a features writer for a local magazine, she sometimes received compliments from readers who were moved by her stories.

As Rita read through the postings, her face suddenly flushed and her heart began to race. One message started out like others that she was used to receiving: a reader shared how he had found her recent article compelling. However, he then proceeded to question whether some parts of the story were true. Intellectually, she knew her source was trustworthy and that she hadn't fabricated anything. Even so, she felt a surge of fear, panic, and shame on reading the reader's accusation. She couldn't work, lost her appetite, and didn't eat the rest of the day.

Although Rita felt pretty bad, she said she would've felt worse if she hadn't already followed coping steps from our work together. By the time she read the harsh message, she had been writing regularly in her RR. Her habit of focusing on self-positives helped protect her from completely giving in to her Negator without question. Although she felt upset, she was able to face her fear and to share what had happened with her supervisor and colleague. After reading the message, they both assured her that her work was excellent and there was no cause for concern.

On further inspection, her colleague noted that he'd received a similar accusatory message about one of his stories from the same email sender. Rita felt some relief at receiving this validation, and later she was able to exercise, to release more stress. That night, she started to write about what had happened in her DDD, but she had a hard time generating self-reassuring messages. However, her efforts did help her get to sleep that night. The next morning, she ate for the first time since reading the message.

By the time Rita met with me later that day, she was still feeling shaky. As we reviewed the helpful coping steps she had taken, she wondered why she didn't feel better. After all of the praise she'd received, how come this one mixed message had rattled her so much? One reason was easy to find. When I asked Rita to describe reprogramming reminders displayed at home and work, she couldn't think of any. She hadn't saved or printed out any of the many complimentary emails she'd received over the years. She'd stuffed away favorite stories she'd written, letters of appreciation, professional certificates, writing awards, and other tangible evidence of her abilities.

Other than the Reprogramming Record she'd recently started, there were no reminders around to strengthen Rita's self-positive focus. Without these consistent reinforcements, she was vulnerable to this Negator trigger, even when the criticism she received was combined with compliments. To resist this trap in the future, Rita agreed to find as many of these boosters as she could and display them where she would see them often.

As we talked further, another deeper reason for her intense anxiety became clear. The reader's unfounded accusation resembled the charges that her mother (and primary ND installer) had leveled to her as a child. Rita was blamed for all sorts of bad things she didn't do—such as gouging a hole in the arm chair, taking money from her mother's purse, and drinking alcohol from the liquor cabinet. With each accusation, Rita became anxious, confused, and uncertain. Eventually, she automatically felt nervous, guilty, and ashamed whenever her mother—or anyone else—blamed her for something wrong that she didn't do.

As she recounted these memories, Rita visibly relaxed. Her strong reaction now made sense as an old response, programmed by the hurtful experiences that she had endured as a child. Now knowing that one component of Rita's anxiety was about her basic morality, I urged her to post a thank-you note she'd once mentioned receiving from a stranger whose wallet she'd found and returned.

Just as Rita and I discovered, weaken your Negator by identifying early experiences that made you vulnerable to negative feedback. You'll understand how your self-harmful reactions were learned and are fundamentally separate from you. By remembering that you were young and defenseless when your responses

**Table 3.7**

| Negator Trigger | Ways to Exorcize Your *Critiquing* Negator |
|---|---|
| Receiving negative feedback. | 1. Strengthen yourself in advance by periodically changing and reviewing your reprogramming reminders and record (RR). |
| | 2. Pause to review the criticisms for validity; seek assistance from knowledgeable and objective others as needed. |
| | 3. When valid, use the information to make beneficial changes. |
| | 4. Identify experiences that created your ND to help forgive your slips and empower your reprogramming efforts. |

were programmed, it'll be easier to stop beating yourself up whenever they're activated. Write about these attacks in your Demon Disrupting Diary to reinforce your efforts. Reassure yourself of what you know to be true. For additional validation, engage outside support—the support that wasn't available to you as a child.

*Accepting Compliments*   How we react to positive feedback is just as important as how we handle criticism. When afflicted with Negator Demons, we may not realize how often we negate the compliments that we receive. I see this so often in clients and in general, especially among women, that this nullifying habit deserves special attention. Rita was no exception. Whenever I complimented her, she immediately discounted what I said, usually providing evidence to counter my observations. This showed me that her response was not simply an attempt to be modest, but a deliberate effort to minimize and undermine her successes. Only when I pointed this out repeatedly, did she realize how strong her negating habit was.

It took many weeks of prompting for her to catch and stop her automatic response, but eventually she did. I encouraged her to accept my compliments verbally even though she didn't believe them. She practiced replacing her negating comments with *"thank you,"* which, although simple, was still difficult for her to say. Here are some other responses you can choose to accept praise:

> Marissa's Reprogramming Record:
> *9/12:* I went with my friend and her husband to dinner, karaoke, and dancing. A lady asked how old I was. I told her I am 40 and she said I looked hot for my age. I said, "Thank you." <u>I am able to accept compliments.</u>

**Table 3.8**

**Options to Accept Compliments**
Thank you.
Thank you for your kind words.
I appreciate your thoughtfulness.
Thank you for your kindness.
Your feedback means a lot to me.
Thank you for saying so.
I'm so pleased to hear you say that.
You just made my day.
Thank you very much; coming from you, it means a lot.

The more you accept praise publicly, the easier it will be to acknowledge it privately. For added reinforcement, write these compliments in your RR. As you install each new layer of positive programming, you'll feel calmer and more confident, shrinking your Negator and Master Demon of unworthiness.

### Facing New Uncertain Experiences

The third chief Negator trigger is activated when we encounter situations that are unfamiliar and uncertain. Some involve major milestones, such as graduating from school, starting a new job, transferring positions, receiving a promotion, moving, getting married, having a child, divorcing, being laid off, or retiring. Others are minor but more frequent occurrences that include giving a presentation at work; changing supervisors, co-workers, or employees; dating; starting a class; taking a test; switching job responsibilities; arranging for child care; joining a group; or getting a pet.

When we're not sure what to expect, our negating demons can prey on our uncertainty, steering us to imagine the worst about how we'll handle these new endeavors. In reality, the worst rarely happens. But if we allow it, it occurs in our imagined fears every time. As my client Diane wrote, *"The truth is easier to deal with than the Negator Demon."*

*Prepare for Unfamiliar Situations*   A primary way to resist your ND is to prepare as much as possible before facing these new situations. Knowledge is power: the more you know, the fewer surprises you'll encounter. Your Negator won't get away with convincing you to accept anxiety-provoking commentary, because you'll be aware of what to expect and how to act.

Learn by asking knowledgeable others for information and resources to help you get ready. Research information in books, publications, and Internet resources that are specifically tailored to the occasion. Take classes, join groups, and/or do self-study to enhance the skills required to maximize your success. Familiarize yourself in advance by surveying novel places involved and meeting new people you'll be interacting with. Take time to practice and rehearse what is required from you. The more prepared you are, the calmer and more confident you'll feel. You'll be in a strong position to disregard your negating agent when it tries to evoke fear, anxiety, and worry.

Ray came to his session with big news. He'd just made a down payment on a home outside the dense urban environment where he'd lived for years. He was pleased about moving to an area with more space to breathe and less traffic and smog. As soon as escrow closed, he planned to move with his wife and stepchildren. Amid his excitement, there was just one thing wrong: instead of his usual 10-minute commute to work, he would soon be driving for an hour or longer each way.

The good news was that Ray had already worked hard with me to purge his Negator Demon, which was often activated by freeway driving. The bad news was that soon his negating force would have the advantage of more opportunities to strike, as he traveled an unfamiliar and much longer freeway route. He knew all too well how rough it could get. His ND would start in while Ray was driving or, sometimes, even the night before: "You can't drive the freeway to work," "You'll have a panic attack," "You're going to crash," "You'll pass out," "You're having a heart attack." On the worst days, Ray listened and responded with sweaty palms, a racing heart, tingling hands and feet, rapid breathing, feelings of panic, and an impending sense of doom.

Fortunately, by the time Ray found his new home, we'd already outed his Negator and developed an array of protective strategies for him to use. We discovered he was vulnerable to attacks because of work demands, his recent second marriage, becoming a new parent of two stepchildren, and arranging visitation with his two children from his first marriage, who now lived with his ex-wife and her new husband.

Our focus to date had covered two fronts: to lower his susceptibility to his ND by reducing the stress of multiple responsibilities and to implement specific steps to refuse his ND while driving. He was already working on managing his time, building parenting skills, communicating assertively with his ex-wife, prioritizing and delegating work and home tasks, and making time for himself. The more effort he made in these areas, the more protected he was in general from his Negator, especially while driving. Because he faced additional stress with the upcoming move, keeping these strategies going would be vital.

Although Ray was committed to continuing these approaches, unexpected stressors sometimes arose that left him vulnerable to his ND; for instance, his teaching assistant slacked off, leaving him with more work, his ex-wife changed the visitation schedule before consulting him, and his father became ill. Unforeseen issues such as these were bound to continue, especially when adding a stressful move to a completely new location.

Because his Negator targeted Ray mostly on freeway drives to work, we paid special attention to preparing ways for him to thwart these attacks on the road. As we'd done with his 10-minute commute, we mapped his upcoming long commute with three driving options: a slow drive circumventing freeways, a medium route taking one freeway and some side streets, and a fast way via connecting freeways.

To master the fast commute, we gradually increased weekly driving goals, starting with the least anxiety-producing slow route. He then practiced getting on and off the freeway, followed by the medium drive. He advanced to connecting from one freeway to the next, until he successfully drove the entire fast route each way during the morning and afternoon hours of his upcoming commute.

Ray timed each driving option, allowing a few extra minutes for possible traffic tie-ups. Ideally, he wanted to take the fast route each day. However, just in case there were times when he felt especially vulnerable to his negating demon, he could choose one of the less stressful, easier commutes and still get to work on time. This type of intervention, involving live exposure to a graduated series of feared situations, is a long-standing and well-documented treatment for anxiety.[9]

For protection while Ray drove, we added tools to ward off his Negator. He took his cellular phone as a back up in case of an emergency. He placed it within easy reach, providing a calming reminder whenever he glanced at it. To prevent his ND from capturing his attention, he listened to favorite music or sports on the radio, chewed gum, and counted telephone poles as he drove past them. When physical signs of anxiety surfaced, he used them as cues to initiate reassuring self-talk: *"It's okay," "I know what this is," "I'm able to breathe," "I'm not having a heart attack," "This will pass," "I can pull off on the side of the road and take a break," "I can call my wife for support."* As he talked to himself, he took deep slow breaths and relaxed his tight grip on the steering wheel.

To reduce stressful overload on workday mornings, Ray switched from taking his shower after waking up to taking it the night before. For better sleep, he cut out sugar and caffeine in the evening. He put out his clothes and shoes and packed everything to take to work before going to bed. Preparing the night before eliminated the morning rush, giving him more time to eat breakfast and read the paper. On difficult mornings, when his anxiety was high, he could choose to leave early. Then, if needed, he was able to pull over on the side of the road until his symptoms subsided and still get to work on time.

Important, but often overlooked, is the advantage gained over the Negator and other Soldier Demons by scheduling routine medical care. Ray was no exception. Although he disliked seeing the doctor, he made himself go to his annual physical. He followed through with recommended blood and treadmill tests and took the cholesterol and blood pressure medications his physician prescribed. He added daily vitamins and made an effort to eat more fresh fruits and vegetables and less fast food.

As Ray adjusted to his new freeway commute, his Negator still got to him at times. However, by preparing his repertoire of strategies in advance and

**Table 3.9**

| Negator Trigger | Ways to Exorcize Your *New Experience* Negator |
|---|---|
| Facing new and uncertain experiences. | 1. Deflate your negating agent by preparing in advance.<br>2. Gain information and resources to help you get ready.<br>3. Survey novel places and meet new people prior to the event.<br>4. Take time to practice and rehearse what is required of you; gradually progress from easy to more difficult steps. |

incorporating them into his routine, his anxiety markedly diminished. When he did experience panic, the episodes happened less often, were milder, and ended sooner. His negating demon was left hungry, even after intense attacks.

## Expel Your Terrorizer Negator Demon

In addition to the common triggers we've covered, stay alert for things that activate an especially virulent type of Negator Demon, the Terrorizer ND (TND). It is similar to post-traumatic stress disorder (PTSD),[10] but it is milder and more difficult to spot because it's dormant much of the time. Like PTSD, it forms when we experience or witness life-threatening ordeals, and it feeds on our fear and helplessness. Initially, it orients us to blame ourselves for what happened and for not being able to stop it. It influences us to replay what happened in our minds, so that we feel afraid and personally responsible again. Our sleep and concentration suffer; we feel edgy, irritable, and easily upset.

However, unlike PTSD, the TND rapidly retreats, lurking in the shadows as we recover and continue with our lives. Instead of causing continual, noticeable emotional upset, the Terrorizer strikes only when a new stress activates it. Because we don't know it's there or see how it operates, it gets away with surreptitiously creating repeated and cumulative distress.

When I've encountered TNDs, they typically formed when clients were children: through medical trauma; physical, sexual, or emotional abuse; or any combination thereof. Some watched a parent or sibling being hurt and were unable to stop it. Others saw their loved ones die in an accident or from an illness. Many don't identify these childhood ordeals as reasons for seeking therapy; instead, they want help with immediate stresses. Only when I ask about previous harmful events do I uncover TNDs. By the time people see me, their TNDs have wreaked havoc by repeatedly attacking as new stressors occur. Through these TND assaults, clients became conditioned to respond automatically to stress, even minor events, with familiar feelings of fear and helplessness regarding everything that could go wrong.

If you've survived traumas and believe that you have a TND, take control by reviewing the experiences that formed it as soon as possible. By shining a spotlight on the roots of your TND, you can dig them up and stop them from growing. You'll avoid what people I see have suffered unnecessarily: years of

## Table 3.10

The Terrorizer Negator Demon
- It forms through experiencing or witnessing life-threatening ordeals, often in childhood; it feeds on fear, helplessness, and self-blame.
- It rapidly retreats but strikes again when a new stress activates it, creating repeated and cumulative distress.

increasingly debilitating reactions to stressors. Write and share what happened, including feelings you have now about the original trauma. Remind yourself as often as needed that it was not your fault. Log TND attacks in your Demon Disrupting Diary and review them to identify patterns.

Prepare for future Terrorizer attacks with the knowledge that they cause the most damage when new stressors resemble those we've previously endured. Assess new situations in advance for danger and put safety precautions in place as needed. Catch your TND when it orients you to fearful thoughts and feelings. Although you don't want to feed your TND with terror, feeling some fear is a helpful reminder to ensure that protective measures are in place. Then follow through with exposing yourself to new situations. The more times you have safe new experiences, the less fright you'll feel and the easier it'll be to disregard your TND.

Write Reprogramming Record entries to reinforce healing steps as you take them. Engage additional resources as needed, to identify and release old hurts; read self-help books, find online information and discussion forums, and attend local support groups. Whether you're bothered intermittently by a Terrorizer ND or suffer severe signs of PTSD, don't hesitate to seek professional therapy, the sooner the better. In addition to general psychotherapies, there are many good specialized treatments for PTSD.[11] The longer you remain isolated from empowering resources, the stronger your TND becomes. Cut off its power source by ending your suffering with outside help.

When Margaret was six years old, she was rushed to the hospital with a serious infection. As her lungs filled with fluid, she gasped for breath, feeling terrified, helpless, and confused. Through this medical trauma, her Terrorizer Negator Demon formed, nourished by her fear. Fortunately, the doctors were able to drain her lungs in time to save her life. However, the infection left her very weak, and she had to learn to walk again. Although she recovered completely and life went on, Margaret secretly believed she must have been a bad girl to get so sick.

The next year, her two-year-old brother Tom was also stricken with a lung infection. He was not so lucky. Margaret vividly remembers one night when her mother hurried her to her neighbor friend Joanne's house so she could drive Tom to the hospital. Margaret felt confused, helpless, and terrified again, just as when she was sick. Her TND feasted on her emotional turmoil. That was the last time Margaret saw her brother. The next day, Joanne's mother told her that Tom had died. Margaret felt very guilty; she didn't know how but she assumed that his death was her fault, nourishing her TND and Master Demon of unworthiness.

After Tom's death, everyone moved on to resume normal routines. Although Margaret appeared to recover too, her TND lay in wait for new stressors to trigger it. Over the years, her father became more irritable and at times was specifically critical of her. After she had left home and married, her husband sometimes snapped at her when he was in a bad mood.

When Margaret received these random put-downs, her TND activated and she responded automatically with familiar feelings of fear, lack of control, and self-blame. She reacted the same way, but much stronger, to her Terrorizer when she or loved ones got sick, even when the malady was mild, such as a common cold. Margaret didn't realize that her intense upset stemmed from her early severe traumas. She believed she was very weak and flawed to react so out of proportion to every new minor illness and criticism.

As I shared the demon model and outed her TND, Margaret was visibly surprised and relieved. She could now start identifying and separating from this fear-mongering bully that kept interfering in her life. She enthusiastically began to write in her RR and DDD. However, over the next few weeks, her writing and other demon-busting efforts grew inconsistent. She sometimes refused her TND and other times let it have its way. She slipped back and forth between conscious awareness of how her Terrorizer operated and her old automatic reactions of fear and self-blame.

In the middle of our work together, Margaret decided to relocate to a more affordable area in another state, near her son and his family. I hope that, after moving, she pursued the therapeutic resources we talked about and continues efforts to catch and deny her TND. What made it especially hard for Margaret was that her TND had been operating for so long before she became aware of it. She was 73 years old when she made her first appointment with me. By then, her TND had been operating unopposed for 67 years. Because Margaret didn't begin therapy 50, 25, or even 5 years sooner, she lost the advantage of starving her TND before it grew massively entrenched, from decades of feeding on her fear. Of course, it's never too late to start taking your power back. But fortunately, now that you know about the Terrorizer Negator Demon, you can avoid Margaret's hardship by outing and resisting yours before it stakes claim on the rest of your life.

**Table 3.11**

**Exorcize Your _Terrorizer_ Negator Demon**

1. Identify the trauma(s) that created it; write and share what happened, including your feelings about it now.
2. Remind yourself often that it wasn't your fault.
3. Log TND attacks in your DDD to identify patterns; take safety precautions for new situations with risk.
4. After catching it; call your TND's bluff by facing your fear and following through with the new experience.
5. Add RR entries to reinforce healing steps; engage informal and professional therapy resources as needed.

**Table 3.12**

| | The Negator Demon |
|---|---|
| Directive | • It orients you to focus on the negative aspects of yourself and your life. (pp. 47–48) |
| Ways to Identify (p. 48) | • You worry often about one or more areas of your life.<br>• It's difficult to relax and enjoy activities because you frequently feel anxious and afraid that you'll do something wrong.<br>• You're habitually nervous and self-conscious when you're with other people because you worry that you might make a social blunder.<br>• When you're successful, you don't praise or reward yourself very much.<br>• Making decisions takes a long time because you're constantly second-guessing yourself.<br>• It's easy to find fault with yourself.<br>• It's hard to forgive yourself. |
| Ways to Exorcize | • Name your negating demon and how it operates (pp. 48–49).<br>• Defeat your skill-focused Negator (pp. 49–51)<br>• Refuse 2 common ND tactics; shifting within and between domains (pp. 51–53).<br>• Tune out your recurring Negator; block your Blocker (pp. 53–55).<br>• Build a personal repertoire of Negator disrupters (pp. 55–61).<br>• Stop debilitating Negator comparisons (pp. 61–63).<br>• Triumph over 3 common Negator triggers: (pp. 64–73)<br>   • Interacting with ND installers<br>   • Receiving negative feedback<br>   • Facing new uncertain experiences<br>• Expel your Terrorizer Negator Demon (pp. 73–75). |

CHAPTER 4

# THE ROUSTER DEMON

Sharon arrived home from work feeling pretty good. She ran two meetings that day and was pleased that both went well. Best of all, she'd refused her Negator Demon, which tried to barrage her with a litany of insults to undermine her confidence and make her anxious about her performance. She'd been documenting previous Negator attacks in her DDD for weeks and was getting good at catching it and following steps to refuse it. She'd also made a special effort to write and review RR entries that reinforced evidence of her positive leadership qualities. Although it had tried before and during her meetings, her negating force was unable to penetrate the shield she'd created by taking these protective steps.

Soon her son and daughter would arrive home from after-school activities and the quiet house would come alive. Sharon's thoughts turned to the upcoming weekend, reviewing everyone's schedules and tasks to be done. Her soft gaze suddenly turned hard as she remembered what her husband Dan mentioned earlier that week, that he planned to ride motorcycles with his friends on Saturday. As she pictured him on the road, thoughts sparked in her head and she gritted her teeth: "Sure, he always gets to do what he wants, going out and playing with his friends while I'm stuck at home. He waltzes in and out of this house whenever he pleases. Plus, he's got a surf trip planned next month. He's so selfish; he never thinks about me, what a jerk!" Her work triumph was long lost as thoughts took over her mind about how self-centered and thoughtless her husband was.

When her children arrived home, they immediately knew that Mom was ticked off when she greeted them with a scowl and barked, "Your rooms are a mess. I'm sick and tired of cleaning up after you. After all I do for you; the least you could do is pick up after yourselves." Stunned, they quickly retreated as far from Sharon as possible, wondering what they had done so wrong that day to upset her so much.

By the time Dan came home, Sharon was fuming. When he greeted her, she ignored him and left the room, slamming the door behind her. He followed and asked, "Is something wrong?" She turned around and exploded, "You're so self-ish, you don't care about me at all. All you care about is doing what you want when you please. Why don't you just go live with your friends? You spend more time with them than me!" Speechless, he quickly retreated to his study in the far corner of the house. They barely spoke the rest of the weekend. He rode motor-cycles all day Saturday with his friends, even going out for drinks with them afterward because he dreaded going home to Sharon's wrath.

Sharon was in very bad shape when she came to see me on Monday. Bags hung under her eyes, her face was red and blotchy, and her body sat stiff in the chair. She immediately spewed out her fury with Dan, recounting in detail his selfish motorcycle escapade, plus his upcoming surf trip. Tears fell as she spouted, "What's wrong with me? Am I that ugly and boring? Why doesn't he want to spend time with me?" After venting her outrage, she looked expec-tantly at me.

---

> Our Rouster Demon steers us to criticize and attack others.

---

I immediately recognized what had happened—a stealth Rouster Demon (RD) attack. The third of the four Soldier Demons, the RD's directive is to make us criticize and attack others. Although Sharon had legitimate concerns about Dan, her Rouster steered her to react by angrily berating and assailing him. It also influenced her to lash out at her children. Its crowning glory came when she felt rejected and unlovable after her family members had distanced themselves from her.

Sharon had unknowingly fed her Rouster and Master Demon of defectiveness a feast of anger and self-blame. She was vulnerable and blindsided by her RD because she was completely focused on defeating her Negator. This is one way the Rouster strikes, when we're unprotected because our attention is on starving a different Soldier Demon. Sharon automatically became angry in response to this Sniper attack; she had no idea her RD was operating on her.

## Root Out Your Rouster

To prevent Sharon's fate, watch for any of these signs that you're beset with a Rouster Demon:

- You often criticize and judge people, especially those you are close to.
- When things don't go as you expect, you get angry and take it out on others.
- It's hard to forgive people, even for minor transgressions.
- You gossip regularly about friends, family, and co-workers.

- When your needs aren't met by someone, you give that person the silent treatment and withhold affection.
- You hold anger about something inside for a long time and then suddenly blow up.
- You get irritated easily and snap at others.
- When anyone criticizes or questions you, you respond by immediately attacking them.
- You explode in physical outbursts toward objects, animals, and/or people.

Significant hazards follow when you're plagued by a Rouster. Every time you repeat these contentious habits, your RD feasts on your anger. Afterward, you beat yourself up for becoming so critical and irate. You feel guilty and ashamed and you regret what you said or did. Your RD consumes and feeds your Master Demon with this stew of negative emotions. Your belief (MD) grows that you're weak and defective for losing control and hurting people you care about.

The more often your rousting force rules, the more likely you are to lose your partner, children, job, health, friends, and even your freedom if outbursts break the law. For example, health research reveals that anger leads to a weakened immune system, heightened vulnerability to illness, increased pain, and a greater risk of death from cardiovascular disease.[1]

---

> When Rousters rule, we risk losing our health, relationships, jobs, and personal freedom.

---

You may not immediately notice Rouster attacks. Sharon didn't recognize her rousting program until I outed it in our session. To avoid this blind spot, stay alert for these signs. Your loved ones distance themselves from you and go out of their way to avoid you. Note that Sharon's entire family steered clear of her after she blew up at them. Your friends stop inviting you over. Your partner no longer confides in you and talks with others instead. You overhear people commiserating that you're judgmental, angry, and/or hard to be around. Managers give you feedback that others at work are complaining about the critical ways you treat them.

Once you identify your Rouster, be wary of getting stuck feeling ashamed about what you did and doing nothing but beating yourself up. Avoid the opposite pitfall too: letting your RD thrive by justifying your actions and doing nothing to change. When I exposed Sharon's Rouster, she vacillated between both traps, feeling ashamed and defending her angry outbursts. Neither approach freed her from her rousting program.

---

> Beware of two inertia traps after angry outbursts: shame and justification.

---

## Be Sure It's Your Rouster

Before proceeding with steps to starve your Rouster, check to be sure it's not actually someone else's. To locate the RD's host, pause and review in detail who acted out in anger. If you're still unclear, ask objective witnesses for their help in locating who's got a Rouster. Engage therapeutic resources as necessary to aid in your discovery.

If your caregivers had virulent RDs and repeatedly blamed you for their angry outbursts, you're especially prone to taking the blame when others explode in anger. Because the demon model applies to those of us who internalize negative events that happen in our lives, we're at risk for taking the blame when others criticize and attack us. You may automatically assume that you're the mean, angry one when someone beset with a Rouster is critical or attacks you and you experience a flaring of anger in response.

Feeling anger is not sure evidence of your RD at work; the anger could be a result of someone else's Rouster in action. It's inflaming it and allowing it to escalate the conflict that has your RD's talon marks all over it. Even if your parents didn't hold you responsible, you may still have blamed yourself for the criticisms and fights you observed and experienced as a child. If you discover a Rouster that belongs to someone else and you've internalized their anger, then you've got a Negator, not a Rouster. If so, go back to Chapter 3 for steps to shrink your Negator Demon.

---

> Check first; the Rouster may not be yours.

---

My client Cynthia habitually felt guilty for her parents' conflicts when growing up. Although they never directly blamed her, she assumed that she must have caused their fights by being an angry, difficult daughter. Because, in her mind, she created the conflicts, she believed that she had the power to stop them. She did everything she could think of to be the best-behaved girl—never talking back or complaining, always obeying the rules, doing her chores, getting good grades, and so on.

Because, in reality, Cynthia didn't cause her parent's troubles, her many efforts never succeeded in ending their discord. However, she believed into adulthood that she was at fault and she criticized herself (ND) whenever others beset with RDs became angry. Once we identified her correct Negator Demon in therapy, we were able to stop her no-win strategy of trying to shrink a nonexistent Rouster.

## Catch Common Triggers to Expel Your Rouster

Through working with clients over the years, I've observed common situations that repeatedly trigger rousting programs. Once you know you've got a Rouster, watch out for these risky scenarios where it may strike. Catch and refuse your Rouster by employing the following strategies tailored to each situation.

**When Your Needs Aren't Being Met**

Anytime you're not getting what you want, you're a target for your rousting agent. Unmet needs include but are not limited to emotional, spiritual, intellectual, creative, physical, sexual, and monetary needs. Your RD focuses your mind on how someone in your life isn't meeting these needs, whether this is true or not. It keeps you dwelling on what you don't have and silently blaming others, locking you into a passive victim role.

Your anger and resentment build, until you lash out at those you hold responsible for your predicament. Ironically, these are usually the people you care about the most. Your RD gulps down your red hot rage, as you alienate your loved ones before you've had the chance to discuss calmly what's upsetting you or to ask for what you want.

To prevent this destructive pattern, identify in detail what you need. Envision exactly how your life will look different once you get these missing things in your experience. Break down what you want into doable actions that both you and others can take to obtain them. When you and your loved ones are calm, share your needs and ask them to take the specific steps you've identified. Through these requests, you create opportunities for others to be successful by giving you exactly what you need.

When I review this process with clients, I find that they often haven't asked themselves what they want. Instead, they've focused exclusively on what they don't want. It's very hard to ask for something you haven't yet identified. In contrast, it's very easy to fall prey to your RD and criticize others for what they're doing wrong. Even when clients know what they want, I discover that many haven't told their loved ones because they assume others already know specifically what to do to meet their needs.

Sharon was furious that her husband was doing activities he enjoyed without her. However, when I asked if she would like to join him, she had no interest in riding motorcycles or surfing. When I asked what she did want, she couldn't answer right away. She was so consumed with anger at Dan that she hadn't focused on identifying specifically what would help her feel better.

Only when I continued questioning did Sharon recognize that what she wanted was not to do more activities with Dan. Rather, it was to have more time on her own to do what she preferred—reading, lunch with friends, and crafts. We then identified specific actions to get these things: perusing the bookstore for books she wanted, scheduling regular quiet time to read, calling friends to set lunch dates, and signing up for a weekly painting class. As we focused on her needs, Sharon's ideas expanded to include a day shopping trip with her daughter and a weekend visiting a girlfriend out of state. In her case, all of these steps were ones that she could take independently. If Sharon hadn't paused to examine what she wanted, her Rouster would have kept her swirling in a vortex of pointless anger and resentment, further alienating her family.

**Table 4.1**

| Rouster Trigger | Ways to Exorcize Your *"Unmet Needs"* Rouster |
|---|---|
| When your needs aren't being met. | 1. Identify in detail what you need.<br>2. Break this down into actions that both you and others can follow to get what you want.<br>3. Begin the self-care activities within your control.<br>4. When calm, share your needs and ask others to take the specific steps you've identified. |

### When You're Doing for Others at Your Own Expense

One reason Sharon's needs weren't met was because she was spending her time taking care of others but doing very little for herself. This is another common Rouster trigger that I regularly encounter in my practice. Although occurring mostly at home with loved ones, it can happen anywhere: at work, school, with friends and extended family, even during leisure activities such as sporting and social events. It frequently develops from saying yes to requests until your obligations snowball and you're lost underneath. You become frazzled, irritated, and easily influenced by your RD to blow up, often at the very people whose requests you agreed to fulfill. Your outbursts may also extend to new people who ask you to do something for the first time.

The best defense against this Rouster trap is to pause and review what you're doing for others, compared to what you're doing for yourself. If you typically take a back seat to everyone else, determine what current obligations you can release, delegate, or renegotiate now. Identify predictable requests to say no to in the future. Use the time and energy you gain from setting limits with others to focus on meeting your needs.

*Use Anger as a Cue*    Foil your rousting program by letting your angry feelings alert you to check whether you're doing for others at your expense. Then follow steps to set boundaries to their appeals before you fall under your Rouster's influence and angrily explode. Here are three different clients who successfully used this approach.

Reprogramming Record Entries:

*April 17:* "I stuck to my guns" and did not give in to a request for an infringement on my time. My sister and I arranged that I would see her at 5 pm. Today she called me earlier, requesting me to arrive three hours earlier. I had things to be done and taken care of and did not give in and stuck to the intended time. <u>I am capable of saying no. My time is valuable.</u>

*October 23:* I didn't let Jay take advantage of my kindness at work. <u>I set boundaries for myself.</u> [This client was asked by her co-worker, Jay, to work overtime for him after she'd made plans with her boyfriend. Plus, Jay habitually left his unfinished tasks for her to do when she arrived at work. She said no to his request.]

*January 29:* Got my student assistants to do the welcome folders for the new students and to organize the study materials for the same. Students will be in on Monday to pick them all up. <u>I can delegate jobs to my student staff to keep them busy during their work shifts.</u>

You may not detect your rousting bully right away. To strengthen your radar, stay alert for behaviors that manifest underlying anger, such as repeatedly criticizing and snapping at others for small or random things. Disengage from your rousting agent's external focus to uncover what you're really upset about and list exactly what you need. Share your requests directly with the people who can help you make this happen.

My client Tina's rousting program activated many times before she spotted it. She was a new mother and worked full-time as a teacher while her husband Ben stayed home with their four-month-old daughter Chloe. Tina's days were a whirlwind of rushing to and from work, coming home at lunch to breast feed and pump more milk for Chloe, attending meetings after school, doing daily chores, running errands, grading papers late at night, and so on.

As she grew weary, attending to everyone else's needs, Tina's RD steered her to criticize Ben silently: "He's not taking care of our family the way he should," "He's not earning any money," "He's such a loser," "He doesn't even do the housework right." She began to snap at him for little things. Her critiques morphed into tirades in which she swore and called him bad names.

**Table 4.2**

| Rouster Trigger | Ways to Exorcize Your *Self-Sacrificing* Rouster |
|---|---|
| When you're doing for others at your own expense. | 1. Compare what you do for others with what you do for yourself. |
| | 2. If you usually come last, choose those responsibilities to stop, delegate, or renegotiate now. |
| | 3. List expected requests to decline in the future. |
| | 4. Use the time and energy you gain from setting limits to focus on meeting your needs. |
| | 5. Let angry feelings cue you to return to Step 1. |
| | 6. Detect latent anger from behaviors (e.g., snapping at others); discover what you're really upset about and calmly request what you want from others. |

As Tina divulged these episodes in therapy, I asked her to describe what she wanted. She hated her job and more than anything yearned to quit and stay home with Chloe. She wished Ben would get a steady paying job to allow this to happen. When I asked if she'd shared her desires with him, she paused and replied with a surprised look on her face, "He must know this is what I want, when I come home every day all stressed out and irritated." As we continued, Tina realized that she hadn't ever directly shared her wishes with Ben. Instead, her Rouster ruled and she repeatedly blasted him randomly for trivial things before having the awareness that she needed to articulate what she truly wanted.

### When Unexpected Irritations Occur

Our rousting programs can quickly catch us off guard whenever unanticipated frustrations happen. Although major stressors are readily identified as RD triggers, more frequently occurring minor annoyances are easier to overlook. Seemingly small problems are easy bait for your RD if they're irritating to you. Typical examples that my clients encounter include aggravating incidents at work, equipment malfunctions and power failures, flat tires, locking keys in the car or home, losing items, inclement weather, travel delays, waiting in line, and varied other schedule disruptions.

> To disempower Rousters, use humor and the self-calming Negator disrupters from Chapter 3.

As you catch and deny your Rouster before and during predictable situations, your anger management skills will improve. It'll then be easier to resist your RD with familiar, well-practiced coping steps when unexpected minor frustrations occur. For generally effective self-calming options, review and routinely schedule the Negator disrupters described in Chapter 3. Fortunately, these strategies also work very well to interrupt Rousters. The more often you feel calm, the harder it is for your RD to get a rise out of you when things go wrong. At times when you do get caught up in destructive angry reactions, another quick and effective release is to engage humor. By laughing at your predicament, you'll weaken your rousting bully and free yourself by cutting off the supply of angry fuel it requires.

Melinda's Reprogramming Record Entry:

*October 10:* Upon arriving at work, Lilly told me the deadline for purchasing requests was moved up to today. Got the requests typed up and electronically submitted to the vendor by noon. <u>I am able to work calmly under pressure. I am able to complete work assignments.</u>

Melinda's Demon Disrupting Diary Entry:

*January 21:* Carpet guys here @ 9 a.m—no warning. My sister Lori started flipping out. Rouster Demon almost won because it was extremely stressful to have them just show up—I wasn't prepared at all. I wanted to scream at her to calm down and shut up! But instead I kept my sense of humor and tried to keep her laughing instead. "Lori, calm down it's gonna get done. I have to pick my dirty underwear off the floor before the carpet guys see it. Let's get the bras out of the living room." It was so rewarding to see our rooms looking so beautiful after we put them back together.

## When Expectations of Others Aren't Met

A major Rouster activator occurs when others do not fulfill what we expect of them. Whether our standards are reasonable or not, when people don't behave the way we anticipate, our rousting bully can quickly influence us to react angrily. Typical complaints I hear are the following: spouses who don't complete home projects, children who skip chores or homework, employees or co-workers who perform poorly, customers who are too demanding, or service personnel who make mistakes. Melinda's DDD entry includes another example. In addition to the irritation of the carpet installers arriving early, she was vulnerable to her RD when her sister did not respond calmly, as she expected.

*Identify Early Warning Signs of Anger*   The sooner you're aware of Rouster attacks, the easier it is to separate from and stop supplying it. When encountering dangerous situations our bodies have evolved to survive by quickly reacting with a fight or flight response. This process involves a general activation of our sympathetic nervous system, which prepares us to attack or flee.[2]

These days we rarely encounter life-threatening events. However, we're still hardwired to react to stressors as though we're in danger and must battle or escape to protect ourselves. When the threat is formidable, we're likely to flee; when there's a good chance of overcoming the hazard, we're more predisposed to fight. Our RD activates in the latter instance, when the combative response is triggered. Because this physiological process occurs rapidly, it's difficult to notice and use fight-provoking thoughts as cues to help avert impending anger outbursts.

Fortunately, your body provides warning signs that your Rouster is preparing to strike. By recognizing early physical symptoms in nonemergency situations, you can derail the automatic fight response and substitute self-calming steps. Common body cues that my clients have identified include pressure in the head or chest; clenched teeth, jaw, or fists; tensed arms or legs; racing pulse; and biting the lip. Your signals may differ from these, so carefully tune into your body to identify your unique alerts.

Once you know your physical signals, let them cue you to pause and reflect before reacting out of anger. If your Rouster has already fully activated, physically leave the situation and take time to cool down. As your body symptoms subside, ask yourself what you're upset about. Uncover feelings beneath your anger, such as disappointment, sadness, or fear. Identify relevant wants, needs, and specific steps to get them met. Review your various choices in responding and the likely consequences for each course of action you consider.

*Let Go and Move On*    After physically calming down, you may discover there's nothing worth addressing. The frustrating event could be an accident, something involving strangers you won't see again, and/or a situation that nothing will make better. In these cases, refocus your attention on something else. If needed, calmly share what happened with supportive others and/or in your DDD. By letting go and moving on, you'll prevent your rousting bully from influencing you to attack and alienate others who aren't responsible or who can't fix what happened.

Tina came to her next session with good news. She had asked her husband Ben to get a job so that she could quit teaching and stay at home with their daughter, Chloe. Although Tina thought it was obvious, Ben was surprised to hear how miserable she was in her teaching job. He listened supportively and agreed to pursue actively a salaried job. By the week's end, he'd updated his résumé and started sending it out to prospective employers. Although Tina was very pleased, her RD was undaunted: episodes of snapping at Ben remained a stubborn habit.

As we reviewed her outbursts, I asked Tina to recall any physical sensations she had before lashing out. Her primary body symptom was tension in her chest. Over the next few weeks, she practiced using this early warning signal as a cue to pause before blasting Ben and ask herself what she was upset about. When too agitated to think clearly, she walked away from Ben and took time to cool down. When the pressure in her chest subsided, she proceeded to identify what was bothering her.

After some times when she had remembered to take these basic steps, Tina correctly identified when she was frustrated by other things and not by Ben. Her stressors continued to be work-related, such as problems with students, unwelcome meetings after school, and loads of papers to grade after hours. However, she now calmed herself by remembering that she had asked for what she wanted from Ben and that he was actively pursuing a job so she could quit and leave these irritations behind.

*Speak Out Calmly*    After identifying what's upsetting you, there'll be many times you need to express your needs and wants to others. A key to getting them to hear you without being defensive or turning off is to deliver your message assertively, not aggressively. Share your feelings, needs, and wants with a positive tone and reasonable volume. Use "I" statements: "I feel," "I need," "I want." Convey a cooperative attitude. Instead of just reviewing what others have done wrong, request reasonable specific actions they can take to fulfill your needs. Research documents well the significance of nonverbal communication.[3] When talking in person, avoid powerful nonverbal provocations of rolling your eyes, pointing your finger, folding your arms, staring menacingly, or looking away.

---

Leon's Demon Disrupting Diary Entry:

*August 30:* Almost had an argument with Jada [his girlfriend]. It was a Rouster Demon attack. We were not able to agree on something silly as whether or not we would go to a movie. I was trying to be sympathetic to her need for getting rest but I feel that old habits got the best of me and the words and actions on my part were not helping and she became defensive. Before I could get upset I took a minute and explained in detail what my intentions were and I made sure I was very clear and kind. We resolved the issue before reverting to arguing and our reward was later going to see Invasion [movie] and a large popcorn and icy for myself.

---

*When Angry Feelings Linger*   Don't be surprised if you still feel angry inside as you're starting to communicate calmly on the outside. It takes time for old, conditioned feelings to fade when you're replacing aggressive with assertive behaviors.[4] If you become frustrated that you don't yet feel calm, remind yourself that your anger will dissipate in time, as you continue to express your needs diplomatically. If, instead, you're impatient and beat yourself up for feeling mad, you lose out—by feeding your Master Demon your personal disappointment and self-blame.

Helen was getting good at asserting her needs with others. She practiced at work, with her friends, and when dealing with service personnel. She was now able to say no to unreasonable demands and speak out to request help when she needed it. Her latest triumph was calmly handling a situation in which a client arrived early, after she'd already told him the meeting room wouldn't be ready by then. Instead of berating or ignoring him, she assertively greeted and kindly ushered him to a seat in the waiting area until the room was available.

After describing her progress, Helen frowned, looked down, and lamented, "But I still felt angry at him. What's wrong with me?" I reassured her that it takes time for old, destructive feelings to fade as new constructive behaviors are established. In the meantime, patience was her best ally. I cautioned her that, if she continues to put herself down for feeling anger, she'll unwittingly be serving her Master Demon of defectiveness.

**Table 4.3**

| Rouster Trigger | Ways to Exorcize Your *"Let Down"* Rouster |
|---|---|
| When expectations of others aren't met. | 1. Let early body symptoms cue you to pause before reacting angrily; when necessary, leave the situation to cool down. |
| | 2. Once you are calm, identify your feelings, needs, and wants; review your options to respond, including possible consequences. |
| | 3. For incidents not worth pursuing, write in your DDD and/or vent with supportive others, and then focus on something else. |
| | 4. For important issues, speak assertively and request specific actions to meet your needs; avoid nonverbal aggressions. |
| | 5. Refuse your Master Demon with self-patience if angry feelings remain after calmly expressing your needs. |

*Avoid Overreacting*   A common way I see clients lose out to their Rousters is when they have a justified reason to be upset but they react with inappropriate anger. Often this occurs when others make mistakes that directly affect them. Instead of getting what they want, such as the errors corrected, my clients' aggression backfires: others react defensively, angrily, and even vindictively. I see this especially when the original transgressors, such as a boss, landlord, or spouse, have power to make my clients miserable in some area of their lives.

George regretted losing his cool after the coordinator for his work seminars made repeated mistakes in scheduling his talks. He stormed into her office, carrying a computer printout highlighting her latest error, holding it up with his clenched fist, and berating her about how incompetent she was. Instead of improving her performance, soon after his tirade, George received word that one of his seminars would soon be discontinued. In his place, a colleague was scheduled to conduct a similar offering. Although he didn't know for sure whether his aggression had led to his loss, rousting episodes such as these are highly likely to facilitate these types of misfortunes. If he'd recognized the first signs of his rousting force, a flushed face and tensed muscles, he could have paused to cool down and avoided alienating the person in charge of scheduling his presentations.

Fortunately, Jacqué caught her RD before suffering major repercussions. She was home much of the time while contractors began to remodel her kitchen. A careful observer, she noticed initial blunders right away. Rather than improving their work, the builders slowed down after she pointed out their errors. As we discussed this, Jacqué realized she was very blunt and her voice carried a

condescending tone when she told the men about their mistakes. Her Rouster installer was her father, who had modeled this harsh, patronizing manner of talking. After identifying signs of her RD, she consciously paused before speaking to the workmen, shifting her words and tone of voice to convey respect and cooperation. Although mistakes continued, Jacqué's new manner of communicating helped her address problems without adding lengthy delays to the project.

*Stop Recycling Anger*   One hazard I see repeatedly in my practice is when clients quickly become angry at current loved ones based on the past sins of others. They're so hurt by the previous transgressors that they're highly sensitive to the smallest new perceived slights. Their Rouster automatically activates at the first hint of injustice, with old familiar anger. Because this process occurs so rapidly, they don't realize they're reacting disproportionately to the current minor incidents. I see this most often with romantic partners, but it can also occur with caregivers, friends, those at work, and others we're close to.

If you've been hurt by someone, prevent your RD from recycling your anger by reviewing your painful history. Identify the transgressions that caused you harm; remind yourself that you're vulnerable to your rousting force when you think that new people are acting similarly, however small the incidents may be. Watch for these high-risk triggers and catch your RD before reacting. Pause and review what just happened. When you gain perspective by separating from your rousting program, you'll typically realize that the current offense is not nearly as severe as what happened previously. You'll be free to choose how to react based on your corrected observation. You'll avoid persecuting loved ones for what others had perpetrated in the past, and you'll prevent losing the trust and affection in your current relationship.

Although Sofia had been dating Jose for four years, she struggled to trust him. From her own accounts, he was a stable, caring boyfriend who hadn't done anything to warrant her suspicion. Unfortunately for Jose, a major reason for her difficulty was her first relationship with Marcos, who repeatedly cheated on her during the three years they were together. Sofia was just 18 when she fell in love with Marcos; she was heartbroken when he betrayed her trust.

Jose was the first man Sofia had allowed herself to get close to after recovering from Marcos. However, the closer they got and the longer they were together, the more fearful she was that he would hurt her as Marcos did. She became hypervigilant and easily angered when he didn't behave the way she expected, for example, not calling or arriving at her apartment exactly on time as planned. As we reviewed her dating history in my office, she realized how much Marcos's transgressions had fueled her RD and MD (that she was unlovable) and damaged her trust in Jose. Her rousting program repeatedly influenced her to overreact to Jose when he'd done nothing to warrant her extremely angry outburst.

In one such incident, Jose planned to meet with a landlord to survey a prospective new apartment. When he first mentioned his meeting, they mutually agreed

that Sofia would go with him, even though they didn't live together and she had no plans to move in with him. However, as the appointment drew closer, he changed his mind and left her a phone message that he didn't think it was a good idea for her to go. When Sofia listened to the message, she'd just returned from running too many errands in one day. She was exhausted and suffering the beginning symptoms of a cold. Her RD took advantage of her weakened state and said: "He isn't taking you because he doesn't love you anymore; he'll date other women there; he's going to dump you."

Sofia listened to her RD without question and became enraged at Jose, driving to his place and accusing him of planning to break up and start a new life without her. Only after he'd taken away her car keys, to prevent her from driving away while angry, did she calm down enough so they could talk rationally. He explained that he wanted to make a good first impression with the landlord, because he'd already explained over the phone that he would be the only tenant. He assured her that he wasn't planning to break up and he wanted her to visit often after he successfully secured the apartment.

If Sofia had paused before reacting to her Rouster's irrational conclusions, she could have reminded herself that Jose was not Marcos. His plan to meet with the landlord alone was a minute issue and not comparable to Marcos's cheating. She could have asked him about it calmly and received his explanation and reassurance. She would've avoided falling prey to her RD and MD and prevented hurting Jose and herself for Marcos's mistakes.

*Catch Rejection Fears*    Sofia's attack is also an example of a rousting program fueled by the fear of rejection. This type of recycled anger happens often to people who've previously been hurt by others they're close to. Their RD steers them to interpret the smallest new incidents as signs that their loved ones are leaving them. They react angrily, even when there's no evidence of rejection. Fortunately, by following the aforementioned steps you can catch and refuse your Rouster when abandonment fears are triggered.

As we worked together, Sofia got better at identifying and refusing to feed her rousting program. However, as she thwarted its attacks in the daytime, it crept into her dreams at night. She enlisted her DDD to record and reinforce her efforts. She told Jose about her RD, and he was pleased to know that she was actively working to stop it from hurting their relationship. The following is one incident she recorded and shared with Jose. After reading it, he reassured her that nothing was real in her fear-inducing Rouster dream.

Sofia's Demon Disrupting Diary Entry:

*February 29:* This morning I woke up with an awful nightmare. It was 4:05 a.m. I was in a cold sweat, yelling. I am surprised my roommate didn't

hear me. I dreamt that Jose had left me for my former best friend Lena. In my dream, they had been carrying on a relationship for almost a year. That was the reason why she stopped being my friend. I feel my Rouster Demon coming back in a big irrational way. My feelings of jealousy were stirred up, but I knew it was just a dream. I told myself this is not possible: it is a dream. I did not allow my emotions to come out onto Jose. I battled my Rouster Demon and told myself that I am stronger than that and much smarter. I rewarded myself with a book, Real Simple Solutions.

*Caring for Children*  A frequent frustration I hear is when children don't meet their caregivers' expectations. Although mostly occurring when the children are young, these disappointments can happen when children are any age through adulthood. Especially difficult are years two through five. Problematic behaviors include making a mess, not following directives, breaking rules, getting hurt, fighting with each other, talking back, crying, throwing temper tantrums, and so on. These aggravations set off the RDs of unprepared hosts, steering them to fits of criticisms, yelling, swearing, inappropriate punishments, and, at their worst, physical outbursts. Afterward, clients feel guilty and ashamed, criticizing themselves for losing control and hurting the very children they love. Their self-flagellation fuels their Master Demon of defectiveness, which swells as it feasts on their misery.

If you experience these stressors and consequent anger episodes, it's crucial to mobilize your resources to reduce them as soon as possible. The risk in doing nothing is high. According to research, parental stress and expressed anger are strong predictors of potential child abuse.[5] For information and guidance in implementing effective parenting skills, seek outside assistance through parenting classes, parenting support groups, psychotherapy, and parenting books.[6] You'll find these parenting resources at therapy clinics, community centers (e.g., YMCA), local churches, hospitals, community colleges, public recreation programs, and on the Internet.

Even if your outbursts are not severe, they can deeply affect your children, who are impressionable and affected by everything you do. Initially mild anger episodes can escalate to verbal or physical abuse if you don't get help to halt your rousting program. You'll learn whether what you're expecting from your children is developmentally appropriate. You'll gain age-specific communication and discipline techniques.

To apply the skills you acquire, identify common behaviors your children repeat that let you down and trigger your Rouster. Practice self-calming steps in advance and engage them as soon as your children exhibit the misbehaviors you've identified. To help create your repertoire, review Negator disrupters described in Chapter 3. After cooling down, use discipline as necessary and as appropriate to the transgressions.

Celeste's Reprogramming Record:
*September 6:* My son did not behave and he escalated his misbehavior then asked to be rewarded by the computer games or going out skating with friends. I was able to say no for the entire week. He knows he will lose computer time or skating time if he misbehaves. I am able to set boundaries.
*September 19:* My son talked back and lost his computer time for one week. He kept coming every day to beg to get on for 5 mins. I reminded him that his talking back was disrespectful & he has been warned about this behavior & the consequences of losing his computer time. I stay firm on consequences.

If you're like many parents I've worked with, you're aware of appropriate behaviors for your children and yourself. You have good intentions in reacting to your children, but you get caught off guard by your Rouster when new problems arise or when you're vulnerable because of fatigue, overload, or other stressors. My client Kim had a flexible part-time job that allowed her to be home with the children when her husband Jerry was at work. When she sought help, they were raising twin boys who'd just turned two. She'd always had a short temper but was able to manage her anger pretty well until now. However, when caring for the boys alone, Kim found herself snapping and sometimes yelling at them. When very frustrated, she became too rough in picking them up or sitting them down. She loved her sons and felt awful after every angry episode. Before things got worse, she wanted help to stop her angry reactions. She was especially vulnerable because her rousting program had been installed in childhood by watching and experiencing her explosive father. The last thing she wanted was to become verbally and physically abusive like him.

Kim identified clenching her jaw, biting her lip, and having a racing heart as early warnings of impending anger outbursts. In addition to body symptoms, we reviewed problematic situations at home to watch out for as common RD triggers. Kim practiced using these body and situational cues to interrupt her rousting bully. She then implemented quick self-calming strategies we devised for her. When the only adult at home, she was limited to methods of cooling down that allowed her to remain attentive to the boys. When Jerry was there, her favorite ways to relax were napping and working on craft projects alone in the study. To boost her success, we additionally came up with actions she could take to reduce RD triggers.

*Kim's Rouster Triggers*

- Times when the boys misbehave, fight with each other, cry, get hurt, don't hear me.
- When the boys squirm in their car seats, while having their diapers changed, or being dressed.

- Staying home all day watching the boys, with no breaks.
- Running late when getting the boys ready to go somewhere.

---

Kim's Quick Self-Calming Strategies
Keep my hands to myself and my voice in control (i.e., volume low and tone neutral).
Turn away when I get mad, so my angry face won't scare the boys.
Tense-release-breathe: clench my fists, release them, and take a deep breath.
Say to myself, *"It's not personal. This too will pass. Things will work out."*
Squeeze stress balls. Jump rope in the hallway for a few seconds.
Run with the boys around the patio one or more times.

---

*Kim's Options to Reduce Rouster Triggers*

- Plan daily outings with the boys, to break up the monotony and get out of the house.
- Take the boys to the gym day care twice a week so I can reduce stress by working out.
- Instead of doing chores, lie down for a rest break when the boys take their nap.
- When possible, give each boy two options to choose from to prevent overcontrol.
- Keep goals for the boys small, to avoid expecting and doing too much.
- Reduce scheduled commitments on the weekends (e.g., stop teaching Sunday school).
- Catch the boys behaving well and praise them to increase desired behaviors.
- Write an RR entry at the end of each day, to reinforce a positive parenting experience.
- Schedule a babysitter at least once a month, to allow a date night with Jerry.
- Ask my mother to watch the boys when I need a reprieve.
- Call a backup babysitter for relief on extremely stressful days.

Some days Kim did very well in catching her rousting force before it fully activated. Other days, she slipped back to old, angry ways. I encouraged her to write RD attacks in her DDD, to reinforce her success and learn from her mistakes. Kim was very hard on herself, so a major challenge was forgiving herself at times when her Rouster prevailed. She practiced reminding herself, *"It's okay to make mistakes, nobody's perfect,"* and I reinforced this in every session. With practice, she got better at diffusing her RD and enjoying more good times with her sons. Kim's greatest satisfaction came from replacing the abusive anger her father had perpetrated on her with these positive approaches.

*Internal Disappointment*    Our rousting program can also steer us to displace our anger unknowingly onto others when we're really upset with ourselves. People who are externalizers habitually blame others when frustrated, especially during those times when they're disappointed in themselves. Although those of us who internalize predominately turn inward to assign blame, we're not immune to finding fault with others inaccurately at times.

As Tina and I continued working together, she learned that she was occasionally mean to her husband Ben when she was really disappointed with herself. Although infrequent, the few episodes that happened were hurting her relationship. She snapped at Ben when she felt like a failure as a teacher, specifically on days the students goofed off or talked back in class. Sometimes she lashed out after trying to accomplish a goal, such as learning a new software program, but becoming dissatisfied with her progress. Other times, she felt bad about herself with no immediate identifiable stressor. Instead of feeling relief, after every outburst, Tina's Master Demon grew, as she felt guilty and beat herself up for being cruel to Ben.

As we reviewed her outbursts, I asked Tina to recall any physical sensations she had before lashing out at Ben. Her primary body symptom was tension in her chest. She practiced using this early warning signal as a cue to pause and ask herself what she was upset about. When too agitated to think clearly, she left the situation physically and took time to cool down. After the pressure in her chest subsided, she reviewed recent events to discover what was bothering her. When she remembered to take these basic steps, she correctly identified that she was disappointed with herself, not with Ben. She stopped being used by her Rouster to hurt Ben (and herself) and redirected her focus toward denying her Negator, the real demon causing her upset.

**Table 4.4**

| Rouster Trigger | Ways to Exorcize Your *Wound-Based* Rouster |
|---|---|
| When expectations of others aren't met (II). | 1. To prevent harmful retaliations, avoid overreacting angrily to others' mistakes. |
| | 2. To stop recycling anger, identify prior hurts (especially rejection) and watch for similar actions, however small, as high-risk triggers; pause and compare current incidents to past offenses to correct biased observations and prevent punishing current loves for the sins of past loves. |
| | 3. To avoid anger outbursts with children, seek community resources for effective parenting skills; identify common misbehaviors and self-calming steps to implement (including Negator disrupters), and then calmly discipline as appropriate. |
| | 4. To stop hurting others by displacing anger toward yourself onto them, identify when you're beset with a Negator, not a Rouster; then refocus on refusing your ND. |

## When Others with Rousters Attack You

A challenging trigger to resist happens when others with active RDs snap at you. These situations are difficult to anticipate and occur all too frequently. Whether incidents are minor or major, if you respond with aggressive anger, you become a pawn, along with your challenger, in service of your RDs. When you suffer the negative consequences of raucous exchanges, your Rouster and Master Demons grow fortified by your anger and self-blame. Although anyone can lash out at you, the most likely people you'll encounter are loved ones you're regularly around. Conflicts are usually initiated in person, but they can also start over the phone, by email, or in a letter.

By pausing before reacting, you can freeze-frame the situation and review what just happened. With practice, you'll spot others' RDs attempting to activate yours. You'll free yourself from both Rousters by refusing to fuel unhealthy conflicts that only hurt you and your loved ones. It's very hard for others to fight unfairly when you refuse to participate. By disengaging, you'll also give them the chance to separate from and stop feeding their rousting bullies.

Although every situation is different, the following are general steps to resist RD affronts. Although they may be obvious, when Rousters are involved, it's easy to lose sight of following these basic civilized behaviors. Tell yourself and others that you're not going to fight destructively. Refuse to raise your voice, call names, or swear. Do not throw items or slam doors. Refrain from physical aggressions, such as pushing, slapping, or hitting. Walk away if needed to prevent altercations, and give the person space to calm down. Remind yourself that their inappropriate anger is not your fault or your responsibility to fix. Only get physical as a last resort if you have to restrain the person or protect yourself from immediate attacks.

Later, after everyone's calmed down, take time to address the incident. Let them tell you what they were upset about and what they want from you. Share how you were affected by their aggressions and ask them to share concerns calmly with you in the future. Kindly request that they take specific actions during discussions, such as using a calm and respectful tone, making eye contact rather than looking away, sitting down instead of standing, and holding hands instead of pointing fingers. If they flare in anger again, step back once more from destructive exchanges to allow time to calm down before proceeding.

People I work with typically encounter verbal aggressions from family, such as curt, gruff, and/or critical retorts. Their loved ones are usually upset by unexpected irritations or other stressors that weren't precipitated by my clients. If people in your life snap at you, it'll take practice to step away from these provocations, especially if they regularly occur in your home. Writing in your Demon Disrupting Diary and Reprogramming Record will help you resist invasive Rousters. Your entries don't need to be long or detailed to be effective. For example, my client John jotted down brief entries to identify the RDs operating in his relationship (DDD) and reinforce his efforts to stop feeding them (RR).

John's Demon Disruptive Diary:

*April 4:* Stacy's been grouchy & mean today & this week. I'm feeding off of her & getting mean too: ROUSTER. Just walk away & don't get caught up in her crap.

John's Reprogramming Record:

*April 7:* I didn't get mad/snap back at Stacy when she was in a bad mood. I am patient.

*April 9:* Again Stacy was in a bad mood. I called her on it without being mean or snapping back. I am a patient person.

At times when you're not sure how to respond, a good rule of thumb is to do less versus more. You'll avoid saying or doing things you might regret later. You'll prevent trying to fix others' problems that aren't your responsibility or within your control. If you already know specific understandable reasons your loved ones are stressed, remind yourself of their burdens. Give them space and remain supportive and empathic.

Sue was concerned that her husband Bob was growing more irritable toward her. He was abrupt and critical of her for things that didn't matter to him before. He became easily frustrated and was rarely satisfied. Sue found herself snapping back at him and didn't like her reactions at all. When I asked if she knew of any recent triggers for Bob's anger, she reflected that he was approaching his 50th birthday—an age he'd always considered old. Plus, he was looking for work after being recently laid off. It also didn't help that his car battery had just died and the shower had started leaking.

As we reviewed these reasons for Bob's irritability, Sue was reminded that none of them had to do with her. She felt empathy for his struggle and was proud that, in spite of everything, he was actively pursuing a new job. As we talked about what she could do instead of snapping back at Bob, I asked her to write these options in a DDD entry. Although she didn't write down a specific incident of Bob snapping at her, I recommend that you describe triggering events in your entries.

---

Sue's DDD Entry:
*January 11:* -Rouster-
*Trigger:* If B's Rouster triggers him & causes him to lash out at me I can stop myself from reacting to my Rouster (lashing out) by
— being sympathetic to how he feels (approaching B-day)
— not being a co-dependent; it is his struggle; I cannot *fix* it .
— just being there for him without doing or saying anything.

**Table 4.5**

| Rouster Trigger | Ways to Exorcize Another's *Bullying* Rouster |
|---|---|
| When others with Rousters attack you. | 1. Spot others' RDs trying to activate yours and resist reacting verbally or physically aggressively; know that it's not your fault or burden to fix, and only get physical if needed for protection. |
| | 2. When all is calm, share concerns about their outbursts and request specific respectful behaviors from them in the future. |
| | 3. Write in your DDD and RR to help steer clear of harmful Rouster exchanges, especially when loved ones snap at you regularly; provide space and empathic understanding when you know of particular stressors affecting them. |

## When to Flee

But what if these ways of handling another's Rouster Demon attacks aren't sufficient because these affronts put you in physical danger? Under these circumstances, you have to leave the situation in order to protect yourself. Before doing so, however, it's wise to plan the hows, whens, and wheres of your escape. During times of overwhelming danger, the flight part of your fight/flight response is activated. Hopefully, you won't encounter this hazard. But if you do, the earlier you detect warning signs of impending assaults, the easier it will be to escape potentially life-threatening traumas.

If you're living with or have constant contact with someone exhibiting increasingly hostile outbursts, you could ask the person to attend individual and/or couples therapy. However, if he/she doesn't agree to go or things don't get better with help, your safety remains a priority. Seek individual therapy and/or the resources of a nearby domestic violence center. Most communities list domestic violence hotlines in their telephone and Internet directories. You can also call a toll-free National Domestic Violence Hotline.[7] If needed, these professionals will help you develop and follow a plan to move yourself (and your loved ones) safely to a secure, private destination. For optimal assistance, also engage the resources of your personal network of family, friends, and other trusted people in your life. If you get stuck in a situation and you're in imminent danger of a physical attack, call 911.

My client Wendy was done trying to fix her marriage and felt ready to divorce. She tried for years to accommodate to and help her husband Noah with his moodiness and escalating temper. She coaxed him into attending an intensive couples retreat. She pleaded with him to go to couples therapy with her. The counselor promptly referred Noah to a psychiatrist for a medication evaluation and individual therapy for anger management. Although Noah attended these appointments and began taking prescribed medication, he continued to fly into rages at home.

Although she was glad he was getting help, Wendy believed that Noah was only going through the motions to prevent her from leaving him. She saw no improvement in his relationship with her and their four-year-old daughter. His outbursts were getting worse, and she couldn't predict what would set him off. Among other things, he blew up about parenting, finances, schedules, home remodeling, and in-laws. She constantly felt as though she was walking on eggshells. He grew louder and more critical of her during tirades, and nothing she tried calmed him down. In addition to being miserable and ready to leave her marriage, she was increasingly worried that Noah would physically harm her and her daughter.

Escalating episodes such as these are important to take seriously, because research findings indicate that verbal arguments precede physical aggression in couples two-thirds of the time. Instead of subsiding, angry outbursts tend to grow more violent and more frequent over time.[8] Noah had already started to act out physically, by angrily throwing the phone down, stomping off, and slamming the door behind him. Once his worst fear was realized and he discovered that Wendy was going to leave him, there was no telling what violence he might perpetrate. Research supports Wendy's serious risk of harm on leaving Noah. Women who leave physically abusive partners are at a high risk of repeat violence and homicide for up to one year after leaving. In particular, the first three months are especially dangerous for these women.[9]

As I worked with Wendy individually, we focused on her primary goal: to leave her marriage safely and start a new life with her daughter. As you read what she did, note that her advance preparations were especially careful and thorough. If you find yourself in Wendy's position, some of the steps that she took may not apply to your situation. If so, undertake only the actions that are relevant to your circumstances.

To prepare financially, Wendy had been secretly setting aside cash for months. To facilitate independence, she privately opened a checking account and post office box in her name only. She hadn't worked since getting married, so her goal was to return to school and pursue a degree to help secure a well-paying job. When she had time alone, she searched the Internet for local college and financial aid options.

Wendy told her parents, siblings, and trusted friends of her plan and gladly accepted their help. Her parents extended an open invitation for her to stay with them as long as she needed. She received an apartment key from her neighbor friend, in case she had to flee quickly on foot with her daughter to a safe place. Wendy was also welcome to fill out divorce paperwork and store items there for safekeeping. Another friend referred her to a divorce attorney, who guided her through the necessary legal steps. Her brother offered to loan her money and provide financial advice.

For education and resources, Wendy called a local domestic violence center and talked with a counselor there. She read information the center provided and followed suggested steps in preparing to leave. When Noah was at work, she made an inventory of the home and the items she planned to move out. She found a rental unit near her parents to store her things when she left.

To minimize disruption to her daughter, Wendy located a preschool close to her parents for her to attend. For financial and personal safety, she copied important monetary documents and made sure there were no weapons in the house. In the case of an emergency, she added 911 and the local sheriff's number to her cellular phone speed dial list and carried it with her at all times. To alert others covertly if she was in immediate danger, she identified a code word and advised everyone that if she said the word during a phone call, they should immediately call the police.

Wendy's instincts about Noah were right. In the middle of her preparations, he lost his temper at home again worse than before. He was walking backward ahead of and facing her as they jointly carried a heavy box upstairs. As he flared in anger, he let go of the box and the full weight of it toppled Wendy painfully down the stairs. He showed no remorse or concern and stayed home while she drove herself to the emergency room. After many hours at the hospital, Wendy emerged with a wrapped sprained ankle and crutches.

Although she declined to alert the police, this trauma fueled Wendy's determination to leave as soon as possible. She told her supports what happened, and her attorney prepared a restraining order to file if necessary. For her daughter's safety, she arranged for her and the dog to stay at a friend's house on the day she planned to leave. She alerted the preschool staff about Noah's angry outbursts and asked them to call if he showed up before letting him take their daughter. To break the news in a public, neutral setting she advised the couples counselor in advance that she was going to tell Noah of her decision to divorce during the next couples session. She asked a friend to remain nearby, in case she needed assistance and support. To prevent isolation, she arranged to attend a divorce support group at the domestic violence center

Fortunately, when Wendy broke the news to Noah, he didn't attack her in the couples session or afterward. She said he initially reacted to her decision as though he didn't believe her and expected her to return home shortly. Because he could have just as easily responded violently, her advance preparations were crucial in protecting her and her daughter. As time went on and Wendy didn't come home, she saw Noah put on his best behavior to try and win her back. By the time he fully realized that she wasn't returning, she was well into pursuing the new life she'd carefully planned for herself and her daughter.

## Emotional Bullies

Less dangerous, but more frequent than physical assaults, are situations in which others beset with Rousters attempt to bully you emotionally. This usually involves pressuring you to do something you don't want to do. Instead of respecting your wish, they keep trying to influence you to comply with their request. Examples include when sales people attempt to sell you things, friends cajole you to drink with them, or romantic hopefuls ask you for dates.

When others become emotional bullies, watch out for your Rouster: it will goad you to react aggressively, not assertively. Resist your RD by remembering that you have control over what you will and will not do. Prevent angry outbursts by assertively saying no and backing up your decision with your actions. If others don't accept it, instead of arguing with them, end the interaction by disengaging. Remind yourself that you'll not be manipulated by anyone's rousting bullies, theirs or yours. Take a look at my client Michelle's RR and DDD to see how she accomplished this and acknowledged herself for doing so.

Michelle's Reprogramming Record:

*February 9:* I didn't let them (car salesmen) talk me into buying a car of another color. I wanted a green car, and I stuck to my guns even though they tried to change my mind. <u>I am assertive. I do not compromise when I know what I want.</u>

*February 12:* Today I picked up my brand-new green Toyota RAV4. I will be leasing it for *three* years. <u>I am an astute consumer. I know what I want and will not give in and get less than what I want.</u>

Michelle's Demon Disrupting Diary:

*February 14:* Brian called me to wish me a Happy Valentine's Day and I told him same to him. He wanted to know how I was doing. I told him I was doing fine, having lunch with friends, going to the gym, and cleaning

**Table 4.6**

| Rouster Trigger | Ways to Exorcize Another's *Lethal* Rouster |
|---|---|
| When others with Rousters attack You (II). | 1. When in physical danger of a lethal Rouster, prepare and follow a plan to leave safely with support and help from family, friends, and domestic violence, therapeutic, legal, and law enforcement resources. |
| | 2. Validate your decision to go by knowing that anger outbursts escalate over time; keep safety measures a priority by remembering that you're still at high risk for harm within the first year after leaving your abuser. |
| | 3. Refuse to fight with emotional bullies; calmly say no and then disengage if they continue efforts to manipulate you. |

my home. He then said he had no phone call from me to invite him to lunch. I said I was busy, and he continued saying his phone must be broken as he had no voice mails or text messages inviting him to lunch. I said I had to go as I did not feel like arguing with him, and he kept being sarcastic with me and I did not want to get upset. I did not give in to the Rouster Demon. I finally told him I had to go and would call him at another time.

Just as others are vulnerable to rousting demons, beware of situations in which you may bully someone else. The sooner you catch it, the quicker you can disengage from your Rouster before hurting anyone. It may be tempting to let your RD rule if you only focus on the immediate benefit of getting others to comply quickly with your controlling efforts. Although, in the short run, you may bully them to do what you want, in the long run, you'll damage your relationships by losing their trust, affection, and positive regard for you.

Calvin yelled at his son Russell when he wanted him to do anything, such as get off the phone, do his chores, focus on his homework, or stop playing on the computer. Calvin was an imposing man, over six feet tall with a large build. His barks grew louder as his son got older and less responsive to his directives. As we talked about his bullying behavior, Calvin recognized that, although he usually got Russell to comply, he felt guilty afterward and beat himself up for being a mean father, feeding his Master Demon of defectiveness. Everyone in the family was turned off by his constant bellowing. Plus, Russell was learning to shout back more forcefully each year. Calvin's wife gave up trying to stop her husband's tirades and grew distant emotionally and physically. His daughter turned away from him too, bonding with her mother over their mutual aversion to his bullying outbursts.

As I introduced and described the demon model to Calvin, he easily recalled situations in which his Rouster Demon had formed in childhood. Growing up with eight brothers and sisters, he had learned from his older siblings to yell to get what he wanted. One recurring fight revolved around whose turn it was to use the single bathroom they all had to share. He watched his older brothers scream at his sisters to force them out of the bathroom whenever they wanted it. From observing and repeating countless battles such as these, Calvin's RD had emerged and thrived from the time he was very young.

After realizing what he was dealing with, Calvin worked on catching his RD and cooling down before reacting to Russell. Instead of yelling, he practiced giving calm directives and taking away privileges when Russell misbehaved. I cautioned Calvin that, because his rousting program had been installed and operating unopposed since early childhood, reprogramming would take time and repeated effort. I encouraged him to forgive himself when his Rouster prevailed and to learn from these slips what to do in the future to refuse his RD. I reminded him that self-forgiveness did not mean excusing himself from his reprogramming efforts; he retained full responsibility for starving his RD.

As Calvin practiced catching his RD at home, he noticed that his bullying behavior extended well beyond his family. He flared in anger while driving if he perceived that someone was impeding his travel goals. Such angry outbursts are very dangerous. High-anger drivers compared to low-anger drivers report more aggressive driving, more extreme and recurring anger episodes, and more auto accidents.[10]

---

Beware of bullying others, especially at home and when driving; catch and resist your Rouster to preserve your relationships and health. Forgive yourself for slips, while remaining responsible for starving your rousting demon.

---

One of Calvin's aggressive driving incidents occurred when he and another driver pulled up to a parking space. His rousting program activated in a split second, as he ignored his wife's pleas to forgo the confrontation and give up the space. He flashed his headlights, put on his turn signal, swore at the other driver, and muscled his car into the space. Although fortunately his car didn't hit anyone else's and he didn't cause an accident, only afterward did he realize that his parking space win was a loss in other ways. His wife turned emotionally cold to him for the rest of the day, and he felt guilty long afterward.

On realizing how often his RD attacked, Calvin expanded his reprogramming efforts to driving and to other public situations. He wrote in his DDD to learn from his slips and reinforce future RD-busting steps. Here's an entry describing another driving RD episode.

---

Calvin's Demon Disrupting Diary
*December 15:* Driving back from the gym, a car cut me off and pulled in front of me. My Rouster Demon influenced me to yell, honk, and swear in righteous indignation, that resulted in nothing but me endangering myself. My RD told me it was appropriate—even necessary—to act out. I've believed it all my adult life. But now I see it's not appropriate or necessary.

**Table 4.7**

| The Rouster Demon | |
|---|---|
| Directive | • It steers you to criticize and attack others. (pp. 77–78) |
| Ways to Identify (pp. 78–79) | • You often criticize and judge people, especially those you are close to. |
| | • When things don't go as you expect, you get angry and take it out on others. |
| | • It's hard to forgive people, even for minor transgressions. |
| | • You gossip regularly about friends, family, and co-workers. |
| | • When your needs aren't met by someone, you give that person the silent treatment and withhold affection. |
| | • You hold anger about something inside for a long time and then suddenly blow up. |
| | • You get irritated easily and snap at others. |
| | • When anyone criticizes or questions you, you respond by immediately attacking them. |
| | • You explode in physical outbursts toward objects, animals, and/or people. |
| Ways to Exorcize | • Name your Rouster Demon and how it operates (pp. 78–79). |
| | • Confirm that it's your Rouster and not someone else's (p. 80). |
| | • Catch common Rouster triggers and follow steps to refuse it (pp. 80–102). |
| |   • When your needs aren't being met (pp. 81–82). |
| |   • When you're doing for others at your own expense (pp. 82–84). |
| |   • When unexpected irritations occur (pp. 84–85). |
| |   • When expectations of others aren't met (pp. 85–94). |
| |     • Stop recycling anger; catch Negator Demons posing as Rousters. |
| |   • When others with Rousters attack you (pp. 95–102). |
| |     • Prepare and follow a plan to safely leave a lethal Rouster. |
| |     • Disengage from emotional bullies, including your own. |

CHAPTER 5

# THE TEMPTER DEMON

When the doorbell rang, Ellen jumped up excitedly to welcome her good friend Ava. She'd looked forward all week to this planned evening of hanging out, popping popcorn, and watching their favorite TV show. Ellen had barely opened the door when Ava burst in, spouting a tornado of complaints about her daughter Casey's recent disrespectful attitude and misbehaviors. Ellen's body stiffened and her stomach clenched as she thought, "Oh no, not again! I've heard this all before, too many times!" She was sick and tired of being Ava's emotional dumping ground. She might have felt differently if her friend had listened even once to her many suggestions to set limits and enforce consequences with Casey. But no, Ava continued in the same negative pattern with Casey and then vented her frustration onto Ellen.

As Ava came inside and sat down, Ellen's roommate Megan emerged from the kitchen and joined in. Megan listened intently, nodded, and validated Ava, expressing her mutual disgust about Casey's inappropriate behavior. Ellen's head pounded and her face flushed, as anger toward her friends surged inside. She instantly recognized these signs of an imminent Rooster Demon attack. She knew that if she stayed in that room any longer, she'd succumb to her RD and lash out angrily. Instead, she quickly excused herself and went outside to cool down.

As Ellen sank into the patio chair, a replay of what had just happened flooded her mind. Her head throbbed as thoughts surfaced, "I get so angry when Ava tells me this stuff! I don't know what to say anymore. I can't take it, oh, the hell with it!" Ellen's resolve to cut back on smoking vanished, as she pulled out a half-pack of cigarettes and matches and lit up. As the nicotine took effect, she physically relaxed and her focus shifted to the steady ritual of inhaling and exhaling. The entire upsetting episode soon became obscured as she finished cigarette after cigarette, in a chain-smoking haze.

When Ellen arrived at her therapy appointment, she pulled out her Demon Disrupting Diary and slapped it on the table. She shook her head in self-loathing and said, "I'm so upset with myself; I let my Tempter Demon get to me again!" She briefed me on her Tempter Demon (TD) attack as I opened her DDD to read her entry out loud:

Ellen's Demon Disrupting Diary:

*July 30:* Ava came over with more tales of woe about how horribly Casey treats her. I can't listen to her anymore because she just seems content to roll over and take the abuse. It has affected my feelings about her daughter. I will always love her, but I don't *like* her very much. I don't know what to say to Ava anymore. I get so angry when she tells me this stuff! (I want to strangle Casey.) But Ava just seems to use me as a dumping ground, never willing to consider advice. Megan (typically) was full of bluster and indignation at Casey, saying how much she wanted to kick her ass, etc. etc. I ended up outside chain smoking. I just couldn't take it anymore. *Tempter Demon.*

---

> The Tempter Demon lures us to do destructive things to ourselves.

---

As Ellen recognized, the Tempter Demon is another of the Soldier Demons, the fourth. Its directive is to tempt us to do destructive things to ourselves. Only after binge-smoking that night did Ellen fully realize how she'd been influenced by hers. While caught up in her goal to refuse her Rouster, her TD lured her with a quick fix—to cool down with a cigarette. One led to two until she lost count. Only after growing cold from sitting outside alone, did she realize that her triumph over her Rouster was really a defeat in service of her Tempter. As with every Soldier Demon, the Tempter can activate this way; when we're vulnerable because we're focused on refusing a different Soldier Demon.

## Tag Your Tempter

To tag your Tempter Demon as quickly as possible, stay alert for one or another of these revealing clues that signal its presence:

- You smoke, drink alcohol, overeat, or abuse other substances, even though it's harming your health, work, or relationships.
- When you're currently stressed or reminded of past hurts, you turn to alcohol, drugs, or food to escape your negative feelings, thoughts, and memories.
- Although you want to, you can't stop at just one drink, cigarette, pizza slice, etc.
- You're repeatedly drawn to the same type of abusive partner; you keep trying to make unhealthy relationships work even when you're constantly getting hurt.

- When you're lonely, you have unsafe sex with someone you don't know very well.
- You often overspend and you've accumulated unpaid debt.
- You've been charged with one or more legal offenses involving alcohol or drugs.
- You sabotage your success by doing distracting activities instead of completing your desired projects.

After succumbing to your Tempter, you feel guilty and beat yourself up for doing the self-destructive act. The TD feasts on your self-hatred and feeds your Master Demon of unworthiness. As your demons grow, you weaken to the Tempter's false promise that, if you follow its directive, you'll get what you want the next time. And the cycle repeats. The costs of addictions are enormous.[1] Debilitating consequences follow in crucial areas of your life, such as your health, job, relationships, and/or finances. Some of the countless possibilities include the following scenarios: you develop high blood pressure and diabetes from being overweight; you're arrested for drunk driving; after smoking for years you're diagnosed with lung cancer; you contract HIV from unprotected sex; you're forced to file for bankruptcy after shopping away your assets; you're fired from your job because your performance is poor and you're absent too often because of drug abuse.

The Tempter is often successful because it focuses us exclusively on instant gratification, not on the negative consequences that we'll suffer afterward. Ellen fell to her TD's promise that she'd get immediate relief from her anger by smoking. She was an easy mark, because her mother had modeled this "nicotine fix" approach when Ellen was growing up. Whenever her mother became upset, Ellen watched her pull out her cigarettes and light up. Through this observational learning, Ellen's smoking TD formed and grew.

> The Tempter promises instant gratification.

If Ellen had paused before pulling out her pack of cigarettes, she could've reflected on how disgusted she'd be with herself after smoking. She'd have time to review and select another option to calm down that wouldn't end up hurting her. She'd deny her Tempter, avoid feeling like a failure, and shrink her Master.

Because her Tempter had already prevailed in this incident, I first encouraged Ellen to stop fueling her Master Demon by forgiving herself for her slip. We then identified self-calming strategies that she could use instead of smoking to refuse her TD when Ava complained about Casey in the future. Because she'd tried to reason with Ava or change the subject many times with no results, Ellen decided that talking was not effective. Instead, leaving the situation was her best option. Her top choice was going to her room to read or to watch TV. She enjoyed these activities and found them to be distracting and calming. Because there was a long-standing rule of no smoking inside the apartment, she was less prone to lighting up inside—versus outside in her familiar patio smoking chair.

For more distance from the situation, she could also leave the apartment and go for a walk or a drive. As we discussed options, Ellen remembered that Ava planned to move out of state within a few months. Soon she wouldn't have to deal with this situation. Simply reminding herself of this fact during visits was another good way to diffuse her anger before Ava relocated.

To help reinforce and implement these self-calming options in the future, I directed Ellen to add them to her DDD entry. When writing in your DDD, remember to document specific strategies that you discover to triumph over your Tempter and other Soldier Demons. With this writing advantage, you'll turn future demon attacks into your gain by reminding yourself to use what you learn to separate yourself from and to refuse your demons.

---

> Always include strategies to deny your Tempter in your DDD.

---

## Catch Common Triggers to Expel Your Tempter

Through working with clients like Ellen over the years, I've witnessed common situations that repeatedly trigger tempting programs. Once you know you've got a Tempter, watch out for these vulnerable scenarios where the demon may strike. Beware, name, refuse, and triumph over your Tempter by utilizing the following strategies tailored to each situation.

### The Tempter Promises Escape from Current Stress

Ellen's TD attacked through one common trigger, promising a fast escape from current stress. When we take this bait and engage in destructive quick fixes, we may feel relief at first. But soon afterward, our stress multiplies. Now we're beset with the negative health, emotional, and other consequences resulting from the self-sabotaging act. Plus, the original stressor remains.

Ellen's Tempter also prevailed when she felt stressed at work. Because her workplace prohibited smoking inside, she had to leave her desk and walk around the building to a designated outside area. To save time, she often stopped to light up behind trash bins closer to her office. This shortcut also concealed her activity and allowed for a longer break. Still, Ellen felt like a pariah having to smoke outside, especially when hiding next to the foul refuse. Afterward, she felt ashamed and upset with herself. She knew that others could smell the smoke on her clothes and hair when she returned. To make things worse, she worked in a health care center. She hated herself for being a hypocrite; promoting healthy practices to others while voluntarily inhaling well-known toxins. Plus, on returning to the problems that she'd escaped, she now had less time to deal with them before the workday ended.

When enticed to flee a stressor through a self-destructive act such as smoking, call your Tempter's bluff instead and face the stressor head on. More often than not, you'll find the problem is not nearly as taxing as your TD led you to believe. Even if the situation is difficult, by addressing it right away you can dispatch it as quickly as possible. For Ellen, this means responding promptly to vendors and employees who leave angry voice and email messages. Initially, she feels overwhelmed and doubts her ability to handle such grievances. However, when she forces herself to address these stressors right away, she handles them much better than she predicted. Plus, she avoids the damages from escaping through smoking, including returning to the burden of unresolved complaints.

Even if you don't do a good job handling something, you can learn from your mistakes and apply this knowledge to the next situation. For errors at work, ask co-workers and supervisors for constructive feedback and answers you didn't know. Seek additional training to learn the skills and information required. Delegate tasks and request assistants to handle work overload.

When Ellen worried that her supervisor thought she was performing sub par, she often succumbed to her Tempter and smoked to distract herself from her concerns. However, after finishing each cigarette, her fears resumed. When she shared this in our session, we discussed asking her supervisor right away for an early performance evaluation. When Ellen followed through with her request, her supervisor did bring up concerns about numerous absences. However, this feedback was much less critical than what Ellen's TD had conjured up. Armed with reality, Ellen could now focus on boosting her work attendance without having to escape a stack of false fears through smoking.

> When stressed, resist TD attacks by addressing problems right away; when your efforts don't work, seek answers, constructive feedback, and guidance from others.

*Get Outside Help*   When pernicious habits, such as smoking, drinking, dangerous eating patterns, or other substance abuses, develop from repeated Tempter Demon assaults, maximize your results by engaging additional resources to help break free. Assistance from others may be crucial to your success, especially when your habit is a full-blown addiction. If you remain alone, you're beginning your battle already compromised from the toxic effects of the substance. When you've got physical cravings and your mind is in a haze, you lose the strength and focus to resist your TD. It easily tightens its grip, keeping you trapped in a debilitating cycle of substance abuse and shame.

A good first step to garner resources is to schedule an appointment with a mental health professional who is experienced in treating your type of substance abuse. To find someone, ask supportive friends, family, or others for suggestions. Insurance, phone, and Internet directories are other fruitful places to look. Many employers also provide referrals through employee assistance programs. During the appointment, the therapist will interview you and provide recommendations, depending on the severity of your usage. Options range from weekly outpatient psychotherapy and 12-step meetings, to structured daily outpatient substance abuse programs, to round the clock detoxification and inpatient substance abuse treatment centers.

If you haven't recently received a full physical exam, you'll be directed to schedule one with a primary care doctor. When you go, shine a spotlight on your Tempter by divulging the substance that you've been abusing; ask for tests to check whether it's caused detectable harm. Results will reveal your current medical status and options to improve your health. If the substance has already caused damage, start suggested medical treatment before the condition worsens.

Depending on your specific needs, your treatment professionals may also refer you to a psychiatrist, nutritionist, chiropractor, acupuncturist, or various other health specialists. This may seem like a lot to do. However, when dealing with resistant addictions fostered by Tempters, the more resources that you work with, the more likely it is that you'll succeed. Assessing and healing your body from the outset provides a big jump-start in detaching from your tempting force and reclaiming control over your life.

Sometimes a routine physician visit becomes your first step to get help. Many physicians regularly screen new patients for drug abuse; those with significant symptoms are often referred immediately to drug abuse treatment.[2] In Ellen's case, she'd just seen her primary care physician for her annual physical and revealed to him that she'd struggled with depression off and on for years. He referred her to me for that reason.

Although in our first appointment Ellen revealed smoking 6 to 10 cigarettes daily, she wasn't feeling able to cut back. Only after we'd been working together a few months and her depression had improved did she consider taking on this challenge. Even now, she vacillates between being ready or not to kick her Tempter out. Although her usage is not a one or two-pack addiction and has

---

**Table 5.1**

When Tempter Attacks Create Serious Addictions

1. To determine the best treatment for you, consult with a mental health professional with experience in your type of substance abuse.
2. To detect health problems from the addiction and learn medical care options, schedule a full physical exam with a primary care physician.
3. For maximum results against virulent TDs, follow through with additional referrals: psychiatrists, nutritionists, chiropractors, and so on.

remained steady for years, it's still cumulatively harmful to her health and self-esteem. So, I suggested additional treatment options, including a stop-smoking program at work, medications such as a nicotine patch and nicotine gum, and self-help reading to assist with this goal.[3] When Ellen is ready, she now knows a host of resources that she can enlist to smoke out her Tempter and Master.

### The Tempter Promises Escape from Old Hurts

The Tempter also lures us into self-harm by assuring us freedom from old hurts. Typically, these hurts are unhealed emotional wounds caused by loved ones. Although the physical, sexual, or verbal abuse may have happened long ago, the damage to our self-worth is still fresh. We drink, overeat, do drugs, and so on, to blot out the painful memories and the feelings of worthlessness and responsibility that remain. Afterward, we reap the negative consequences and beat ourselves up for doing the harmful acts, further nourishing our Master Demon of defectiveness. As we feel awful, the hurtful memories stay strong.

To detach from your Tempter's grip, instead of self-medicating through destructive habits, first identify and heal old emotional wounds. Face what happened by telling yourself, those close to you, and, if possible, a psychotherapist about them. Shrink your Master Demon by releasing self-blame. Remind yourself that it wasn't your fault and that you are worthy. Because this is difficult, for childhood traumas, remember how old you were when you were hurt. Imagine that the same thing happened to another child of the same age. Would you blame that child for what happened? For adult traumas, such as physical or sexual abuse, would you blame your best friend or family member if the same thing happened to him or her? Now treat yourself just as you would others by releasing personal blame. Repeat these steps as often as needed. Add efforts to deny your Tempter; replace harmful addictive patterns with healthy self-enhancing approaches.

Alyson was molested by her uncle when she was 12 years old. She blamed herself and kept it a secret until, in high school, finally gathering the courage to tell her mother. Nothing was done. As she shared her "dirty" secret again with me, I spotted a Tempter. She described soothing her pain with food: first the upset from her uncle's abuse and then the despair from her mother's inaction. As we talked, it also became clear that Alyson's TD was subconsciously assuring her that being overweight would protect her from future unwanted sexual advances. However, her "fat overcoat," as she called it, didn't always work; some men continued to show an interest. Plus, her excess pounds were now contributing to high blood pressure, joint pain, and frequent fatigue.

Alyson had already tried many weight loss approaches. Although she had learned much about healthy nutrition and exercise, her knowledge never materialized into desired results. One reason was that her MD thrived on her self-blame for the hurtful events. Deep down, she believed that she was defective and not capable of being physically or emotionally healthy. Every time she started to make progress and lose weight, her belief of unworthiness surfaced. For relief from self-loathing, she succumbed to her tempting program's phony claims that she'd receive comfort and safety through her old familiar fix of food. Afterward, she beat herself up for sabotaging her diet. If she was going to successfully lose weight this time, she needed to reject proactively both her Master and her Tempter.

To help Alyson heal from her original wound, we focused on helping her stop blaming herself for her uncle's abuse. Because she'd never told anyone the details, I asked her to tell me, in order to pull her shame out of the closet. As she recounted what happened, I interrupted many times to point out evidence to support why she was not at fault. To strengthen my case, I asked, "Would you blame your niece (a preteen) if the same thing happened to her?" For extra support, I suggested a nearby group for survivors of sexual abuse. To aid in recovery, I directed her to reading resources specifically for adult survivors of sexual abuse.[4] Alyson declined the group and book options, but now she knows that these resources are readily available if she changes her mind.

To reinforce tangibly that she wasn't at fault, I asked Alyson to write a letter to her uncle, holding him accountable for the many ways he'd hurt her. She agreed to express her anger, betrayal, grief, and other reactions with no holds barred. Because she didn't want to confront him, I assured her that she didn't have to send him the letter. After we read it together in our next session, she could destroy it in whatever way that she wanted, such as shredding, burning, or the option she chose—mashing it down the garbage disposal.

I then asked Alyson to write a letter to herself as if it was written by her uncle. The letter said everything she wanted to hear from him but hadn't. Important messages included taking responsibility for the abuse and apologizing in detail for the harm that he'd caused her. In subsequent weeks, she wrote similar letters to and from her mother—this time to hold her mother accountable for doing nothing after Alyson had told her about the abuse. Writing letters such as these, both to and from the perpetrators, is often employed as an effective healing tool in psychotherapy.[5]

As we worked together to shrivel her Master Demon, I cautioned Alyson that it had grown massive from her years of self-flagellation. Shrinking it would not be instantaneous; she needed to remind herself repeatedly that she wasn't to blame for what her uncle had perpetrated. Equally important, she needed to establish new, healthy, self-care habits to starve her well-entrenched Tempter Demon.

A top priority was refuting her Tempter's claims that she must remain overweight for protection. Contrary to when she was a child, she was now an adult and able to protect herself in ways she couldn't back then. Verbally, she could refuse men's advances and end unwanted conversations. Physically, she could leave or defend herself if necessary. For education and practice in protective strategies, a local community center offered an evening self-defense course that she could take after work. We also reviewed preventive steps, such as staying mindful of her surroundings, carrying aids to use if needed (e.g., loud whistle, pepper spray, cellular phone), avoiding walking alone at night, parking in well-lit and well-traveled areas, and installing home and car security systems.

To replace overeating, we identified other self-nurturing activities that she could choose instead. Her top choices were getting a massage, gardening, taking a bath, calling a friend, asking her husband to hold her, sitting in her lawn chair and reading a novel, and doing yoga. To enhance the effectiveness of these soothing strategies, I encouraged Alyson first to write DDD entries describing her TD attack and what she chose to do instead of overeating. To ensure that she didn't restrict healthy eating, she agreed to check whether she was physically hungry or not before substituting a different activity.

During many stressful situations, her Tempter tried, through criticisms, to drive her to binge-eat. When this happened, she recorded the TD's put-downs, countered them with her own words, and then engaged in a self-care activity.

> TD: "You're fat, you're always going to be fat."
> Alyson: "Okay, GET OUT NOW! I'm done with you, good-bye. I'm not going there. I don't need that (fat overcoat) to protect me. I can take the coat off."
> TD: "You might as well have the hamburger and fries because you'll probably never lose weight anyway."
> Alyson: "I deserve to be healthy. I can take care of myself and eat the food that is the best for me."

To facilitate her goals, Alyson agreed to rejoin Weight Watchers and Curves, the weight loss and exercise programs that she'd experienced the most success with previously. However, unlike before, now she was actively focused on depleting both her Master and Tempter Demon. This multipronged approach placed her in a strong position to heal past hurts and build healthy habits from the inside out.

For reinforcement, I directed Alyson to document her new healthy eating and exercise efforts in her Reprogramming Record. I encourage you to use your RR similarly to weaken the Tempter and other Soldier Demons. By recording the steps that you take to replace self-sabotaging behavior with self-enhancing alternatives, you'll facilitate new positive habits. You'll also build evidence to counter your TD when it tries to sabotage your progress and make you slide back. For example, here are RR entries written by various clients to strengthen desired habits and diminish their food Tempters:

*August 10:* Went for a 1-hour walk with Phil. It felt good. <u>I am able to exercise and take good care of myself.</u>

*May 13:* Going to Weight Watchers for 9 weeks. Lost 9 lbs. I prepare each day in the kitchen and my mind what I am going to eat. Jello is my friend. <u>I am working toward a healthy body, keeping strong, and not giving in to the Tempter Demon.</u>

*May 14:* Only getting what's on the list at the grocery store. <u>I'm making healthy choices and becoming more disciplined.</u>

*September 20:* Went to the fair today. Did a lot of walking. Got rained on several times, but it certainly didn't dampen my enthusiasm! Didn't eat a whole lot of fair food. <u>I have strong willpower. I plan and follow through with fun activities that include walking.</u>

*November 3:* I make healthy lunches to bring to work. <u>I am taking care of my body.</u>

*March 12:* 50 sit-ups at home. <u>I am determined to have great abs. I have determination.</u>

**Table 5.2**

| Tempter Trigger | Ways to Exorcize Your *Open Wound* Tempter |
| --- | --- |
| When you're beset with old emotional hurts. | 1. Identify, confront, and share old hurts with close others.<br>2. Release self-blame repeatedly; write letters to hold perpetrators accountable in order to let go of negative emotions.<br>3. Replace damaging habits with self-enhancing behaviors; engage boosters of therapeutic groups, self-help reading, and, for food TDs, healthy eating and exercise programs.<br>4. Write down Tempter criticisms, replace them with your own kind words, and then reward yourself with a self-care activity.<br>5. Document slips and triumphs over your Tempter in your DDD; reinforce successful reprogramming steps in your RR. |

As with all of the Soldier Demons, remember to beware of the Tempter flaring as you make progress. When threatened, it will attack, to keep you in the same negative patterns. Because its very survival requires a constant supply of your misery and self-blame, it will repeatedly activate, to retain you as an emotional fuel source for itself and for the Master Demon.

### The Tempter Lures Us into Unhealthy Relationships

The TD also influences us to pursue relationships that aren't good for us. I encounter this often in my practice. One frequent scenario occurs when clients are attracted to romantic partners who, similar to the clients' parents, are emotionally unavailable to them. Clients keep trying to make these one-sided relationships work—consciously, to mend the current detachment and, unconsciously, to heal emotional hurts that began in childhood. Their efforts don't work because no one has the power to fix someone else, partners and parents included. Their Tempters keep them locked in an impossible quest, attempting to get love from those who don't have it to give.

To break free from this TD trap, let go of trying to change someone who isn't putting effort into having a relationship with you. Use your energy instead to follow the steps that we discussed earlier to identify and heal old emotional wounds. Fortunately, unlike trying to fix others, healing yourself is a process within your control. Resist the urge to revolve your life only around that person. Identify specific personal goals and interests. Build activities, professional pursuits, and social contacts into your schedule to help you meet your needs and objectives. As you focus on fulfilling yourself outside of your relationship, your elusive partner may make an effort to connect more with you. Or nothing could change. Either way, by creating a life that extends beyond that person, you'll feel stronger and better able to decide whether to stay or leave the relationship.

Melissa came to her session stressed out and fatigued. She lamented, "I've been dating Ryan for months now and we're not moving forward in our relationship. I'm doing everything I can to get closer to him, but I feel like I'm his lowest priority." As she reviewed her numerous phone calls, long drives to see him, and offers to attend his baseball games, I recognized and revealed her Tempter's influence. Melissa was doing all of the work in the relationship and losing herself in the process. Everything in her life had taken a back seat to Ryan. The less responsive he became, the more she tried to engage him.

If the relationship had a chance, Melissa needed to back off and allow Ryan the opportunity to pursue her. Just as important, she needed to refocus on other aspects of her life. Priorities included school, work, and friends, all of which she'd been neglecting. She used to enjoy running outside, afterward feeling energized and happy. A while ago, she had started to create several short stories to submit for publication. These activities fell by the wayside when she began to see Ryan.

As we talked about resuming her running and writing, Melissa grew animated. She still had her running shoes, clothes, and familiar route to follow. She resolved to find her unfinished stories and select one to complete first. She decided to start writing an Internet blog about daily events that she observed. I encouraged her to make time every week for these pursuits. In addition to meeting her needs, they would help her ignore her Tempter's pleas to contact Ryan.

---

Beware: Tempter statements are often in the first person.

---

Melissa was prone to pursuing unavailable men, just as she'd tried unsuccessfully to gain her father's attention. As we focused on healing from her father's neglect, we spotted a familiar Tempter message that had been created back then. This time Ryan's name replaced her father's: "If Ryan doesn't want to be with me, then no one else will. I'm worthless on my own." Note that this message is in the first person. As discussed previously, the Tempter and other Soldier Demons often operate this way, through statements that sound as though you're talking to yourself. Don't be fooled; recognize this as old programming, not you. Do what Melissa did and replace it with your own words: *"I have enough worth on my own; if it works out with Ryan, he is a complement to me."* Reprogram in this way every time that you spot a self-sabotaging Tempter declaration.

As Melissa stopped pursuing Ryan, he did not go after her. Although she fell back sometimes to chasing him, she mostly refocused on the other areas of her life that we'd identified. Their relationship faded until he broke it off. Although Melissa was sad and upset, she wasn't as devastated as in previous breakups. Instead of losing her whole world when Ryan disappeared, she retained the people, commitments, and activities that she'd reconnected with.

If you find yourself in a similar situation to Melissa's, keep your guard up. Even after you're out of an unhealthy relationship, your Tempter will try to pull you back in. Use your DDD to catch and refuse it. Learn your vulnerabilities and adjust your environment to avoid being an easy target for your tempting force. If you slip, write in your DDD to learn what to do next time and then forgive yourself.

Although Melissa began to date other men after Ryan, her TD activated whenever she was weakened by boredom, loneliness, or alcohol. Its directive was always the same—to urge her to contact Ryan in the hopes of getting him back. Here is one such attack that she recorded in her DDD:

*February 20:* Bored in class with laptop and wireless Internet. Browsing through bookmarks and see Ryan's site. Didn't go to it, but thought about it and thought a lot about him. Sad that his life is going on without me, most likely untouched and unaffected. Miss him a lot and wish there was an email or something from him. Not necessarily thinking bad thoughts about myself, just general, sad, empty thoughts. Loneliness. I don't know which demon this is. (11:00 p.m.) I wanted to go to his site instead of going to bed. —Tempter. I turned off my computer instead.

Melissa initially wasn't sure which demon was operating when she was at school. However, when she paused that night to record a similar attack at home, she realized it was her Tempter. As she discovered, the more often you document attacks in your DDD, the easier it will be to identify and ignore the demons that operate on you. As you can see, entries don't have to be long or time-consuming to be effective.

Melissa didn't include in her DDD how she had rewarded herself after successfully refusing her TD. When I pointed this out, she said she'd forgotten all about it. I hear this often from clients; most of whom aren't accustomed to celebrating their triumphs. To avoid similar losses, remember to reinforce your victories by treating yourself to something special. Once reminded, Melissa rewarded herself with a luxurious bath, complete with aromatherapy candles—something that she loved but rarely did for herself.

---

Remember to reward yourself after you triumph over your TD.

---

The Tempter can also lure you to other types of self-sabotaging relationships. For those that you're at risk for, identify specific TD triggers and adjust your environment to avoid them. By removing outside factors that make you vulnerable, you'll increase your resistance against your TD. A major trigger for Melissa was alcohol. When she went out to bars drinking with her friends, her tempting force was at its maximum advantage.

Once revealed, we recorded what Melissa could do in the future to avoid her TD's tactics. Because she was the most vulnerable when drunk, her best defense was to limit alcohol. Although an optimal solution, she didn't want to stop going out drinking with her friends. She also wasn't ready to forgo alcohol at the bars. However, she was willing to set a limit of drinking no more than two alcoholic drinks all night. For outside reinforcement, she asked a girlfriend who didn't drink to help monitor her intake and prevent her, if necessary, from ordering a third drink.

Note that Melissa's plan worked because she didn't have an alcohol addiction. Stopping at two drinks was not excruciating for her, unlike someone fully engulfed in alcoholism. If you struggle with a substance addiction, Melissa's plan may not work for you. Instead, read on for other strategies to use.

**Table 5.3**

| Tempter Trigger | Ways to Exorcize Your *Unrequited* Tempter |
| --- | --- |
| When you're attracted to someone who is emotionally unavailable. | 1. Redirect your energy from chasing that person to identifying and healing old emotional wounds.<br>2. Set personal goals and initiate activities, professional pursuits, and social contacts to meet your needs and objectives.<br>3. Catch and replace old Tempter sabotaging messages with your self-enhancing affirmations.<br>4. Learn your vulnerabilities and adjust your environment to avoid falling back into pursuing a one-sided relationship. |

### The Tempter Says, "Go Ahead; Have Just One"

When you are beset with an addiction, the Tempter can entice you into using with the assurance that you can stop after one drink, one cigarette, and so on. As soon as you partake, the TD's work is done. When your body feels the addicting effects again, you're hooked back into physically craving more. Stopping now is incredibly difficult. You blame yourself for breaking your abstinence. You feel like a failure and say, "What the heck, I've already blown it," and continue using. Through your defeat, your Tempter and Master Demon thrive.

The best way to avoid this downfall is to say no to the first drink, cigarette, or other substance. Prepare for vulnerable situations with strategies to prevent using. Well-known addiction programs advocate this tactic, having long incorporated abstinence-based approaches in their treatment protocols.[6] Major events that are scheduled far in advance, such as vacations, weddings, and parties, lend themselves well to early planning.

However, small immediate incidents may be more likely to catch you off guard. Identify and remain alert for these sudden triggers that may otherwise slip you up. The following are examples that my clients in recovery have confronted. Unfortunately, they learned what to do after falling off the wagon to their TD's appeals. By taking preventive steps before and during high-risk situations, you can avoid how they had to learn, the hard way:

- While at home making dinner. TD: "You're working hard; pour yourself a glass of wine."

  Prevention: *Remove all alcohol from the house.*

- When on a first date. TD: "Go ahead. Have just one beer: you'll feel more relaxed."

  Prevention: *Practice relaxation strategies before and during the date. Order club soda with lime.*

- At night, when you're keyed up and worried about work. TD: "You'll relax and stop worrying after you have a drink."

  Prevention: *Write down the worries and list action steps to take to resolve concerns at work. Take a long hot shower.*

- After a day of skiing. TD: "You deserve to reward yourself with a nice hot Baileys and Cream; after all, this is your vacation."

  Prevention: *Make an agreement in advance with your spouse to have an alcohol-free vacation. After skiing, relax in the hot tub instead.*

- Arriving home feeling overwhelmed with things to do. TD: "Sit down and pour yourself a glass of wine first. You'll relax and it'll be easier to get your chores done."

  Prevention: *Recall that drinking impairs productivity. Start with one chore, such as folding the laundry or making a phone call. Remember that getting things done is the key to feeling relaxed.*

My client Max carefully had planned a weekend in Mexico with his wife. This was a very high-risk situation, because he used to go there often to get drunk before becoming sober. Together, they set goals to remain abstinent, to avoid bars, and to eliminate any alcohol from their room. Max looked up AA meetings that were held close to their hotel and chose in advance which ones to attend. They identified activities to enjoy as a couple instead of drinking, such as walking, lying on the beach, swimming, dining at various restaurants, and taking a local bus tour. Aided by this preparation, Max stayed sober and had a good time.

However, after arriving home, his Tempter almost got to him through an alluring Sniper assault. One hot afternoon, while he was working in the yard, it subtly suggested, "It sure would be nice to have a beer to cool down." Although it was a minor incident, Max was highly vulnerable. Unlike during the Mexico trip, this time his guard was down because he hadn't anticipated or prepared for this. Drinking beer after working outside used to be his routine. Without thinking, he went inside and opened the fridge. A few beers were there, left over from entertaining guests.

Fortunately, Max caught and refused his TD before popping open the first beer. In addition to therapy, he was fortified by months of AA meetings, regular sponsor contacts, and working through the 12-step program. In place of a devastating relapse, he cooled off with a tall glass of lemonade.

For double reinforcement, record your triumphs over your Tempter in your RR in addition to your DDD. Here's an example from another client's RR:

Derek's Reprogramming Record:

*May 9:* Walked to the coffee shop. Mixed tracks. Went to Erica's, played outside, and went to a movie. She offered me a beer, but I didn't drink. <u>I am social, productive, and it's becoming easy to play music with others. I'm more powerful than the demons. I'm stronger than the Tempter.</u>

**Table 5.4**

| Tempter Trigger | Ways to Exorcize Your *Addiction-Based Tempter* |
|---|---|
| When you're abstinent from your addiction and tempted to have just one. | 1. Say no to the first drink, cigarette, or other substance.<br>2. Plan ahead for vulnerable situations by preparing your environment, activities, and coping tools to prevent using.<br>3. Stay alert for unexpected small triggers; catch and refuse your TD before partaking in the substance. |

### The Tempter Says, "You Must Buy It Right Now!"

Our society is filled with advertisements promoting quick access to what we want, usually through available credit. In this atmosphere of instant gratification, the Tempter can easily thrive, and this presents a problem for those of us who are in debt or close to it. Whether it's overspending through shopping, gambling, investing, or something else, the end result is the same. We feel ashamed afterward for losing two things: self-control and money.

A good defense against this tempting program is to create a budget and stick to it. If you have a partner, do this together. Do not keep secrets. Allow your partner to monitor what you're spending to help put a stop to TD activity quickly. To avoid complete deprivation, which sets you up to binge, allot some money to spend how you want each month. Find ways to get desired items by spending less. Look for sales and promotions, comparison shop, use discount coupons, substitute generic for brand-name items, cook at home more often, and use other creative approaches.

To gain freedom from draining interest payments, use some income to pay off debt each month. Save up for major items, such as college tuition for your child, vacations, or home remodeling, to prevent future debt. Accumulate up to six months' worth of living expenses as a backup in case of a major financial hardship, such as getting laid off or developing a serious illness.

Olivia was beset by a tempestuous divorce. Although relieved that her husband Luis had moved out, she was facing a financial challenge at home, caring for their two daughters. Legal proceedings were dragging on, and Luis was growing unreliable in sending the agreed upon support checks. Although Olivia was a responsible parent and worked full-time, she'd never been a careful shopper. Although shopping had been a source of contention in the marriage, her spending had never created a financial hardship. Luis earned a high income, which had always covered her liberal purchases.

In addition to coping emotionally, we focused on building careful spending habits. Olivia first created a budget of income and expenses. By examining current spending, she saw how quickly her purchases accumulated, even minor ones. The following DDD entries describe resourceful means by which she foiled her TD and found less expensive ways to have the things she wanted.

Olivia's Demon Disrupting Diary:

*April 8:* Starbucks (*Tempter*). Every day, I am tempted to go to Starbucks and buy a tall caramel macchiato, which costs $3.15. That multiplied by 365 days totals $1,149.75 yearly. That would be the equivalent of airplane tickets for 3 for our summer vacation. I bought coffee, coffee creamer, and coffee filters that cost much less. I will make my own coffee and allow myself one Starbucks per week on my office day, Wednesdays. I am able to budget myself and stay on my budget.

*April 21: Tempter.* I was tempted to buy new furniture, knowing full well that I have my credit card debt at $9,000 and need to pay any extra money to the credit card to bring it down to zero. My current sofas look bad as they are 8 yrs old and the cushions are torn, so instead of giving in to the Tempter I washed the cushions and took them to an alteration shop to have them sewn so they will look good again without spending money I don't have. I am responsible with my money.

*June 16: Tempter.* I bought 2 dresses online from Macy's.com and spent $200.00 dollars. The Tempter Demon said it was ok to buy these dresses even though I can't afford them right now. I bought the dresses; however, once I got them, I decided this was not a positive financial decision and I marched into Macy's and returned them both as they did not fit anyway and they were too expensive. I went dancing and wore my pretty blue dress that I had bought last year.

In her third entry, Olivia initially succumbed to her Tempter and bought dresses she couldn't afford. However, after realizing what she'd done, she quickly returned the items for a refund. If you're swept up by your spending TD, as soon as you realize it, explore all options to reclaim your funds. By using your time trying to fix the situation instead of beating yourself up, it may not be too late to undo what you've done.

For extra reinforcement of her new careful spending practices, Olivia documented her successes in RR entries. Because she was already using a one-page per day computer calendar (Outlook) to schedule activities, she added her RR entries there. She typed each entry next to the hour it occurred. By incorporating her RR into her routine, she facilitated writing daily. As she referred to her calendar during each day, she saw her RR entries, which reinforced her triumphs and cued her to write more. (Instead of underlining, she substituted parentheses because they were easier for her to type.) Here are some of her examples:

Olivia's Reprogramming Record:

*April 8:* 7:00 a.m. Every morning, I make my own coffee with flavored creamer—the smell of freshly brewed coffee especially made just for me, tastes great. I am saving $3.15 daily for other pleasures. (I am staying disciplined and only allow one coffee away from home per week as a treat.)

*April 10:* 6:00 p.m. Dinner with girlfriend at her house. We did not spend any money buying food and ate all of her leftovers. (I am conscientious about money.)

*April 16:* 1:00 p.m. Washed car. (I take care of my car and saved $14.00 in the process.)

*April 19:* 10:00 a.m. $2.57. Bought lip liner using coupon. (I take care of my needs while taking advantage of coupons.)

*April 20:* 12:00 p.m. Starbucks. (I treat myself to one Starbucks per week.)

*April 21:* 5:00 p.m. Soap opera. (My treat for the day that does not cost money.)

To create a hard copy of her RR, Olivia regularly printed out the calendar pages and organized them in a binder. She liked being able to flip through this tangible version of her RR for a mood boost whenever she wanted. She remarked that she had no idea how many constructive things she was doing until she started documenting them. As Olivia experienced, the more you write in and review your RR, the more you engage this power of positive reprogramming.

**Table 5.5**

| Tempter Trigger | Ways to Exorcize Your *Overspending* Tempter |
|---|---|
| When you're lured to overspend because you want it right now. | 1. Set a budget and stick to it; let your partner monitor your spending to help stop any Tempter activity quickly. <br> 2. Allow some discretionary spending monthly to prevent binges. <br> 3. Save through smart and creative shopping strategies. <br> 4. Pay some income monthly to reduce debt and interest payments; save up for major expenses to prevent future debt; save up to six months' worth of living expenses to use in case of hardship. |

### The TD Says, "Have Fun instead of Meeting Your Goal"

When we're working toward a goal, TDs can sabotage our efforts by tempting us to do something enjoyable instead. Breaks in moderation and at the right time are healthy and not a problem. In contrast, our tempting agents convince us to enjoy ourselves in excess or at the wrong time. As a consequence, we fail to reach our goals on schedule, if at all. When we do, our finished project is lacking because we've wasted too much energy goofing off. As we blame ourselves for falling short, our Master Demon of defectiveness grows.

The best way to thwart your distracting TD is to stay in control over your projects and schedule. Set goals and manageable steps to reach them. Create a reasonable time frame for completion. Build in fun breaks at optimal times to enhance your productivity. As with all Soldier Demons, identify vulnerabilities to your TD and stay alert to these high-risk situations. When it strikes, refuse your TD as planned and write about it in your DDD. If it succeeds, forgive yourself for slipping and resume your efforts as quickly as possible. Here's how another client reacted to one of his TD attacks:

> Jordan's Demon Disrupting Diary:
> *May 10:* I have a problem with delayed gratification and would do fun stuff before work stuff. In this case, anything is fun rather than work on my proposal. The Tempter was strong to go dancing instead of finishing my proposal for the Friday deadline. I was ill Sun, Mon, Tue, Wed, so Thursday I worked on it as much as I could and also on Friday and I sent it out by 5:00 p.m. that day. I am able to stay on track even though I was sick and tempted to go dancing and watch TV instead of my proposal. I am able to resist the Tempter.

Jordan told me afterward that refusing his Tempter was especially difficult because his friends called him three nights that week to go salsa dancing. They had all met and formed a bond while taking salsa lessons together. They had so much fun that when the class ended, they continued dancing together at various salsa clubs. By sticking to his goal, Jordan didn't have to wait too long to do what he loved. After completing the proposal, he danced with his friends later that night. Because he forgot to write it down, I directed him to add his reward to his DDD entry.

In DDD examples like Jordan's, the Tempter's messages are not written down. However, by pausing to identify TD dialogue, you can more easily tailor your thoughts and actions to reject its specific manipulations. Take, for example, Derek's DDD entry:

*June 29:* I don't know if Erica is good or bad for me. I like hanging out with her but I'm afraid that the situation is gonna consume me. The Tempter wants me to lose myself in the relationship: "Let music go. Erica will fulfill your needs." True me says: "The situation doesn't have to consume me. I can still focus on music and personal goals. I don't have to revolve my life completely around her and I'm not going to. Only I can fulfill my needs and I'm gonna keep playing music because it fulfills me."

Although detailed entries are optimal, the most important thing is to make a habit of writing in your DDD and RR. If brief entries help you stop your Tempter and other Soldier Demons effectively, then write those entries. Anita included many short entries in her DDD. These brief references were enough for her to remember and to reinforce the healthy steps that she took to halt her food Tempter.

> Anita's Demon Disrupting Diary:
> *July 12:* Tempter. Wanted pie, said it wasn't worth it.
> *July 14:* Tempter. Exercised instead.
> *July 22:* Tempter. Wanted more food, resisted.
> *July 28:* Tempter. Hungry after dinner. Diet more important. Looked at dresses instead.

This last entry was especially effective, because looking at dresses offered dual rewards for Anita. First, it was a desirable substitute for overeating. Second, she enjoyed browsing dresses to show off the results of her healthy eating and exercising.

**Table 5.6**

| Tempter Trigger | Ways to Exorcize Your *Distracting* Tempter |
|---|---|
| When you're tempted to have fun instead of completing your goal. | 1. Control your projects and schedule by breaking goals down into doable steps with reasonable completion dates.<br>2. Program enjoyable breaks at ideal times to boost your efforts.<br>3. Write TD dialogue in DDD entries to help tailor effective statements and actions to refuse it; write habitually in your DDD and RR for maximum results in shrinking your TD. |

## Oust Your Tempter with Passion and Purpose

A powerful deterrent for tempting demons is pursuing healthy passions. The old adage "An idle mind is the devil's playground" is particularly relevant to this strategy. When activated, TDs quickly dominate our thoughts and behaviors, trapping us into mental and physical addictions. Once we stop these destructive habits, we're highly vulnerable. Because the TD previously occupied much of our time and attention, we're now at a loss for what to do. If we don't substitute beneficial things to focus on, we're sitting ducks for our TDs. Left idle, we easily succumb to old physical and emotional cravings, falling back to familiar self-sabotaging habits. Addiction programs include this approach in their treatment protocols, replacing addictive behaviors with healthy activities to help prevent relapses.[7]

If you're like many clients I've seen, you don't know what your Tempter-free passions are. To find out, ask yourself these questions:

---

- What topics and causes interest me?
- Is there something I'd enjoy learning?
- What do I look forward to doing?
- Which activities make me feel good when I do them?
- What have I always wanted to do but was afraid to try?
- Is there anything that I used to enjoy doing but stopped?
- What do I like to do that I'm good at?

---

If this is difficult, ask close confidants to help you answer these questions. Think back to when you were a child. What were your early interests? What did you want to be when you grew up? Was there anything you were passionate about but were discouraged from doing? Did unexpected obligations or choices sideline any pursuits?

After identifying possible passions, try them out and see how you feel. Start with small steps to avoid overload. Know that you are in charge and that you can change your mind anytime. You're not required to do anything you don't want to do. What you prefer is up to you. The important thing is to discover what excites and inspires you. Once you discover a passion, this may well lead you to a special purpose.

---

Ask key questions to identify potential Tempter-free passions; sample each one to discover what energizes you.

---

Among my clients, one passion that turns into a purpose is learning something new. Often, this happens during addiction recovery programs. By focusing on self-enhancing endeavors, they build confidence and keep their TDs at bay. After sustained personal success, they share what they've learned, in order to help others. In addition to providing assistance, mentoring helps them feel useful and stay on track with self-affirming steps. It's hard to tell who's gaining more, the clients or the people they're aiding. I often hear that making a positive difference—not only in their lives but also in others' lives—is extremely rewarding.

For example, while in recovery, Claire grew passionate about attending AA meetings and learning to follow the 12-step program. After much hard work and successful sobriety, she became a sponsor to assist a new AA member. While Paul was recovering from drug dependence, he became interested in learning to meditate. We'd done some relaxation exercises during sessions, which spurred his interest in taking group meditation classes. He liked it so much that he proceeded to enroll in advanced classes to become a meditation trainer.

> Find purpose through sharing your passion to help others.

Other clients reconnected with a passion they'd previously learned. They first pursued the interest for themselves and then expanded their efforts to assist others. Here are some examples:

- Bill started riding his bicycle for exercise, to build up his lung capacity and to remain smoke-free. He used to enjoy bike riding as a boy but hadn't ridden since college. Bill enjoyed it so much that he decided to train for a bicycle race to raise funds for AIDS.

- Judy began walking as part of an exercise and eating program to lose weight. Soon after, she signed up to participate in an arthritis walk and began raising donations. Judy was passionate about this walk because her sister had suffered with arthritis since childhood.

- Cathy created art in therapy to help avoid alcohol binges and to heal old emotional wounds. She was reminded how much she relished painting, which she'd stopped during a painful childhood. After reconnecting with her passion, Cathy resolved to add art to her classroom activities as an elementary education teacher.

- While in recovery from heroin dependence, Jason took vocal lessons to reconnect with his early passion for singing and to help stay clean. He loved it so much that he recorded songs at home with heartfelt lyrics he'd written before and after he started in recovery. Jason eventually added these songs to his My Space page for other listeners' benefit.

## Defeat the Tempter's Quick-Switch Tactic

Once you've successfully identified and refused your TD, it may try to steer you to a different self-sabotaging habit. Addiction substitution is a well-known phenomenon in the therapeutic community.[8] I see this all the time in practice. People become so focused on stopping one bad pattern that they're caught off guard when their TDs influence them to engage in a different problematic activity.

To prevent falling prey to this tactic, know that your tempting program is always seeking to pull you back into destructive behaviors. This is the only way it survives, by feeding off your negative emotions when you act out in debilitating ways. Once you disconnect from it by stopping one harmful habit, it will automatically attempt to plug you back into another one.

Identify addictive vulnerabilities in addition to the one that you're focused on right now. Take steps as soon as possible to prevent falling into these damaging actions. Program your day to replace old addictive routines with new healthy patterns. As always, write daily in your Reprogramming Record. Tailor entries to reinforce successful steps to deny your Tempter. If your TD succeeds, follow the steps discussed earlier: write about it in your DDD, learn what to do next time, forgive yourself, reset, and move on. Here are two examples of this quick-switch TD tactic that I've witnessed.

After stopping a long-standing pattern of overeating, Beth began smoking cigarettes daily instead of occasionally. She was susceptible to smoking because nicotine helped curbed her appetite. Cigarettes also provided a comforting replacement to binging—a ritual involving her hands and mouth to ingest a substance.

After attending an alcohol abuse program and becoming sober, Alexis began dating men who treated her poorly. She met them all through an Internet dating Web site. The men she pursued were critical of her, called her at the last minute for dates, and then stopped contact after she was physically intimate with them. Instead of alcohol, Alexis was now chasing toxic men.

The TD has no limit to its quick-switch ploy. In the case of my client Brenda, as a teenager she began overeating and throwing up. After much help and hard work, she stopped this binge/purge cycle in her twenties. Becoming pregnant with her first child provided a timely motivator to kick out her food Tempter. However, instead of leaving, it switched her attention to shopping. Although initially harmless, her spending eventually grew frequent and out of control. She ran up thousands of dollars of credit card debt. She hid it and told no one, not even her husband.

To curb her TD, Brenda resolved to window-shop only when she went to the mall. As she browsed items she was used to buying, her Tempter quick-switched her from spending to shoplifting. She stuffed a blouse in her purse and proceeded to leave. Brenda's theft was witnessed via a store video camera. Two security officers appeared and escorted her to the back room of the department store. They questioned her and quickly recovered the stolen blouse from her purse.

Because Brenda had no previous record, she avoided incarceration and was instead punished with a stiff fine. She was banned from shopping at that department store and her name was sent on a watch list to security at other store locations. As she confessed this to me, she said the worst part was the humiliation and self-blame that she heaped on herself for doing something she knew was so very wrong. The only thing that would have made it worse was if one of her children had been with her that day. Score 0 for her and 100 for her Tempter and Master Demons.

Brenda did well to share honestly what happened and to take full responsibility for stealing. As always, we remain accountable for stopping our demons from creating misery in our lives. However, I cautioned Brenda about getting stuck in self-blame and doing little else. Because the demon model is designed for those of us who habitually blame ourselves (internalize), we're prone to falling into this inertia trap of unrelenting self-flagellation. To regain control and stop feeding her Master Demon of worthlessness, Brenda needed to forgive herself. Studies show that people with high self-compassion are able to acknowledge their mistakes without feeling overwhelmed with negative emotions.[9] By being kind and self-forgiving, Brenda could hold herself accountable without getting mired in self-hatred. She'd stop fueling her MD and be able to turn her full attention toward refusing her tempting demon.

Brenda also needed to reprogram her routine actively in order to resist her shoplifting Tempter in the future. Being publicly humiliated in the store was already a helpful deterrent. In addition, she agreed to tell her husband, other family members, and her pastor at church about the incident. From now on, there would be no more window-shopping. She would never go to a department store alone and only take enough cash for planned purchases. Because she was very religious, she resolved to put a small bible in her purse as a TD deterrent. She also planned to read her bible and pray every day.

I cautioned Brenda about her TD's quick-change maneuvers. Now that her shoplifting Tempter was exposed and dealt with, it could easily switch back to food and/or spending. Or it could steer her to a different destructive activity. For protection, I reminded her to continue healthy eating and exercise habits and to keep her credit cards in check. As additional substitutes for her addictions, Brenda became passionate about volunteering at her church and attending bible study.

To reinforce her TD-busting steps, she agreed to write them down in her RR every day. To prevent her TD from quick-switching, I reminded Brenda to include efforts to refuse all three major temptations: food, spending and shoplifting. She also agreed to write Tempter successes and slips in her DDD.

**Table 5.7**

Prevent the Tempter's Quick-Switch Tactic
1. Identify negative habits that you're vulnerable to in addition to the one that you're actively focused on.
2. Reprogram your routine to avoid switching habits.
3. Forgive yourself for slips and go back to Step 2.
4. Boost reprogramming with your DDD and RR.

The more that Brenda sticks with these reprogramming efforts, the more she'll deplete her TD. Through her triumphs, she'll gain self-worth and automatically shrink her Master Demon of unworthiness.

## The Tempter Says, "You Can Stop Now. You're Cured!"

As you become successful in thwarting your Tempter, it will try to convince you that you're cured of the destructive habit and you don't have to continue the reprogramming steps anymore. If you listen to its false assurance, you'll set yourself up for a slip. Once you stop your TD-busting efforts, at first you may not notice how vulnerable you're becoming. Your strength will fade gradually, especially if no new stressors are testing your resilience. However, your defenses will continue to weaken until some problem eventually occurs. Bang! The Tempter fires a Sniper attack and you fall back into the sabotaging behavior.

Although you can always recover, it's much easier to keep positive steps going than relapsing, suffering the consequences, and then having to piece back together your protective steps. For example, research shows that patients who attend at least one 12-step meeting every week after completing substance abuse treatment have much lower levels of substance use (almost 50% lower) compared to patients who don't go to meetings as often or at all.[10]

Julie was making great progress in therapy. When she first came to see me, she'd been sober for more than three years and was regularly attending AA meetings. By sticking with her recovery program, she hadn't relapsed to drinking. This time, instead of problems related to alcohol, she wanted help dealing with a difficult breakup. We'd identified her old habit of pursuing unhealthy relationships, and she was getting good at steering clear of abusive men. She'd begun dating men who were kind and respectful, and her confidence was growing. Instead of losing herself in potential relationships, she was now prioritizing her needs and goals.

During each session, I always asked Julie about her AA meetings and she shared which one she'd attended that week. One week, she casually mentioned that she didn't go. Although skipping one meeting didn't seem like a big deal, I advised Julie not to let her TD gain the advantage. The more meetings she missed, the more separated she would be from the resources that help her prevent alcoholic slips. Julie quickly agreed to go to a meeting that week. Because she was due to get her four-year chip, she offered to show it to me at her next session.

This scenario was replayed in the next three sessions. Each week, Julie offered different reasons for not following through. First, she didn't feel well; then, she forgot; and then, her friend canceled plans to go with her. Each week, I stressed how not attending AA made her vulnerable to her tempting force. This danger was difficult to convey because Julie was making progress everywhere else. She was writing in her RR and DDD, asserting herself with men, and building in weekly self-care steps. She'd just ordered cable TV service, something she'd wanted for a long time but until then did not feel she deserved. Even so, Julie's Tempter Demon was poised to exploit any weakness and tempt her to drink. Once she fell back to drinking, her progress in other areas would also fall down.

---

*Warning:* Do Not Listen
When your Tempter assures you that you're cured, instead continue positive reprogramming steps to avoid slipping back into old self-sabotaging habits.

---

Finally things came to a head. I confronted her about her pattern of making a commitment, not following through, and showing no concern for how this affected her. Just as she felt hurt when past boyfriends had shown no regard for her, she was repeating this pattern by treating herself with little respect. Julie was stunned to recognize that she was hurting herself as others had hurt her before. She became tearful and she resolved to honor her commitment by going back to AA.

At the next session, she brought the four-year chip that she received at an AA meeting that week and proudly showed it to me. We paused to review her success and celebrate her triumph. Fortunately, Julie disarmed her TD before it pulled her back into drinking. She avoided the losses that come from falling back and having to climb out of an addictive pit. However, I reminded her that her Tempter Demon would activate the next chance it got. To keep it at bay, she needed to continue her self-care steps, including going to AA. Like the popular AA saying advises, *"Keep coming back; it works if you work it!"*

**Table 5.8**

| | The Tempter Demon |
|---|---|
| Directive | • It lures you to do destructive things to yourself. (pp. 105–106) |
| Ways to Identify (pp. 106–107) | • You smoke, drink alcohol, overeat, or abuse other substances, even though it's harming your health, work, or relationships.<br>• When you're currently stressed or reminded of past hurts, you turn to alcohol, drugs, or food to escape your negative feelings, thoughts, and memories.<br>• Although you want to, you can't stop at just one drink, cigarette, pizza slice, etc.<br>• You're repeatedly drawn to the same type of abusive partner; you keep trying to make unhealthy relationships work, even when you're constantly getting hurt.<br>• When you're lonely, you have unsafe sex with someone you don't know very well.<br>• You often overspend and you've accumulated unpaid debt.<br>• You've been charged with one or more legal offenses involving alcohol or drugs.<br>• You sabotage your success by doing distracting activities instead of completing your desired projects. |
| Ways to Exorcize | • Name your Tempter Demon and how it operates (pp. 106–108).<br>• Catch the following common Tempter triggers and follow steps to refuse it.<br>  • You're experiencing current stress (pp. 108–109).<br>  • When Tempter attacks create serious addictions (pp. 109–111).<br>  • You're beset with old emotional hurts (pp. 111–115).<br>  • You're attracted to someone who is emotionally unavailable (pp. 115–118).<br>  • You're abstinent from your addiction and tempted to have just one (pp. 118–120).<br>  • You're lured to overspend because you want it right now (pp. 120–122).<br>  • You're enticed to have fun instead of meeting your goal (pp. 123–124).<br>    • Oust your Tempter with passion and purpose. (pp. 125–126).<br>    • Defeat your Tempter's quick-switch tactic. (pp. 126–129).<br>• When your Tempter assures you that you're cured. (pp. 129–130). |

CHAPTER 6

# UNHOLY ALLIANCES

Steve met his friends at a local sports bar. He hoped this diversion would help him get over Valerie, the woman he'd been seeing for months. From the beginning, their relationship was shaky. They had met soon after Valerie's boyfriend Rick broke up with her. Although she was very sad and preoccupied by her loss, Steve thought she would recover as they continued to date and grow closer. However, after just a few weeks, Rick contacted Valerie. They started talking and then casually meeting. At first, she told Steve that she and Rick were just friends, but eventually she admitted to having feelings for Rick. When she repeatedly refused to stop spending time with Rick, Steve ended their relationship. He told her he was sick and tired of feeling second place in her heart. Although relieved from the constant stress, his self-esteem was shot and he missed Valerie terribly.

Although he felt very sad, Steve sat down and told no one at the bar about his heartache. Instead, he proceeded to hang out with his friends. He ordered a beer, with the intention to drink just one. He had to get up early for work tomorrow and didn't want to wake up feeling lousy. Although he'd never had an alcohol problem, on the few occasions when he did drink too much, he felt tired and blue the next day.

As Steve told me in his therapy session what had happened, he pulled out his corresponding Demon Disrupting Diary entry:

*July 24:* I was spending time with friends at a bar when I received a message from Valerie telling me that she missed me and she would like to talk with me if I was available. I started to feel bad about my situation with her. My Negator Demon said, "Your relationships never work out. You will always be unhappy." I felt as if I had just been knocked down. My Tempter Demon then said, "You should get drunk. What does it matter if you are self-destructive?" I then proceeded to buy more drinks. The next day, I had a hangover and felt as if I had let the demons get the better of me. In the future, I would like to recognize before the fact that I am upset and that drinking will just make me more upset.

---

| Beware of demon pairs striking in a one-two punch. |
| --- |

---

As Steve realized, two of his Soldier Demons had teamed up to attack him in a classic one-two punch. His Negator first oriented him to be self-critical about his failed relationship, and his Tempter then coaxed him to hurt himself by binge-drinking. I see group demon attacks such as these all the time in my practice. They strike in various combinations, in pairs, threesomes, and sometimes all four. In this chapter, we'll highlight common Soldier Demon alliances and methods of attack.

As you read on, see if you can identify the coalitions that are most likely to team up on you. Use the tailored strategies that follow and then review and combine those from solo demon chapters to exorcize your Solider Demon combinations. As they shrivel and fade away, so will your Master Demon of unworthiness, freeing you to live as the powerful, loving, and worthy person you truly are.

## Negator-Tempter Duo

Steve was hit by the Negator-Tempter duo. As he experienced, one common scenario is when both demons triumph, one right after the other. His Negator brought him down first and then his Tempter delivered the knockout punch. As he and I reviewed his DDD, Steve added one important detail that had made him highly vulnerable to his ND. He called Valerie back immediately from the bar on receiving her text message. His Negator had attacked after their conversation, when he realized that nothing had changed. Valerie asked to see him but, when he inquired, maintained that she had no plans to stop seeing Rick.

For protection against future ND-TD attacks, Steve needed space and time away from Valerie in order to heal from the breakup. As we discussed options to facilitate his recovery, he agreed to ask her not to text or call him unless she stopped seeing Rick. If and when he was ready to be friends, he would contact her. As long as Valerie honored his request, Steve wouldn't have to experience this major Negator trigger of her reaching out to him when nothing had changed. With his ND inactivated, Steve's TD would have a harder time pulling him down to drink self-destructively.

If Valerie did contact him, Steve set a goal to not respond if he was in a situation where alcohol was readily available, such as at a bar. If he did succumb to talking with Valerie, he resolved to remember what he had written in his DDD: drinking when upset just makes him more upset. Instead of drinking, we reviewed coping

**Table 6.1**

| For each Demon Disrupting Diary entry, include: | | |
| --- | --- | --- |
| • Date | • Demon name | • When and how it attacked |
| • How you responded | • What you learned | |

steps that he could take, such as replacing harmful ND and TD dialogue with his own self-affirming messages, talking with his friends or sister, going to the gym, and pursuing healthy interests such as watching and playing sports.

As Steve discovered, writing in your DDD helps you identify triggers and plan ways to bust your demons in the future. Like him, at first, you may often find yourself writing only after your demons have prevailed. Remember to write your entries according to the DDD format first presented in Chapter 2 and reproduced here.

Do not write on and on about how terrible the situations or people were or how awful you felt. Focusing too much on negatives is draining and it sets a potential Negator and Rouster trap. When caught in it, you're diverted from effectively identifying and replacing demon programming with your self-enhancing steps. Instead of starving your demons, you end up unwittingly feeding them.

When the ND and TD team up, either one can activate first, based on the situation and your vulnerability. Watch out for changes in their sequence and remember their directives in order to help foil their ploys. If you defeat the first one, stay alert for the second one to step in and attack. Here's a DDD example of a Tempter striking first, followed by a Negator. My client Lea writes how she prevailed over both:

*January 22:* Today I had to send out résumés. I was home and had just finished tutoring. My Tempter Demon was telling me to sit and watch a movie. But when I told myself and Keith [her boyfriend] that I needed to get these résumés out, my Negator Demon began to kick in and tell me that I was incapable of applying to any position and that I was unqualified. But I had drafted my cover letters last and read them aloud, telling myself that I am qualified and an excellent potential employee. Since it was too late to reward myself, I am going to reward myself tomorrow. I think I will make myself a fresh berry smoothie or get a new CD.

| |
| --- |
| Watch out for changes in demon attack sequences. |

By refusing both her TD and ND, Lea felt very good about herself. She stayed focused on her résumés and strengthened her confidence as a job candidate. As planned, she successfully sent her résumés out that day. If she'd watched the movie instead, as her Tempter had directed, she would've lost valuable time that she'd set aside for the résumés. If she had been weakened by falling behind her schedule, her Negator would've had an easier time convincing her that she was not good enough to be hired. If both her ND and TD had won, her Blocker Demon could've easily joined in and stopped her from fulfilling her career goal of getting résumés out to prospective employers.

## Negator-Rouster Duo

Another formidable demon pair is the Negator-Rouster. I encounter them frequently in my practice. They team up especially when ambiguous situations occur. The Negator orients us to be self-critical and feel inadequate. The Rouster steers us to assume the worst about others and inappropriately lash out against perceived transgressions. I see this ND-RD pairing often in situations involving desirability to one's partner and competency at home or work.

### Desirability

For instance, consider my client Lynn's DDD concerning desirability to her husband:

*October 10:* Came home from work to Glen. [He] got off the Internet fast. [I was] immediately suspicious and worried. What was he doing?
*Rouster:* "That bum."
*Negator:* "It's because I'm getting old that he's looking at other girls more."
*Demon Disrupter:* Called Glen [later, at work] and told him what I'm thinking and asked if any basis to that, which brought rational conversation. He told me nothing was going on, that he would try hard not to look at other girls.
*To Rouster:* "Glen has given me no reason to believe anything is up."
*To Negator:* "I look good for my age, no reason for him to look elsewhere."
*Reward-* Take a nap!

In this example, Lynn refused both her ND and RD. A key to her success was that she caught them soon after they had struck. She thwarted her RD by pausing before reacting to Glen and taking time to cool down. She spotted her ND even when it used the first person (e.g., "I'm getting old"). She then examined its criticisms for veracity. When she was calm, she asked Glen in a nonaccusatory tone if he was finding her less attractive and pursuing other romantic connections. He assured her that he found her beautiful and he wasn't looking for anyone else. He did acknowledge briefly glancing at other women when they walked by, saying he'd do his best not to look in the future.

Lynn already knew that Glen looked at other women and reminded herself that it had never upset her before. She also reflected that, in all of their years of marriage, he'd done nothing to raise her suspicions. She remembered the many compliments she continued to receive about her attractiveness, especially those from Glen. With these steps taken, she confidently wrote rebuttals to both her rousting and negating agents. After triumphing, she remembered to reward herself with a nap, a welcome pleasure that she usually skipped.

Although catching Soldier Demons right away is optimal, chances are that they'll slip beneath your radar at least some of the time. Although your first reaction may be to blame yourself for failing, remember that you're bound to fall back, especially at first. By not beating yourself up, you'll be able to focus fully on reviewing what just happened. Take credit for partial successes, however small, and for writing down what you learn, in order to stop similar attacks in the future. Include helpful ways that you recover after your demons have prevailed. By pausing to write the incidents down, you may realize that your recuperation efforts are the most empowering steps that you take.

Remember that—unlike other therapeutic approaches that direct us to look inward for the source of damaging thoughts, actions, and beliefs—the demon model orients our attention away from ourselves, in order to recognize and catch our demons, the destructive patterns we have learned through early aversive life experiences outside our control. Instead of depleting ourselves by feeding our Soldier Demons and Master Demons with self-blame and self-criticism, we are empowered by the demon model to use our resources to gain freedom from these external foes.

My client Kelli fell victim repeatedly to her Negator-Rouster duo. She had discovered, through writing in her DDD, that they kept inflaming her fear that her boyfriend Wes would lose interest and leave her. Here is an entry Kelli wrote soon after identifying this type of ND-RD attack. The triggering incident happened when she was out with Wes and other friends at a dance club. Note that DDD entries can be as long or short as you need to assist your demon-busting efforts.

*March 10:* My boyfriend Wes was sitting next to me; then he got up and left and was gone for a while. I sat there and then decided to go to the bathroom. As I was walking to the bathroom, I ran into Wes and Monique hugging hello. I first thought that she must be walking in and that they encountered each other as I was meeting up with them; then, in a flash, my Rouster Demon told me that they probably had made plans to meet and he probably had exchanged phone numbers with her and they had called each other to meet up at the club. I went to the bathroom and while there I tried to think rational. I have learned to take a time out and try to cool off before making rash decisions. However, I couldn't and my Negator told me that Neil [her ex-husband] had left me for a woman who had a beautiful body like the one Monique has and that probably Wes would also leave me for her just as Neil had done. I tried my best to rationalize the logical case scenario—that they met on the way to the dance floor by chance—rather than what my Negator was telling me, that he probably likes her better because she has a perfect figure. I could not recuperate and think logically and my only alternative was to leave. I was livid and jealous of one of my group friends only because of her figure. The Rouster wanted me to fight so instead of saying good-bye to everyone at the table I grabbed my purse and coat and left, making a scene and people were left asking what had happened to me as I was noticeably angry. I learned next time to say good-bye to my friends, regardless of my anger as they should not have to deal with my personal Rouster Demon.

Kelli started out strong, by spotting her rousting and negating agents as soon as they had struck. She thwarted her Rouster, by taking time out to cool down instead of lashing out at Wes and Monique. She documented these successes to take credit for and reinforce her efforts. When her Negator tried to convince her that she was undesirable, she did her best to counter its criticisms. She lost ground when her ND prevailed and her RD joined back in, steering her to leave in an angry huff.

When I asked what happened later with Wes, I was surprised to hear that Kelli had quickly recovered from her ND-RD attack. She called Wes an hour after leaving the club. They had a long talk and she apologized for angrily leaving without saying good-bye. She shared her negative assumptions and how hurt she felt. He explained that running into Monique was not planned and that he had no desire to dump her for Monique. He was upset that she didn't trust him, but what hurt him the most was her rude exit. Kelli knew from our sessions that her Master, Negator, and Rouster had been created in part by being abandoned by her mother as a child. To help Wes understand why she reacted so irrationally, she shared her trauma with him. To her surprise, he confided that he too had been abandoned in childhood, which explained why he was so wounded when she suddenly left him.

---

| Include efforts to recover from demon attacks in your DDD. |
|---|

---

I encouraged Kelli to add her successful recuperation to her DDD entry. Not only did she bounce back, but she'd grown closer to Wes as they shared similar hurtful experiences that had created their demons. Empowered by this knowledge, they could now help each other to catch and detach from their NDs and RDs. If Kelli didn't document her recovery, she'd forgo taking the credit that she deserved. With no tangible record to review, she'd be less likely to reflect on or feel good about her revitalizing steps. As the popular saying foretells, out of sight is out of mind.

### Competency

Sometimes you'll realize well after an incident that your demons have struck. Know that it's never too late to go back and write about what happened in your DDD. You'll reinforce your successes and learn how to prevent future demon attacks. My client Jim wrote the following DDD entry late one night. He'd been feeling lousy ever since that morning. As he reviewed what had happened that day, he realized that his ND-RD duo had attacked during an early staff meeting at work. Although he'd disabled his Rouster, his Negator had continued unchecked. This is another common pattern I see, stopping one Soldier Demon but not the other.

---

Jim's DDD Entry:

*August 26:* Tonight I recognized a trigger that may have (but didn't) release my Rouster Demon. When Craig [his supervisor] said, "Well, Joe has spoken on this, and he knows because he has . . . I heard my Negator totally put me down: "You can't really speak with authority on this. You don't really know. Your opinion and thoughts are not as right or important as Joe's thoughts." Baloney. The lessons: 1. My thoughts are valid. 2. I don't have to convince others for my opinions to be valid or for me to have worth. 3. I can let it go.

---

Note that Jim wrote his DDD well after the meeting. Pausing to review what had happened allowed him to take credit for blocking his RD by not reacting angrily toward his supervisor. He also identified his ND's criticisms as the source of his upset. When the Negator is involved, its personal put-downs are often difficult to recognize and detach from right away. If Jim hadn't paused to explore why he felt so bad, he wouldn't have detected his negating bully or replaced its denigrations with his own affirming statements. His ND would have clandestinely continued to feed off Jim's anxiety and self-doubt.

## Negator-Blocker Duo

The Negator-Blocker twosome is extremely toxic. The Negator criticizes our qualities and abilities related to self-enhancing activities. The Blocker stops us from following through with these self-positive steps. Like other demon pairings, they attack together or sequentially, with either one striking first. They show up in virtually every session I have with clients, while we're talking as well as in DDD entries. If one strikes out, the other steps up to bat. In the case of my client Liz, her Blocker tried to stop her from exercising. When it failed, her Negator tried to criticize her for wasting time exercising instead of doing household chores:

> *June 15:* At home this morning, my Blocker Demon attacked me. It said, "You don't have time to exercise. You've fallen off the wagon. You're too busy since you're babysitting." No, I realize this is *for me*—it's good for me and will make me happy. I made time and feel great. It made me more ready to be there in a good mood for the kids. The Negator Demon tried to make me feel guilty for exercising and not doing other more important chores. It said, "Well, but you should have done these other chores." I overcame it by valuing myself and saying, "This is for me." For next time, I'll remember to say that I am important and this makes me feel great. -Reward myself for catching the demons.

When Liz ignored her blocking program, her negating program tried to make her punish herself for exercising. Fortunately, she caught and refuted it right away. She reminded herself at the end of her entry to reward herself for her success. Although it's best to reward yourself every time you catch your demons, if you forget, you'll still come out ahead. By following through with your self-promoting actions and thoughts, you'll automatically receive the intrinsic payoffs they produce.

If you, like Liz, view writing as one more undesirable duty in a long list of "have-to's," consider what she did. Initially, she struggled to complete her RR and DDD homework. On one typical night, she reluctantly sat down to write. As she reviewed her day—filled with work, child care, cooking, and cleaning— she realized that, unlike these tasks, her journals were exclusively for her. Taking time to self-reflect was nurturing and revitalizing. She always felt better afterward. After this mind shift, she began to look forward to this time just for her. Now whenever her old mind-set of having to do homework creeps back in, she remembers that writing in her journals is a way to pause and take care of herself for a change.

---

> Approach writing in your RR and DDD as a time to pause and nurture yourself.

---

To help catch your BD-ND duo, know that their directive is to ruin any constructive endeavor. In addition to exercising and other personal care efforts, my clients often log attacks as they pursue creative and professional goals. For example, Derek's BD-ND duo activated every time that he played his music for others. He wrote the following DDD entry after playing his self-recorded CD for his friend Mark:

> *September 19:* I felt embarrassed for playing it [CD] for Mark. Negator told me Mark's response to my music meant he thought it sucked and that he lost interest in playing music with me. That's probably why he never called. Blocker told me that I'm not ready to put my music out there. True me/Reality: Mark never said he thought it sucked and wasn't critical at all. He said he still wants to jam. I don't know why Mark didn't call, and it's not important. It's best to let this go and keep playing and doing my best. This is a learning process. It's not about what other people think. I feel ready to put my music out there, so I'm going to. I have nothing to lose, and there's no reason to be embarrassed.

Derek told me that, although he didn't feel 100% better right after challenging his Negator-Blocker duo, his DDD entry did help him to stop his Blocker and to keep playing his music. As he repeatedly listened to and improved his songs, he showed himself that his music was good enough. By taking these self-enhancing steps, he diffused his Negator and increased his confidence. As Derek's example illustrates, overcoming one demon strengthens your ability to stop the other one.

## Tempter-Blocker Duo

In addition to the demon duos we've already highlighted, be on the lookout for others. For more examples, recall the clients that were beset by demon pairings in previous chapters. In those cases, as clients expelled one demon, another one took over. Gloria was introduced in Chapter 3. After winning over her Blocker by going to dinner with friends, her Negator spoiled her fun by criticizing her social skills and desirability. Chapter 4 started with Sharon's experience. After diffusing her negating force while conducting work meetings, her rousting force influenced her to lash out angrily at her family when she arrived home. Ellen was profiled in Chapter 5. She successfully denied her Rouster by not exploding at her best friend and sister. However, immediately afterward she fell to her Tempter's promise of a quick calming fix and she self-sabotaged by smoking.

The Tempter-Blocker is another destructive twosome I've encountered. The Tempter sabotages our goal-oriented efforts by luring us to do something enjoyable instead. The Blocker stops us from following through with steps to reach our goal. Here's my client Sara's DDD entry describing one such attack:

> *April 13:* 1) "I should go out."
> This is the [distracting] Tempter Demon trying to stop me from being productive. It's best to focus on homework tonight, so I don't have to deal with the stress of procrastination.
> 2) "I'm not gonna have the energy to work on the paper."
> I always think that, but once I start, I become energized. This is the Blocker Demon.

Sara identified her demons, even though they had hidden behind the camouflage of "I" statements. By outing them, she was able to refuse them and finish her paper. By proving her demons wrong, she avoided the stressful consequences of not completing her project. Here's another one of Sara's DDD entries. This time her Blocker struck first, followed by her Tempter:

*April 15:* 1) "I'm getting old and becoming hopeless."

I am not getting old. I am very young. I am not hopeless; no one is, no matter how old they are. Age isn't important and there is no reason to worry about this. This is the Blocker Demon trying to make me think it's too late to do anything with my life. It isn't the truth and isn't me.

2) "I should give up on my goals and focus more on having a social life."

This is the Tempter Demon. I don't have to choose one or the other. I can find a balance between the two. It's best to focus on my goals and make more of an effort to socialize. There is no reason to worry about this. Just go with the flow and do my best.

In both DDD entries, Sara condensed her description of how her blocking and tempting demons operated. For a full discussion of this strategy, see Chapter 7, page 151. She already knew from previous DDD entries that these attacks occurred when she was home alone at night, with the goal to study. Although the demons' words changed, their intent was the same: to sabotage her studies and feed on her depressed mood and self-blame. Fortunately, in these cases, Sara identified and separated herself from both Soldier Demons. When she refused to supply them, they had nothing to nourish her Master Demon. While her demons shriveled from starvation, her confidence and self-worth grew.

## Demon Triads

Sometimes three Soldier Demons gang up against us. Although any combination is possible, one tag team that I've seen in action is the Tempter, Negator, and Blocker. The Tempter strikes first, enticing us to take on too much work, activity, or obligation. The Negator then criticizes us for not being able to do it all. As we become weakened from exhaustion and self-doubt, the Blocker stops us from doing anything constructive to change the pattern, and so we feel miserable and depressed. This trio gorges on our negative emotional energy and, as always, feeds our Master Demon of defectiveness.

Here's a DDD entry that my client Mike wrote after he was assaulted by these demons. His Tempter had lured him to overload on tennis matches and work projects, assuring him that he could easily handle it all. Mike was vulnerable to his tempting agent because his tennis teams were winning and his company was downsizing because of a poor economy. He fell prey to the TD's false promises, that adding these extra commitments would ensure continued tennis victories and protection from job layoffs. However, when Mike couldn't fulfill his overwhelming work projects and hurt his arm overplaying tennis, his Negator criticized him for failing. His Blocker kept him from doing anything right away to recover. Although he didn't catch this demon triad immediately, writing helped Mike reinforce what he had learned—to set limits, take breaks, and slow down:

*November 10:* Tempter getting me to take on more and more. More matches, more projects. Strikes at my weakest moment, when layoffs are looming and managers need more hands on deck and tennis teams winning. Tempter tells me, "I can do it all. I'm good enough to handle it all." But then Negator shows me, "Ha, ha, I can't do it all!" So then I start feeling bad and nervous because I can't keep up. Perfect storm. I finally collapse- Blocker Demon. Arm fell apart, stomach hurts, nausea. Then feeling depression, sleeping a lot. Worthless? Failure? But within a couple weeks, I realize I needed a break. I was taking it too fast. Need to slow down. I'm sleeping more and sleeping better. . . . No more tennis for now, taking a break. Told my manager I needed a week break from the computer. When I get back into tennis, I need to slow it down. Tennis team can win without me.

In addition to demon pairs and triads, watch out for attacks from all four Soldier Demons. Although we've examined the most common of these gangs, every combination and strike pattern is possible, depending on your specific vulnerabilities and situations. As virulent as these gangs are, remember that you are much more powerful than your Soldier Demons and your Master Demon because they have no power source of their own. The only way they survive is by surreptitiously feeding off your negative emotional energy. By identifying and replacing their destructive programs with your constructive ones, you'll cut off their fuel supply. As they shrink from starvation, you'll effectively exorcize them and reclaim your freedom.

---

Demons have no power source of their own.

---

**Table 6.2**

| Common Soldier Demon Gangs | |
| --- | --- |
| **Name** | **Directive** |
| Negator-Tempter Duo | The Negator puts you down and makes you feel inadequate. The Tempter lures you to do something self-destructive. |
| Negator-Rouster Duo | The Negator puts you down and makes you feel inadequate. The Rouster steers you to lash out inappropriately against perceived transgressions. |
| Negator-Blocker Duo | The Negator criticizes your abilities related to self-enhancing activities. The Blocker stops you from following through with these self-positive steps. |
| Tempter-Blocker Duo | The Tempter sabotages your goal-oriented efforts by luring you to do something enjoyable instead. The Blocker stops you from following through with steps to reach your goal. |
| Tempter-Negator-Blocker Triad | The Tempter entices you to take on too much. The Negator criticizes you for not being able to do it all. The Blocker stops you from doing anything constructive to change the pattern. |

CHAPTER 7

# TIPS FOR SUCCESS

To maximize the strategies you've just acquired from previous chapters, routinely incorporate the tips that follow. They emerged from years of working with clients to implement the demon model and exorcize their demons. You'll learn optimal ways to create and write RR and DDD entries. Common errors are flagged, including what to do instead. Tips help you tailor your journals to achieve specific goals and prepare for anticipated demon attacks. You'll read how to avoid triggering negative feelings by condensing demon descriptions in your DDD. The imagery rehearsal tool helps you boost reprogramming and stop demon-induced nightmares. Additional pointers describe how to use reminder messages, add a separate vent journal, and privatize your journals.

## Correct for the Contrast Effect

After making progress starving your demons, you'll feel much better. Instead of mostly feeling lousy, you'll be happier, calmer, more confident, and so on. Even as you raise the bar to a new normal emotional set point, you'll still experience demon attacks. Although they'll be fewer, when they occur, you'll feel bad, but you'll think you're feeling much worse. This perceptual error is a well-known phenomenon called the contrast effect. Your appraisal of something changes because of your immediate frame of reference.[1] Within the context of feeling terrible most of the time, you won't feel significantly worse because of a demon attack. When you feel neutral or good much of the time, you'll feel much worse after getting hit, because it's such a contrast from your initial mood state.

To correct this contrast effect error, remind yourself of this phenomenon after demon attacks, especially the Sniper variety. Remember that you used to feel awful much of the time and now you don't. When you take a dive emotionally, it seems more severe in comparison to your new state of feeling better. When I remind clients of this in sessions, they're immediately relieved. Instead of beating themselves up for emotionally plunging, they view their experience as a temporary side effect of the excellent progress that they're making.

My client Lea didn't realize when she was swayed by the contrast effect. She was making great progress shrinking her Blocker. In addition to sending her résumé to employers, she'd secured an internship at an art gallery, submitted her paintings to an art show, and talked about professional goals with her professor at school. With each success, she felt happier, calmer, and more confident. Her new normal of feeling good much of the time was very different from how depressed and uncertain she felt when she first came to see me.

One thing Lea didn't do was to record these positive steps in her RR. By not reinforcing her efforts, her new mood and self-concept remained vulnerable to her Negator. It continued Sniper attacks, criticizing her qualities and abilities. When hit, she felt way worse in comparison to her recent peaceful, confident state. After I alerted her to the contrast effect error, she resolved to correct for this after future Negator attacks. She also agreed to log her successes in her RR, including descriptions of what they mean about her. By continuing empowering actions and reprogramming record entries, she'll more effectively thwart both her blocking and negating forces. She won't have to bother much with the contrast effect because it'll occur a lot less frequently.

## Reprogramming Record Pointers

### Generating Entries

If you have a hard time coming up with positive RR entries, start with a different approach. Imagine that you are your best friend. Now give yourself compliments from the perspective of your best friend. To facilitate this process, remember what your best friend has actually told you and repeat these flattering statements to yourself. I've found that clients can more easily generate and give self-praise when doing so as if they were someone else.[2]

Here are some RR entries that Lea identified using this approach. She imagined that she was her boyfriend Keith, praising her. By remembering and repeating his compliments, she used them as a guide to generate additional self-positives:

*January 29:* Met with my internship director. I was on time. I was comfortable in my own skin. We spoke for an hour. <u>I have the drive to do what I want to do. I am capable of being punctual. All my hard work is paying off. I am worth her time.</u>

*January 30:* I reevaluated my goals and found that I have accomplished most of them. I am taking time regarding graduate school to really nail down what I want. <u>I am capable of making a decision.</u>

*February 9:* I went on my first interview today as a program assistant. I was entirely myself. Ultimately, I feel good about my interview. <u>I am a good person to speak to. I have a great sense of self. I will be an excellent employee.</u>

## Using Active, Present Tense

To empower your RR, use active, present tense when describing what each entry means about you. Replace phrases such as "I can be," "I can," and "I am able to" with "I am," "I have," or just "I." By repeatedly describing *"what is"* instead of *"what is possible,"* you'll provide compelling evidence for effective reprogramming. For good examples, reread Lea's RR entries. Notice how strong her statements sound because she used the active, present tense phrases *"I am"* and *"I have."*

Here are more RR entries that I helped clients to edit. The deleted words are crossed out:

> *November 19:* Sam and I cleaned the labs. <u>I can keep my staff busy. I am able to give clear instructions.</u>
> *June 2:* I helped Vanessa at work with some problem she had with her new husband. <u>I can offer support and advice to friends and family.</u>
> *June 3:* My nephew came over and I went to dinner and played a game. <u>I can be am happy and have fun.</u>

## Expanding to New Areas

To build confidence about abilities and qualities that you don't yet feel good about, tailor RR entries to those areas. By expanding your focus to what you're not yet self-assured about, you'll step outside your comfort zone. As you look for and write specific supportive examples, your self-worth will grow to include these different aspects of yourself.

The following issue often comes up when I go over RR entries with clients: without realizing it, they fall into a pattern of writing about areas that they already feel confident about. This repetition is great, especially at first when they're building a daily habit of writing. However, then they get stuck reviewing the same qualities that they're already self-assured about. When I ask them to identify a different attribute, they're quickly able to name one or more that they'd like to boost. Although the newly focused RR entries take more effort at first, they yield more benefit, because clients expand their confidence to new areas.

Tyler felt very good about his musical and writing abilities. His RR entries were excellent, detailed, and well written. However, they were almost always about these two strengths. When I asked, he didn't take long to name social skills as one area he didn't feel confident about. After shifting his focus to look for evidence of this ability, here's an entry he wrote:

> *June 10:* We went to Todd and Jen's today for dinner and I enjoyed it. I talked a lot and wasn't nervous (as I can be at social occasions). I had fun and spoke a lot. <u>This means I'm a good conversationalist and people like me. I'm more sociable than I give myself credit for.</u>

### Adding Visuals

To enhance reprogramming record entries visually, add drawings, stickers, highlighting, or other creative additions. Every time you review your journal, these visuals will remind you of the self-affirming examples you've described. You don't have to be an artist, create elaborate pictorials, or spend much time or money. The main thing is to supplement your writing with images that reinforce your favorable statements.

The following are two such examples. In addition to underlining her positive descriptions, my client reinforced them with a yellow highlighter. Beneath each entry, she drew a picture that complimented her affirming statements.

*November 20:* Today I paid bills and ran errands that were put off due to surgery and my recovery. <u>I am a very organized person and one that can get a lot accomplished once I put my mind to it.</u> [a simple drawing of a "to do list" with each item checked off]

*November 21:* My 1st day back at work. I got most of the Dr's schedules done and was able to jump back into work like I hadn't been absent. <u>I'm a hard, diligent worker.</u> [a basic drawing of the front desk at work, a welcome back sign, and stick figures of co-workers welcoming her back]

### Using the RR for a Specific Goal

To obtain an explicit goal, such as a job promotion or raise, use your RR to document evidence supporting the outcome you desire. By writing specific examples with descriptive information, you'll amass compelling, timely data to assert your case. Tailored RR entries can be accumulated and presented to support requests at work, home, school, or other places. Here are some examples that clients wrote describing their work successes, including qualities that made them excellent employees. RR entries such as these can be shared as persuasive supplemental information to facilitate desired evaluations, promotions, raises, transfers, and so on.

*September 9:* My co-worker has been sick this week, so I've handled the supply deliveries and set-ups for future deliveries myself. I was able to reassure her that the deliveries are proceeding normally. <u>I am organized and efficient and self-motivated.</u>

*September 10:* Sent out emails for price quotes for equipment for new lab equipment. <u>I get tasks done in a timely manner. I do not procrastinate.</u>

*February 2:* I flew to Atlanta and visited 5 stores. <u>I work well under pressure.</u>

*February 4:* I gave a successful formal training in front of 35 people. <u>I am an effective trainer.</u>

*November 4:* I set up the billing/invoice system at work, organized a binder for it, set up the process for other employees, and presented it to Don [boss], who was very happy with it. <u>I am efficient and do well at my job.</u>

### Creating a Group RR

An effective way to assist the people whom you care about to replace their debilitating messages with self-enhancing messages is to create a group Reprogramming Record. Group RRs are good for everyone, but they're especially helpful for people who struggle to come up with daily self-positive RR entries. They provide a collage of tangible, validating feedback from those who know the person best. Because each person contributes just one entry, this task doesn't require much time or effort. Birthdays, holidays, office parties, or any occasion involving the group are optimal times to give this RR. Entries don't have to follow the RR format exactly, but, for maximum effect, they should include the latter part, describing in some detail the recipient's positive qualities. Group RRs may be elaborate or simple. They can be written in something as small as a birthday card, as long as there's enough room for each person's contribution.

Here's an example of a group RR that my client Jeff received at his 50th birthday party. It was typed on the computer, with festive clip art designs inserted. Each person's entry was printed in a different font. The two-page RR was stapled inside a multicolored jacket, with birthday decorations adorning the cover. It was entitled *"Jeff, We Adore You!"* At the end, it said, *"We Love You. Happy Birthday!"* Here are a few of the entries written by Jeff's friends:

"Jeff's always generous, he's extraordinary, kind, giving, unique, a great friend and an excellent dad. He's truly one of a kind."— Art

"I've never had a friend like Jeff. He's a wonderful son, giving, brilliant, hard-working and endlessly reliable."— Collette

"He's so intelligent, warm, loving, generous, goofy and always loyal." — Ruben

"He's a wonderful father, conscientious, loyal, and truthful. Best friend of my life."— Jack

"Jeff is lively and a master at making cocktails. He's an amazing dad and husband, he's outgoing, and he always shines."— Sydney

## Demon Disrupting Diary Pointers

### Adding Pictures

To supplement your DDD, draw pictures depicting what you describe. As with the RR, these visuals will reinforce your efforts to exorcize your demons. Start by drawing how the demons attack you. Then draw you triumphing over your demons. Include each Soldier Demon that afflicts you, plus your Master Demon. Depending on your unique demon strike patterns, you can create individual and/or group demon pictures.

For example, Karen drew a picture of her Negator attacking while her Master loomed in the background. She was a small figure in the middle, crying, with her hands over her ears. Her Negator was bigger, with horns and wings. A bubble surrounded its criticisms: "You're stupid," "You're ugly," "No one likes you!" Her Master had sprouted huge horns, wings, and a goatee. Its bubble said, "Yes! Feed me!" Karen also drew a second picture of her Tempter, which falsely promised relief from worry and self-doubt through drinking alcohol.

In her third drawing, Karen included her Negator, Tempter, and Master. She was much larger than all three demons and smiling. Her arms and hands were outstretched and held up in victory. On her shirt were the words *"Strong,"* *"Confident."* She was standing very straight and tall atop her Soldier Demons. Her right foot crushed her shriveled up Tempter and her left foot smashed her puny Negator. Her deflated Master was off to the side; its bubble said, "I'm shrinking!" Although she didn't include this, I recommend that you draw your own bubble filled with empowering messages: *"You are not me," "I'm not listening to you," "I'm stronger than you," "I'm smart," "I'm attractive," "I'm sober and confident."*

### Writing Tips

As you write each DDD entry, check whether you're inadvertently using any shame-inducing words such as "should" or "should have." If so, replace them with encouraging words such as *"will"* and *"next time."* This cleanses your writing of critical, punishing messages. Instead of shaming, the proactive words aid in self-forgiveness and help you apply what you have learned to future situations.

If writing about demon attacks is an unwelcome reminder that you have problems, change your orientation to this task. Think of your DDD as a tool that gives you an advantage in reaching your goals. Whether at work, home, in relationships, or elsewhere, you'll get ahead by using this booster. Remember too that negatively focusing on having problems is a sure sign of your Negator attacking. If you slip into this self-critical mode, register this as your negating bully at work. Instead of listening to it, take your power back by viewing your DDD as indispensable in helping you get what you want.

## Condensing Demon Descriptions

After you've identified common attack patterns of your demons, you may wish to shorten the part of your DDD entries where you describe how they operate. Shorthand, summaries, or abbreviations are all methods that you can use to condense well-known demon assaults. Or you could do what one of my clients did: she marked out the demon maneuvers and dialogue right after she had written them. This reduces the risk of old negative feelings or beliefs being triggered from repeatedly focusing in detail on the old demon programs. Instead, most of your time and attention goes toward writing and reinforcing your new positive reprogramming steps.

Before following this suggestion, be sure that you're well-informed about the demon program you're referring to. Remember that to expel your demons effectively, you first need to know exactly how they operate on you. My clients write a number of similar DDD entries in order to identify a frequent demon attack pattern. Only then do they shorten their depictions of these well-established demon tactics.

Here is an example of a DDD where my client Sara summarized an attack and simply named her ND-BD duo. The rest of her entry was focused on constructive steps to shrink her demons. Sara had worked for many months to identify and thwart this common ND-BD program. After writing many DDD entries, she knew in detail how her ND-BD duo targeted areas of school, money, and family. The demon-depleting steps that she wrote were similar to ones that she'd written before. Instead of giving attention to that well-known demon program, this DDD entry reinforces Sara's new reprogramming approaches.

*January 14:* I feel anxious about school and the situation with my family and the issue of money.

This is the Negator and Blocker Demon.

I have a schedule for school figured out. It will be OK. Just go with the flow for the next week and trust my intuition, one step at a time. If I become overwhelmed with the Blocker, it's best to take action.

As far as money, I'll be getting financial aid soon and will also apply for more scholarships. It will all work out.

I can only control myself. I can't control my family. I can give them my input and try to help in whatever ways I can, but stressing out or feeling guilty won't help anyone and is destructive to me. I've suffered enough. I deserve to feel good.

### Using the DDD for Anticipated Attacks

To prepare for predicted demon assaults, write future-oriented entries in your DDD. Describe where you'll be, describe the situation, and name anyone else who'll be involved. Add specific descriptors to make the scenario as realistic and vivid as possible. Most important, include in detail the strategies that you'll use to thwart your demons. By proactively using your DDD to rehearse your reaction, you'll be well prepared to triumph when the actual demon attack occurs.

Tami dreaded her co-worker Edith's first day back to work. Edith was scheduled to return the following day, after being away on a leave of absence. Tami said most everyone had been affected by Edith's negative attitude and critical words. Unfortunately, Edith's desk was near Tami's. On bad days, Edith's Rouster Demon triggered Tami's Negator and Tami internalized the curt comments and excessive complaints. As we discussed strategies, Tami decided her best protection from Edith's RD was to remind herself of her own happiness and her determination not to let anyone take that away. I asked her to include this in a DDD entry predicting what would happen the following day when Edith returned to work.

> *October 10:* Tomorrow will be the first day Edith returns from her month-long leave. I know her Rouster Demon will try to attack me, but I will not allow that to happen. I'm at one of the happiest times in my life and will not allow her or her demons to take that from me. When her demon does try, I will not only remind myself of how unhappy she is, but also of my own happiness and how sacred that is to me.

Although Tami didn't explain why she was happy, I encourage you to include specific affirming details in your DDD. In addition to providing a mood boost, documenting this supportive data protects you from Negator attempts to discredit your vitalizing assertions. Tami had two major reasons for feeling good: she'd recently become engaged and was preparing to graduate from college at the end of that semester.

## Imagery Rehearsal

As you read future-oriented DDD entries and prepare reprogramming steps, enhance your efforts with imagery rehearsal. Visualize yourself successfully implementing demon-depleting strategies in specific situations that are likely to occur. As you watch yourself, experience the positive feelings that accompany your successful behaviors. Play these virtual videos as often as you wish. With each replay, you'll practice acting and feeling the way you desire.[3]

I regularly assist clients in using this visual/feeling tool. It helps deplete all demons and doesn't require anything other than imagination. Videos don't even have to be creative or elaborate to work well. For example, Theresa imagined changing one behavior in her routine to refuse her Negator and Tempter. She was vulnerable to both immediately after dinner, when she tended to worry about things outside her control and then drink wine in a futile attempt to self-calm. Because Theresa didn't have a serious drinking problem, the following strategy had a good chance of working well.

Instead of her usual habit of staying seated at the dinner table after eating, Theresa pictured getting up and starting a task, such as clearing the table or sweeping the floor. Doing and focusing on this simple activity protected her from sitting and wallowing in Negator ruminations. By not worrying, she prevented the need for a drink to self-calm, thwarting her Tempter. As Theresa visualized completing her chore, she felt the satisfaction of getting it done. She imagined giving herself credit and feeling proud for moving past this demon danger zone unscathed. Through this imagery rehearsal, Theresa also strengthened her belief that she would turn her imagined success into a reality.[4]

### Stopping Nightmares

As you become savvy at banishing your demons throughout the day, they may resort to striking when your guard is down, during sleep. To put a stop to unwelcome recurring nightmares, use imagery rehearsal to change them into self-positive dreams.[5] Right before going to sleep, visualize the nightmare as it usually starts. As soon as you wish, alter it so that the dream proceeds and ends how you want. Empower yourself to disable, destroy, or banish any perpetrators; bring in other people to help you; change the horrific outcome; and/or anything else to transform the nightmare into your victory. As you play the revised dream in your head, feel the relief, happiness, confidence, and other beneficial emotions that accompany your success. Replay this modified dream in your mind every night before going to sleep.

Before using this tool, reflect on whether the nightmare stems from traumatic events that you thought you'd put behind you, such as sexual or physical abuse. If so, your subconscious may also be alerting you of unhealed psychological wounds. Listen to this message and seek psychotherapy and/or supportive groups to assist in your healing.

When I help clients alter nightmares using imagery rehearsal, they're already working to heal traumatic wounds in therapy. Their nightmares are no longer needed as signals of these old hurts. Unfortunately, their Terrorizer Negator

Demons keep these dreadful visions alive during sleep. To stop them, we revise the nightmares, adding empowering strategies to help clients confront and triumph over their abusers. Before going to sleep, they rehearse the modified dreams. When we meet again, clients report one of two outcomes. Most often, they don't have the nightmare. Other times, the nightmare begins and then changes as they visualized it before going to sleep.

Alyson had persistent nightmares of a man assaulting her sexually. Her vain struggles to fight off the attacker woke her up each time. She was vulnerable to this Terrorizer ND attack as a result of her uncle's molesting her when she was 12 years old. Sleeping was especially difficult, because the abuse had happened at night when she was in bed. As we focused on healing Alyson's psychological wounds, we added imagery rehearsal to stop her terrible ordeals during sleep. She modified her nightmare so that she kicked the man off her with superhuman strength. He went crashing into the wall, hit his head, and was knocked out. She then called 911 using the phone by her bed. Help arrived soon after, and she felt relieved, safe, and very proud of herself. Each night, Alyson rehearsed this revised dream before sleep; after adding this strategy to her therapy work, she reported no nightmares.

## Reminder Messages

To remember specific incidents to write in your DDD and RR, use reminder messages. Sometimes you'll think of something, but you won't have time to write the full entry immediately. As an alternative, leave a short message on your day planner, email, cellular phone, or landline phone. As long as the memo jogs your memory of the event, you don't need to include more than a descriptive word or two. When retrieving messages later, you'll be reminded not only to write in your journals but exactly what to write about.

This memory aid is especially useful when trying to remember and record your successes. In my experience, clients' Negator programs keep them very oriented to their mistakes. In contrast, triumphs and RR entries are forgotten quickly because clients aren't yet in the habit of noticing or giving themselves credit.

For example, Ellen called her home phone from work and left a brief voice mail message reminder. She'd just thought of something to write in her DDD; she'd refused her Rouster the night before. Instead of lashing out in anger, she was calm when dealing with her roommate Megan, who'd been difficult to live with all week. To ensure that she didn't forget, she simply said, "Write in my RR about not yelling." She didn't say Megan's name to preserve privacy. Even so, this reminder was sufficient to jog Ellen's memory of the incident. When she arrived home and played her messages, her personal memo reminded her to describe her anger management success. Here's what she wrote in her DDD:

> *November 15:* At one point during the week, during a conversation M and I were having, she asked me, "How have I been this week?" And I replied, "Awful." Instead of allowing my Rooster Demon to come up by just going off on M, I answered her honestly. Nothing more was said about this until a while later when she asked, "Have I really been that awful this week?" I replied, "Yes." By not going off on her, I overcame an attack on me by my Rooster Demon. A big step.

## The Vent Journal

If extensive upsetting details related to demon attacks keep swirling in your head and cloud your focus, use a separate journal (not your DDD or RR) to vent and release these concerns. Then go back to your DDD and follow the protocol as described. This is what I tell people who bring in long DDD entries that veer off into self-perpetuating debilitating ruts. To avoid getting sucked back into fixating on these complaints after discharging them, I also caution clients never to reread their vent journals.

In contrast, your Reprogramming Record is always good to read again. Even when your demons prevail, you can use your RR, in addition to your DDD, to turn their successes into your gain. To do this, simply document your recuperation efforts in your RR. Such entries will boost your resilience and speed of recovery. Here's what Steve wrote in his RR after his ND-TD attack:

> *July 25:* Though I was upset on Monday, I was able to recover my inner strength throughout the week. <u>I am strong. I am gaining emotional stability. I am willing to try new methods to achieve success. The more self work I do, the easier I will be able to deal with my problems. I can take control of my life.</u>

Even if you don't fully believe the self-positive descriptions you underline, keep writing them. The more times you repeat them, the easier it will be to accept them as true.[6] Because the Negator and other demons play the same debilitating messages over and over, effective reprogramming requires that you replace them with just as many, and preferably more, of your own self-enhancing statements.

## Privatizing Your DDD and RR

If you're concerned that others may find and read your journals without your permission, one solution is to develop a unique, personal coding system to record your entries. Then if anyone discovers your writing, he or she won't be able to understand what it means. You'll retain the benefits from writing and reviewing your entries without worrying that your privacy might be invaded.

This is what one of my clients did. Although he had nothing incriminating to hide, he was an intensely private person. He didn't want anyone to read his journals and was concerned that he might misplace them for someone to discover. He routinely took his journals back and forth to work and home and didn't want his co-workers, teenage daughter, or even his wife to read them. He developed his own abbreviation system that only he understood. This allowed him to write freely and honestly, taking full advantage of the benefits, without worrying about losing his privacy.

**Table 7.1**

## Tips for Success

- To avoid feeling miserable and punishing yourself, correct for the contrast effect error after your demons successfully attack.

Reprogramming Record Tips
- To help generate entries, start from the perspective of your best friend.
- Strengthen entries by using active, present tense.
- Expand entries to build confidence in new areas.
- To enhance reprogramming visually, add visuals to entries.
- Tailor entries to support a specific goal, such as a job promotion or a raise.
- Create a group RR to facilitate others' successful reprogramming.

Demon Disrupting Diary Tips
- To enhance demon-disrupting efforts visually, add visuals to entries.
- Replace shame-inducing words with encouraging words: for example, replace "should" with *"will."*
- Condense demon descriptions to avoid triggering old negative feelings and beliefs.
- Write future-oriented entries to prepare for anticipated demon attacks.
- Use imagery rehearsal to enhance your demon depleting efforts.
  - Engage imagery rehearsal before sleep to stop recurring nightmares
- Employ reminder messages to help write RR and DDD entries.
- Add a separate vent journal to release upsetting details of demon attacks.
- To privatize your RR and DDD, use a unique coding system that only you understand.

# AFTERWORD

I wish you great success as you engage the demon model to exorcize your psychological demons. By sticking with your strategies and making them routine, you'll starve out your demons, even when they repeatedly resurface. Remember, Sniper demon assaults are common, even after you think you've banished them for good. Do not let them shut you down. Use these strikes as cues to reengage your exorcism efforts.

With personal and financial stressors increasingly bombarding us,[1] we quickly become vulnerable if we stop our demon-depleting efforts. I believe that major hardships will continue around the world as well as where we live. We'll face events that test our strength and resilience, such as economic failures, escalating violence, political unrest, and natural disasters. In these times more than ever, we need to stay vigilant and consistent in our exorcism efforts.

Remember that you are far more powerful than your demons, because they have no power source without you. By continuing your informed efforts, the cards are overwhelmingly stacked in your favor. Love and positive emotions are much stronger than fear and negative emotions. Do not let demon maneuvers deter you; when threatened, they'll do and say anything to survive. Their directive is to keep you imprisoned and feeding them your misery. By replacing their old programs with your new ones, you'll naturally grow in confidence, self-love, and self-worth. As their negative emotional energy is cut off, your demons will starve and be forced to leave, freeing you to live as the self-assured, loving, and strong person that you truly are.

# NOTES

## Chapter 1

1. In a two-year, face-to-face household survey of Americans, data revealed that about half of Americans meet the criteria for a mental disorder sometime in their life (Kessler, Berglund, et al., 2005). One in four adults suffers from a diagnosable mental disorder in a given year (Kessler, Chiu, et al., 2005). When applied to the U.S. Census population estimate for adults, the latter figure translates to 57.7 million (U.S. Census Bureau, 2005).

2. A fuller description of these findings can be found in the market report of Marketdata Enterprises for October 14, 2008 (Marketdata Enterprises Inc., 2008).

3. Survey data show that the number of adults aged 18 to 54 who received treatment for emotional disorders increased by 65% from 1990 to 2003, but the prevalence of mental disorders remained the same (Kessler, Demler, et al., 2005).

4. In a comparison of two large cross-sectional surveys of the adult U.S. population, conducted 10 years apart, the prevalence of major depression more than doubled. This increase was statistically significant for whites, blacks, Hispanics, and for all age groups (Compton et al., 2006).

5. The *Los Angeles Times* reported in October of 2008 that close to 2,000 people had jumped off the Golden Gate Bridge to their deaths since the bridge opened in 1937. To end the infamous distinction of being one of the world's most popular suicide sites, officials voted to install a suicide barrier for the bridge (Chawkins, 2008).

6. Oprah Winfrey reported this finding on her television show (Winfrey, 2006).

7. Such psychological theories exist within behavioral, cognitive, and psychoanalytic approaches. A widely used diagnostic classification of mental illness is

the *Diagnostic and Statistical Manual of Mental Disorders, Fourth Edition, Text Revision*, DSM-IV-TR, (American Psychiatric Association, 2000). A standard manual of general medical conditions that includes mental disorders is the *International Classification of Diseases, Ninth Revision, Clinical Modification*, ICD-9-CM 2009 (American Medical Association, 2008).

8. One popular treatment is cognitive therapy, developed by Dr. Aaron T. Beck. This approach focuses on a person's dysfunctional thoughts as the cause of emotional distress and destructive behaviors (Beck, 1967, 1976). Another established therapy is rational-emotive therapy (RET), developed by Dr. Albert Ellis. RET assumes that a person's irrational beliefs create emotional suffering and unhealthy actions (Ellis, 1984, 1995). Behavioral therapy locates the source of problems in a person's dysfunctional behaviors (Lewinsohn and Gotlib, 1995; Jacobson, Martell, and Dimidjian, 2001) Problem-solving therapy targets a deficit in a person's problem-solving ability (D'Zurilla and Goldfried, 1971). Solution-focused therapy is oriented to a person's difficulty in constructing solutions (Walter and Peller, 1992). Self-efficacy approaches work to correct a person's deficit in expectation and experience of personal mastery (Bandura, 1977, 1997). Note that all of these approaches locate the problematic feature within the person. This orientation is problematic in itself, because it reinforces the fundamental problem of self-blame that the person has.

9. To review the history of possession and exorcisms around the world, see Goodman (1988) and Nevius and Ellinwood (2003).

10. Research confirms that emotional maltreatment leads to feelings of hopelessness and depression in children (Gibb et al., 2001). Another study found that negative events are related to the intensity of suicidal crises (Joiner and Rudd, 2000). Other research shows that adolescents whose parents are overprotective and rejecting of them are more likely to suffer from anxiety (Lieb et al., 2000). In general, negative life events, such as humiliating incidents, are strongly related to the onset of mood and anxiety disorders (Kendler et al., 2003; Kessler, 1997; Kendler, Karkowski, and Prescott, 1999; Mazure, 1998).

11. To read more about these studies, you may wish to consult Nolen-Hoeksema, Girgus, and Seligman (1992) and Alloy et al. (2001).

12. The University of Chicago's National Opinion Research Center surveyed 1,340 people about negative life events and found that people reported more troubles in 2004 than in a 1991 survey (Jayson, 2006).

13. For evidence of the greater tendency of women to internalize blame, see Hankin and Abramson, 2001; Just and Alloy, 1997; Kleinke, Staneski, and Mason, 1982; Nolen-Hoeksema, 1987, 2000; Nolen-Hoeksema and Girgus, 1994; Nolen-Hoeksema, Larson, and Grayson, 1999; and O. Williams (personal communication, June 1, 2006).

14. The power of modeling or vicarious learning was demonstrated by Dr. Albert Bandura through a series of observations and research studies (Bandura, 1977, 1986, 1997).

15. Operant conditioning, introduced systematically by Dr. B. F. Skinner, is the type of learning in which behavior changes as a function of the consequence that follows the behavior. He studied many aspects of reinforcement. He proposed that the most effective way to develop new behavior is to reinforce desired behavior positively (Skinner, 1938, 1953, 1971).

16. Many studies provide evidence that depression, anxiety, and alcoholism tend to run in families (Barlow, 2002; Chassin et al., 1999; McGue, Pickens, and Svikis, 1992).

## Chapter 2

1. Research studies and articles report findings that behavioral approaches are effective in reducing depression (Dimidjian et al., 2006; Jacobson et al., 1996; Martell, Addis, and Dimidjian, 2004). Many cognitive and behavioral therapies incorporate behavioral approaches in their protocols (Beck et al., 1979; Ellis, 1995; Lewinsohn and Gotlib, 1995; Jacobson, Martell, and Dimidjian, 2001).

2. To review research and discussion regarding the effect of moods on the retrieval and encoding of memories, you may wish to consult the following resources: DeSteno et al., 2000; Esses, 1989; Fiedler et al., 2001; Johnson and Magaro, 1987; Mayer and Salovey, 1988. For example, when depressed, it's easier to remember negative memories compared to positive ones. The things we learn in one state—such as feeling happy—are easier to remember when we're in that same state (happy) again. This research finding is called state-dependent memory.

3. In a landmark study, researchers found that people automatically assumed what authors wrote reflected their beliefs. This occurred even when people knew the authors were required to write the information (Jones and Harris, 1967).

4. Researchers have long known that people adjust their actions to remain consistent with what they write down and share with others (Deutsch and Gerard, 1955). A recent study showed that people with low self-esteem could feel as positively about compliments they received from romantic partners as did people with high self-esteem. The key to feeling good was that they were directed to describe the meaning and importance of the compliments they were given (Marigold, Holmes and Ross, 2007).

5. Self-affirmation theory, developed by Dr. Claude Steele, describes processes for coping with self-image threat. Research studies provide supportive evidence. When subjects identified positive aspects of themselves before a self-image threat, they were protected from negative reactions that typically occurred after a threat (Steele, 1988, 1997; Steele, Spencer, and Aronson, 2002).

6. Research found that self-affirming writing led to better physical health for cancer survivors, compared to writing general thoughts about their situation (Creswell et al., 2007).

7. The mental and physical health benefits of social support are described in the following research studies: Cohen and Wills, 1985; Haber et al, 2007; Hogan, Linden, and Najarian, 2002; Olstad, Sexton, and Sogaard, 2001.

8. Detailed information documenting the mental and physical health benefits of exercise appears in the following research studies: Arent, Landers, and Etnier, 2000; Berger and Motl, 2000; Babyak et al., 2000; Dubbert, 2002; Kujala et al., 1998; Powell et al., 1987; Richardson et al., 2005; Thayer, 1987, 1993; Watson, 2000.

9. Examples of action-oriented approaches are cognitive-behavioral therapies (see Chapter 2, Note 1) and self-efficacy theory (Bandura, 1977, 1997).

## Chapter 3

1. Researchers conducted eight separate studies to investigate negative self-thinking as a mental habit. To review their findings, see Verplanken et al., 2007.

2. For research evidence that role-play and rehearsal increase social skills and reduce anxiety, see Turner, Beidel, and Cooley-Quille, 1995; Turk, Heimberg, and Hope, 2001.

3. For a full description of this research, including three separate experiments that reduce or eliminate subjects' negative attention bias, you may wish to consult Smith et al., 2006.

4. See Chapter 2, Note 5.

5. Some experimental studies that reveal the anxiety-reducing effects of music are Khalfa et al., 2003; Knight and Rickard, 2001; Labbe et al., 2007.

6. Reviews examining the effectiveness of these anxiety reducing strategies are found in Baer, 2003; Barrows and Jacobs, 2002; Jorm et al., 2004.

7. To peruse research findings that support writing as a therapeutic practice, you may wish to consult Kerner and Fitzpatrick, 2007.

8. See Chapter 2, Note 7.

9. Strong evidence confirms the efficacy of live (in vivo) exposure to reduce anxiety. For detailed reviews and discussions of these research findings, see Chambless and Ollendick, 2001; Craske and Barlow, 2001; Hazlett-Stevens and Craske, 2009; Tryon, 2005.

10. Post-traumatic stress disorder (PTSD) is classified as an anxiety disorder in the *Diagnostic and Statistical Manual of Mental Disorders, 4th ed. Text Revision (DSM-IV-TR)*. To consult this manual for detailed information on PTSD prevalence, symptoms, and diagnostic criteria, see American Psychiatric Association, 2000.

11. Specialized psychological treatments with good evidence of effectiveness for PTSD are collectively called exposure therapies. These interventions use behavioral and cognitive strategies to expose clients to what they fear, whether in the real world or imagined. Relaxation, stress inoculation, medications, and cognitive restructuring techniques may be used in combination with the exposure

therapies. To review these therapeutic options in detail, see Adshead, 2000; Chambless and Ollendick, 2001; Foa, Keane, and Friedman, 2004.

## Chapter 4

1. In a review of health research studies, evidence links anger to numerous health hazards (Suinn, 2001).

2. The fight or flight response is a phenomenon we've known about for decades, described as early as 1915 by the American physiologist Walter Cannon (Cannon, 1915).

3. Research findings validate the many powerful and efficient ways we communicate nonverbally using gestures, postures, movements, and other nonverbal signals (Mehrabian, 2007).

4. When a new response is elicited to an existing stimulus, this form of relearning is called counter conditioning. To facilitate learning, repeated pairings of the new response with the stimulus are optimal. This principle is integral to a behavior therapy technique called systematic desensitization, developed by Joseph Wolpe (Wolpe, 1958).

5. For research studies that examine the strong relationship between parental stress and expressed anger with potential child abuse, you may wish to consult the following resources: Rodriguez and Green, 1997; Mammen, Kolko, and Pilkonis, 2002.

6. For good examples of useful self-help books on parenting, see Borba, 2006; Christophersen and Mortweet, 2002; MacKenzie, 2001.

7. The National Domestic Violence Hotline telephone number is 800-799-SAFE (7233). Additional information and resources are available at their Web site www.ndvh.org.

8. To review research findings demonstrating that verbal conflicts in couples precede physical aggression and that outbursts escalate over time, see Dobash and Dobash, 1984; Cascardi, Vivian, and Meyer, 1991; Campbell, 2007.

9. To review evidence of the high risk of violence experienced by women who leave their partners, you may wish to consult Campbell (2007). This book provides a comprehensive review of research assessing the predictors of different types of interpersonal violence in a variety of settings.

10. For detailed findings of studies that compared high- and low-anger drivers in terms of aggressive driving, auto accidents, and episodes of anger, see Deffenbacher et al., 2000, 2003.

## Chapter 5

1. For evidence of the debilitating effects of substance abuse in the workplace, including absenteeism and high turnover, see Larson et al., (2007). Information on the prevalence of drug-related emergency room visits is available from the

U.S. Department of Health and Human Services (2004). A review of health service usage and the cost of eating disorders is found in Simon, Schmidt, and Pilling (2005). Harmful consequences of sexual addictions are detailed at the Web site for The Society for the Advancement of Sexual Health http://sash.net.

2. A national survey of primary care physicians revealed the percentage of physicians who screen and refer patients with drug abuse problems. For these detailed findings, see Friedmann, McCullough, and Saitz (2001).

3. A comprehensive review of experimentally validated tobacco dependence treatments is available from the U.S. Department of Health and Human Services (Fiore et. al., 2008). This clinical practice guideline was developed by a panel of 37 experts and sponsored by a consortium of eight federal government and nonprofit organizations.

4. Good examples of self-help books for adult survivors of sexual abuse are *Beginning to Heal* (Bass and Davis, 2003) and *The Courage to Heal* book and workbook (Bass and Davis, 2008; Davis, 1990).

5. For a review and discussion of writing letters as a therapeutic tool to heal from abuse, see Scott and Palmer (2003).

6. Alcoholics Anonymous (AA), the first self-help 12-step program, promotes abstinence as a key to recovering from alcoholism. This program has become the model for many other 12-step addiction programs. For information on AA and its effectiveness, see Owen et. al, 2003. Hazelden, a well-known drug and alcohol treatment center, is an example of a professional addiction program that incorporates abstinence-based approaches. For a description of their treatment model and outcome data, see Stinchfield and Owen, 1998.

7. Information on preventing relapse by substituting healthy activities for addictive behaviors is included in Landry's (1996) overview of addiction treatment effectiveness.

8. A discussion of addiction substitution is available in Buck and Sales, 2000.

9. For research demonstrating that self-compassionate people are able to assume personal responsibility without being overwhelmed by negative emotions, consult Leary et. al, 2007. Five studies reveal how people with self-compassion deal with various negative life events.

10. Researchers in two separate studies interviewed patients in drug and alcohol abuse treatment programs during and after treatment. Data showed that attending at least one weekly 12-step meeting after completing treatment greatly reduced drug and alcohol abuse compared to less or no meeting participation. To review these findings, see Fiorentine, 1999, and Gossop et al., 2003.

## Chapter 7

1. Researchers have long known about this perceptual error; as early as 1905, the eminent Harvard psychologist William James reviewed scientific evidence supporting the contrast effect in his classic text *The Principles of Psychology* (James, 1905).

2. This strategy is especially useful for women, who consistently demonstrate in research studies a tendency to behave more modestly than men—for example, taking less credit for their successes and more responsibility for their failures (Wosinska et. al., 1996).

3. Numerous research findings support imagined practice as an effective tool to increase performance in a variety of settings, including sports, counseling, music, and work (Neck, Nouri, and Godwin, 2003).

4. This finding is well documented by systematic research. For example, a classic series of studies demonstrated that when people imagined experiencing certain events, they believed more strongly that those events would happen to them (Gregory, Cialdini, and Carpenter, 1982).

5. Research studies provide significant evidence to support the effectiveness of imagery rehearsal to stop nightmares (Forbes et. al, 2003; Krakow et. al, 2000).

6. See Chapter 2, Note 3.

## Afterword

1. According to the American Psychological Association's 2008 Stress in America survey (Martin, 2008), money and the economy were the top two stressors for 8 of 10 Americans. Almost 50% reported increased stress about their ability to provide for their family's basic needs.

# BIBLIOGRAPHY

Adshead, G. (2000). Psychological therapies for post-traumatic stress disorder. *The British Journal of Psychiatry,* 177: 144–148.

Alloy, L. B., Abramson, L. Y., Tashman, N. A., Berrebbi, D. S., Hogan, M. E., Whitehouse, W. G., Crossfield, A. G., and Morocco, A. (2001). Developmental origins of cognitive vulnerability to depression: Parenting, cognitive, and inferential feedback styles of the parents of individuals at high and low cognitive risk for depression. *Cognitive Therapy and Research,* 25(4): 397–423.

American Medical Association. (2008). *AMA physician international classification of diseases, ninth revision, clinical modification, ICD-9-CM 2009.* Chicago: American Medical Association.

American Psychiatric Association. (2000). *Diagnostic and statistical manual of mental disorders (4th ed. text revision) DSM-IV-TR.* Arlington, VA: American Psychiatric Association.

Arent, S. M., Landers, D. M., and Etnier, J. L. (2000). The effects of exercise on mood in older adults: A meta-analytic review. *Journal of Aging and Physical Activity,* 8: 407–430.

Babyak, M., Blumenthal, J. A., Herman, S., Khatri, P., Doraiswamy, M., Moore, K., Craighead, W. W., Baldewics, T. T., and Krishnan, K. R. (2000). Exercise treatment for major depression: Maintenance of therapeutic benefit at ten months. *Psychosomatic Medicine,* 62: 633–638.

Baer, R. A. (2003). Mindfulness training as a clinical intervention: A conceptual and empirical review. *Clinical Psychology: Science and Practice,* 10(2): 125–143.

Bandura, A. (1977). Self-efficacy: Toward a unifying theory of behavioral change. *Psychological Review,* 84: 191–215.

Bandura, A. (1986). *Social foundations of thought and action: A social cognitive theory.* Englewood Cliffs, NJ: Prentice-Hall.

Bandura, A. (1997). *Self-efficacy: The exercise of control.* New York: Freeman.

Barlow, D. H. (2002). *Anxiety and its disorders: The nature and treatment of anxiety and panic* (2nd ed.). New York: Guilford Press.

Barrows, K. A., and Jacobs, B. P. (2002). Mind-body medicine: An introduction and review of the literature. *Medical Clinics of North America,* 86(1): 11–31.

Bass, E., and Davis, L. (2003). *Beginning to heal: A first book for men and women who were sexually abused as children.* Rev. ed. New York: Collins Living.

Bass, E., and Davis, L. (2008). *The Courage to heal: A guide for women survivors of child sexual abuse.* 4th ed. New York: Collins Living.

Beck, A. T. (1967). *Depression: Clinical, experimental and theoretical aspects.* New York: Harper & Row.

Beck, A. T. (1976). *Cognitive therapy and the emotional disorders.* New York: International Universities Press.

Beck, A. T., Rush, A. J., Shaw, B. F., and Emory, G. (1979). *Cognitive therapy of depression.* New York: Guilford.

Berger, B. G., and Motl, R. W. (2000). Exercise and mood: A selective review and synthesis of research employing the profile of mood states. *Journal of Applied Sports Psychology,* 12: 69–92.

Borba, M. (2006). *12 simple secrets real moms know: Getting back to basics and raising happy kids.* San Francisco: Jossey-Bass.

Buck, T. and Sales, A. (2000). Related addictive disorders, in *Substance abuse and counseling,* (ed.) A. Sales. Education Resources Information Center #ED440345, CG 030 037, ERIC Clearinghouse on Counseling and Student Services, University of North Carolina, Greensboro: NC. www.eric.ed.gov.

Campbell, J. C. (2007). *Assessing dangerousness: Violence by batterers and child abusers.* 2nd ed. New York: Springer.

Cannon, W. (1915). *Bodily changes in pain, hunger, fear and rage: An account of recent researches into the function of emotional excitement.* New York: Appleton.

Cascardi, M., Vivian, D., and Meyer, S. (1991). *Context and attributions for marital violence in discordant couples,* Paper presented at the 25th Annual Convention of the Association for the Advancement of Behavioral Therapy in New York.

Chambless, D. L., and Ollendick, T. H. (2001). Empirically supported psychological interventions: Controversies and evidence. *Annual Review of Psychology,* 52: 685–716.

Chassin, L., Pitts, S. C., DeLucia, C., and Todd, M. (1999). A longitudinal study of children of alcoholics: Predicting young adult substance use disorders, anxiety, and depression. *Journal of Abnormal Psychology,* 108: 106-119.

Chawkins, S. (2008). Golden Gate to get suicide net, *Los Angeles Times,* October 11. www.latimes.com

Christophersen, E. R., and Mortweet, S. L. (2002). *Parenting that works: Building skills that last a lifetime.* Washington D.C.: American Psychological Association.

Cohen, S., and Wills, T. A. (1985). Stress, social support, and the buffering hypothesis. *Psychological Bulletin,* 98: 310–357.

Compton, W. M., Conway, K. P., Stinson, F. S., and Grant, B. F. (2006). Changes in the prevalence of major depression and co-morbid substance abuse disorders in the United States between 1991–1992 and 2001–2002. *The American Journal of Psychiatry,* 163: 2141–2147.

Craske, M. G., and Barlow, D. H. (2001). Panic disorder and agoraphobia. In *Clinical handbook of psychological disorders,* edited by D.H. Barlow, 1–59. New York: Guilford Press.

Creswell, J. D., Lam, S., Stanton, A. L., Taylor, S. E., Bower, J. E., and Sherman, D. K. (2007). Does self-affirmation, cognitive processing, or discovery of meaning explain cancer-related health benefits of expressive writing? *Personality and Social Psychology Bulletin,* 33: 238–250.

Davis, L. (1990). *The Courage to heal workbook: A guide for women and men survivors of child sexual abuse.* New York: Collins Living.

Deffenbacher, J. L., Huff, M. E., Lynch, R. S., Oetting, E. R., and Salvatore, N. F. (2000). Characteristics and treatment of high anger drivers. *Journal of Counseling Psychology,* 47(1): 5–17.

Deffenbacher, J. L., Lynch, R. S., Filetti, L. B., Dahlen, E. R., and Oetting, E. R. (2003). Anger, aggression, risky behavior, and crash-related outcomes in three groups of drivers. *Behaviour Research and Therapy,* 41(3): 333–349.

DeSteno, D., Petty, R. E., Wegener, D. T., and Rucker, D. D. (2000). Beyond valence in the perception of likelihood: The role of emotion specificity. *Journal of Personality and Social Psychology,* 78: 397–416.

Deutsch, M., and Gerard, H.B. (1955). A study of normative and informational social influences upon individual judgment. *Journal of Abnormal and Social Psychology,* 51: 629–636.

Dimidjian, S., Hollon, S. D., Dobson, K. S., Schmaling, K. B., Kohlenberg, R. J., Addis, M. E., Gallop, R., McGlinchey, J. B., Markley, D. K., Gollan, J. K., Atkins, D. C., Dunner, D. L., and Jacobson, N. S. (2006). Randomized trial of behavioral activation, cognitive therapy, and antidepressant medication in the acute treatment of adults with major depression. *Journal of Consulting and Clinical Psychology,* 74(4): 658–670.

Dobash, R. E., and Dobash, R. P. (1984). Nature and antecedents of violent events. *British Journal of Criminology,* 24(3): 269–288.

Dubbert, P. M. (2002). Physical activity and exercise: Recent advances and current challenges. *Journal of Consulting and Clinical Psychology,* 70: 526–537.

D'Zurilla, T. J., and Goldfried, M. R. (1971). Problem solving and behavior modification. *Journal of Abnormal Psychology,* 78: 107–126.

Ellis, A. (1984). Rational-emotive therapy. In *Current psychotherapies* (3rd ed.), edited by R. J. Corsini, 196–238. Itasca, IL: Peacock Press.

Ellis, A. (1995). Changing rational-emotive therapy (RET) to rational emotive behavior therapy (REBT). *Journal of Rational-Emotive and Cognitive Behavior Therapy,* 13: 85–89.

Esses, V. M. (1989). Mood as a moderator of acceptance of interpersonal feedback. *Journal of Personality and Social Psychology,* 57: 769–781.

Fiedler, K., Nickel, S., Muehlfriedel, T., and Unkelbach, C. (2001). Is mood congruency an effect of genuine memory or response bias? *Journal of Experimental Social Psychology,* 37: 201–214.

Fiore, M. C., Jaen, C. R., Baker, T. B., Bailey, T. B., Benowitz, N. L., Curry, S. J., Dorfman, S. F., et al. (2008). *Treating tobacco use and dependence: 2008 update.* Clinical Practice Guideline. Rockville, MD: U.S. Department of Health and Human Services, Public Health Service, http://www.surgeongeneral.gov/tobacco.

Fiorentine, R. (1999). After drug treatment: Are 12-step programs effective in maintaining abstinence? *American Journal of Drug and Alcohol Abuse,* 25(1): 93–116.

Foa, E. B., Keane, T. M., and Friedman, M. J. (2004). *Effective treatments for PTSD: Practice guidelines from the International Society for Traumatic Stress Studies.* New York: Guilford Press.

Forbes, D., Phelps, A. J., McHugh, A. F., Debenham, P., Hopwood, M., and Creamer, M. (2003). Imagery rehearsal in the treatment of posttraumatic nightmares in Australian veterans with chronic combat-related PTSD: 12-month follow-up data. *Journal of Traumatic Stress,* 16(5): 509–513.

Friedmann, P. D., McCullough, D., and Saitz, R. (2001). Screening and intervention for illicit drug abuse. *Archives of Internal Medicine,* 161(2): 248–251.

Gibb, B. E., Alloy, L. B., Abramson, L. Y., Rose, D. T., Whitehouse, W. G., Donovan, P., Hogan, M. E., Cronholm, J., and Tierney, S. (2001). History of childhood maltreatment, negative cognitive styles, and episodes of depression in adulthood. *Cognitive Therapy and Research,* 25(4): 425–446.

Goodman, F. G. (1988). *How about demons? Possession and exorcism in the modern world.* Bloomington and Indianapolis: Indiana University Press.

Gossop, M., Harris, J., Best, D., Man, L., Manning, V., Marshall, J., and Strang, J. (2003). Is attendance at alcoholics anonymous meetings after inpatient treatment related to improved outcomes? A 6-month follow-up study. *Alcohol and Alcoholism,* 38(5): 421–426.

Gregory, W. L., Cialdini, R. B., and Carpenter, K. M. (1982). Self-relevant scenarios as mediators of likelihood estimates and compliance: Does imagining make it so? *Journal of Personality and Social Psychology,* 43(1): 89–99.

Haber, M. G., Cohen, J. L., Lucas, T., and Baltes, B. B. (2007). The relationship between self-reported received and perceived social support: A meta-analytic review. *American Journal of Community Psychology,* 39(1–2): 133–44.

Hankin, B. L., and Abramson, L. Y. (2001). Development of gender differences in depression: An elaborated cognitive vulnerability-transactional stress theory. *Psychological Bulletin,* 127(6): 773–796.

Hazlett-Stevens, H., and Craske, M. G. (2009). Live (in vivo) exposure. In *Cognitive behavior therapy: Applying empirically supported techniques in your practice,* (2nd ed.), edited by W. O'Donahue and J. E. Fisher, 309–316. New York: Wiley.

Hogan, B. E., Linden, W., and Najarian, B. (2002). Social support interventions: Do they work? *Clinical Psychology Review,* 22: 383–442.

Jacobson, N. S., Dobson, K. S., Truax, P. A., Addis, M. E., Koerner, K., Gollan, J. K., Gortner, E., and Prince, S. E. (1996). A component analysis of cognitive-behavioral treatment for depression. *Journal of Consulting and Clinical Psychology,* 64(2): 295–304.

Jacobson, N. S., Martell, C. R., and Dimidjian, S. (2001). Behavioral activation therapy for depression: Returning to contextual roots. *Clinical Psychology: Science and Practice,* 8(3): 255–270.

James, W. (1905). *The Principles of psychology.* New York: H. Holt & Company.

Jayson, S. (2006). Unhappiness has risen in the past decade. *USA Today,* January 8. www.usatoday.com.

Johnson, M. H., and Magaro, P. A. (1987). Effects of mood and severity on memory processes in depression and mania. *Psychological Bulletin,* 101: 28–40.

Joiner, T. E., and Rudd, M. D. (2000). Intensity and duration of suicidal crises vary as a function of previous suicide attempts and negative life events. *Journal of Consulting and Clinical Psychology,* 68(5): 909–916.

Jones, E. E., and Harris, V. E. (1967). The attribution of attitudes. *Journal of Experimental Social Psychology,* 3: 1–24.

Jorm, A. F., Christensen, H., Griffiths, K. M., Parslow, R. A., Rodgers, B., and Blewitt, K. A. (2004). Effectiveness of complementary and self-help treatments for anxiety disorders. *The Medical Journal of Australia,* 181(7): 29–46.

Just, N., and Alloy, L. B. (1997). The response styles theory of depression: Tests and an extension of the theory. *Journal of Abnormal Psychology,* 106: 221–229.

Kendler, K. S., Hettema, J. M., Butera, F., Gardner, C. O., and Prescott, C. A. (2003). Life event dimensions of loss, humiliation, entrapment, and danger in the prediction of onsets of major depression and generalized anxiety. *Archives of General Psychiatry,* 60: 789–796.

Kendler, K. S., Karowski, L. M., and Prescott, C. A. (1999). The assessment of dependence in the study of stressful life events: Validation using a twin design. *Psychological Medicine,* 29(6): 1455–1460.

Kerner, E. A., and Fitzpatrick, M. R. (2007). Integrating writing into psychotherapy practice: A matrix of change processes and structural dimensions. *Psychotherapy: Theory, Research, Practice, Training,* 44(3): 333–346.

Kessler, R. C. (1997). The effects of stressful life events on depression. *Annual Review of Psychology,* 48: 191–214.

Kessler, R. C., Berglund, P., Demler, O., Jim, R., Merikangas, K. R., and Walters, E. E. (2005). Lifetime prevalence and age-of-onset distributions of DSM-IV disorders in the National Comorbidity Survey Replication (NCS-R). *Archives of General Psychiatry,* 62(6): 593–602.

Kessler, R. C., Chiu, W. T., Demler, O., and Walters, E. E. (2005). Prevalence, severity, and comorbidity of twelve-month DSM-IV disorders in the National Comorbidity Survey Replication (NCS-R). *Archives of General Psychiatry,* 62(6): 617–627.

Kessler, R. C., Demler, M. A., Frank, R. G., Olfson, M., Pincus, H. A., Walters, E. E., Wange, P., Wells, K. B., and Zaslavsky, A. M. (2005). Prevalence and treatment of mental disorders, 1990 to 2003. *The New England Journal of Medicine,* 352(24): 2515–2523.

Khalfa, S., Bella, S. D., Roy, M., Peritz, I., and Lupien, S. J. (2003). Effects of relaxing music on salivary cortisol level after psychological stress. *Annals of the New York Academy of Sciences,* 999 (November): 374–376.

Kleinke, C. L., Staneski, R. A., and Mason, J. K. (1982). Sex differences in coping with depression. *Sex Roles,* 8(8): 877–889.

Knight, W. E., and Rickard, N. S. (2001). Relaxing music prevents stress-induced increases in subjective anxiety, systolic blood pressure, and heart rate in healthy males and females. *Journal of Music Therapy,* 38(4): 254–272.

Krakow, B., Hollifield, M., Shrader, R., Koss, M., Tandberg, D., Lauriello, J., McBride, L., Warner, T. D., Cheng, D., Edmond, T., and Kellner, R. (2000). A controlled study of imagery rehearsal for chronic nightmares in sexual assault survivors with PTSD: A preliminary report. *Journal of Traumatic Stress,* 13(4), 589–609.

Kujala, U. M., Kaprio, J., Sarna, S., and Koskenvuo, M. (1998). Relationship of leisure-time physical activity and mortality: The Finnish twin cohort. *Journal of the American Medical Association,* 279: 440–444.

Labbé, E., Schmidt, N., Babin, J., and Pharr, M. (2007). Coping with stress: The effectiveness of different types of music. *Applied Psychophysiology and Biofeedback,* 32(3–4) (December): 163–168.

Landry, M. J. (1996). *An overview of addiction treatment effectiveness.* U.S. Substance Abuse and Mental Health Services Administration. Office of Applied Studies, Darby, PA: DIANE Publishing.

Larson, S. L., Eyerman, J., Foster, M. S., and Gfroerer, J. C. (2007). *Worker substance use and workplace policies and programs.* (DHHS Publication No. SMA 07–4273, Analytic Series A-29). Rockville, MD: Substance Abuse and Mental Health Services Administration, Office of Applied Studies.

Leary, M. R., Tate, E. B., Adams, C. E., Allen, A. B., and Hancock, J. (2007). Self-compassion and reactions to unpleasant self-relevant events: The implications of treating oneself kindly. *Journal of Personality and Social Psychology,* 92(5): 887–904.

Lewinsohn, P. M., and Gotlib, I. H. (1995). Behavioral therapy and treatment of depression. In *Handbook of depression,* edited by E. E. Becker and W. R. Leber, 352–375. New York: Guilford Press.

Lieb, R., Wittchen, H.-U., Höfler, M., Fuetsch, M., Stein, M. B., and Merikangas, K. R. (2000). Parental psychopathology, parenting styles, and the risk of social phobia in offspring. *Archives of General Psychiatry,* 57(9): 859–866.

MacKenzie, R. J. (2001). *Setting limits with your strong-willed child: Eliminating conflict by establishing clear, firm, and respectful boundaries.* Roseville, CA: Prima Publishing, Random House Inc.

Mammen, Oommen, K., Kolko, D. J., and Pilkonis, P. A. (2002). Negative affect and parental aggression in child physical abuse. *Child Abuse and Neglect,* 26(4): 407–424.

Marigold, D. C., Holmes, J. G., and Ross, M. (2007). More than words: Reframing compliments from romantic partners fosters security in low self-esteem individuals. *Journal of Personality and Social Psychology,* 92: 232–248.

Marketdata Enterprises Inc. (2008). *The U.S. market for self-improvement products and services,* October 14, 2008. http://www.marketdataenterprises.com/FullIndustryStudies.htm#SELF.

Martell, C. R., Addis, M. E., and Dimidjian, S. (2004). Finding the action in behavioral activation: The search for empirically-supported interventions and mechanisms of change. In *Mindfulness and acceptance: Expanding the cognitive-behavioral tradition,* edited by S. Hayes and V. Folette, 152–167. New York: Guilford.

Martin, S. (2008). Money is the top stressor for Americans. *Monitor on Psychology,* 39(11): 28–29.

Mayer, J. D., and Salovey, P. (1988). Personality moderates the interaction of mood and cognition. In *Affect, cognition, and social behavior,* edited by K. Fiedler and J. Forgas, 87–99. Toronto: Hogrefe.

Mazure, C. M. (1998). Life stressors as risk factors in depression. *Clinical Psychology: Science and Practice,* 5(3): 291–313.

McGue, M., Pickens, R. W., and Svikis, D. S. (1992). Sex and age effects on the inheritance of alcohol problems: A twin study. *Journal of Abnormal Psychology,* 101: 3–17.

Mehrabian, A. (2007). *Nonverbal communication.* New Brunswick: Transaction Press.

Neck, C. P., Nouri, H., and Godwin, J. L. (2003). How self-leadership affects the goal-setting process. *Human Resource Management Review,* 13(4): 691–707.

Nevius, J. L., and Ellinwood, F. F. (2003). *Demon possession and allied themes*: Being an inductive study of phenomena of our own times. Whitefish, MT: Kessinger Publishing.

Nolen-Hoeksema, S. (1987). Sex differences in unipolar depression: Evidence and theory. *Psychological Bulletin,* 101(2): 259–282.

Nolen-Hoeksema, S. (2000). Further evidence for the role of psychosocial factors in depression chronicity. *Clinical Psychology: Science and Practice,* 7(2): 224–227.

Nolen-Hoeksema, S., and Girgus, J. S. (1994). The emergence of gender differences in depression during adolescence. *Psychological Bulletin,* 115(3): 424–443.

Nolen-Hoeksema, S., Girgus, J. S., and Seligman, M. E. P. (1992). Predictors and consequences of childhood depressive symptoms: A 5-year longitudinal study. *Journal of Abnormal Psychology,* 101(3): 405–422.

Nolen-Hoeksema, S., Larson, J., and Grayson, C. (1999). Explaining the gender difference in depressive symptoms. *Journal of Personality and Social Psychology,* 77(5): 1061–1072.

Olstad, R., Sexton, H., and Sogaard, A.J. (2001). The Finnmark Study. A prospective population study of the social support buffer hypothesis, specific stressors and mental distress. *Social Psychiatry and Psychiatric Epidemiology,* 36: 582–589.

Owen, P. L., Slaymaker, V. J., Tonigan, S., McCrady, B. S., Epstein, E. E., Kaskutas, L.E., Humphreys, K., and Miller, W. R. (2003). Participation in Alcoholics Anonymous: Intended and unintended change mechanisms, *Alcoholism: Clinical and Experimental Research,* 27(3): 524–532.

Powell, K. E., Thompson, P. D., Caspersen, C. J., and Kendrick, J. S. (1987). Physical activity and the incidence of coronary heart disease. *Annual Review of Public Health,* 8: 253–287.

Richardson, C. R., Faulkner, G., McDevitt, J., Skrinar, G. S., Hutchinson, D. S., and Piette, J. D. (2005). Integrating physical activity into mental health services for persons with serious mental illness. *Psychiatric Services,* 56(3): 324–331.

Rodriguez, C. M., and Green, A. J. (1997). Parenting stress and anger expression as predictors of child abuse potential. *Child Abuse and Neglect,* 21(4): 367–377.

Scott, M. J., and Palmer, S., eds. (2003). *Trauma and post-traumatic stress disorder.* Thousand Oaks: Sage Publications, Ltd.

Simon, J., Schmidt, U., and Pilling, S. (2005). The health service use and cost of eating disorders, *Psychological Medicine,* 35(11): 1543–1551.

Skinner, B. F. (1938). *The behavior of organisms.* New York: Appleton-Century-Crofts.

Skinner, B. F. (1953). *Science and human behavior.* New York: Macmillan.

Skinner, B. F. (1971). *Beyond freedom and dignity.* New York: Knopf.

Smith, N. K., Larsen, J. T., Chartrand, T. L., Cacioppo, J. T., Katafiasz, H. A., and Moran, K. E. (2006). Being bad isn't always good: Affective context moderates the attention bias toward negative information. *Journal of Personality and Social Psychology,* 90(2): 210–220.

Steele, C. M. (1988). The psychology of self-affirmation: Sustaining the integrity of the self. In *Advances in Experimental Social Psychology,* edited by L. Berkowitz, 21, 261–302. New York: Academic Press.

Steele, C. M. (1997). A threat in the air: How stereotypes shape intellectual identity and performance. *American Psychologist,* 52: 613–629.

Steele, C. M., Spencer, S. J., and Aronson, J. (2002). Contending with group image: The psychology of stereotype and social identity threat. *Advances in Experimental Social Psychology,* 34: 379–440.

Stinchfield, R. and Owen, P. (1998). Hazelden's model of treatment and its outcome. *Addictive Behaviors,* 23(5): 669–683.

Suinn, Richard, M. (2001). The terrible twos: Anger and anxiety. Hazardous to your health. *The American Psychologist,* 56(1): 27–36.

Thayer, R. E. (1987). Energy, tiredness, and tension effects of a sugar snack versus moderate exercise. *Journal of Personality and Social Psychology,* 52: 119–125.

Thayer, R. E. (1993). Mood and behavior (smoking and sugar snacking) following moderate exercise: A partial test of self-regulation theory. *Personality and Individual Differences,* 14: 97–104.

Tryon, W. W. (2005). Possible mechanisms for why desensitization and exposure therapy work. *Clinical Psychology Review,* 25: 67–95.

Turk, C. L., Heimberg, R. G., and Hope, D. A. (2001). Social anxiety disorder. In *Clinical handbook of psychological disorders,* edited by D. H. Barlow, 114–153. New York: Guilford Press.

Turner, S. M., Beidel, D. C., and Cooley-Quille, M. R. (1995). Two year follow-up of social phobics treated with Social Effectiveness Therapy. *Behaviour Research Therapy,* 33(5): 553–555.

U.S. Census Bureau, Population Division. (2005). *U.S. census bureau population estimates by demographic characteristics.* Table 2: Annual estimates of the population by selected age groups and sex for the United States: April 1, 2000 to July 1, 2004 (NC-EST2004-02). Release Date: June 9, 2005. http://www.census.gov/popest/national/asrh/.

U.S. Department of Health and Human Services, Substance Abuse and Mental Health Services Administration, Office of Applied Studies (2004). *Drug abuse warning network 2003: Interim national estimates of drug-related emergency department visits,* December.

Verplanken, B., Friborg, O., Wang, C. E., Trafimow, D., and Woolf, K. (2007). Mental habits: Metacognitive reflection on negative self-thinking. *Journal of Personality and Social Psychology,* 92(3): 526–541.

Walter, J. L., and Peller, J. E. (1992). *Becoming solution-focused in brief therapy.* Levittown, PA: Brunner/Mazel.

Watson, D. (2000). *Mood and temperament.* New York: Guilford.

Winfrey, O. (host). (2006). *Why I hate myself: Mothers confess.* Oprah: The Oprah Winfrey Show (television show, originally aired May 11, 2006), Harpo Productions, Inc., Chicago: Harpo Studios. http://www.oprah.com.

Wolpe, J. (1958). *Psychotherapy by reciprocal inhibition.* Stanford, CA: Stanford University Press.

Wosinska, W., Dabul, A. J., Whetstone-Dion, R., and Cialdini, R. B. (1996). Self-presentational responses to success in the organization: The costs and benefits of modesty. *Basic and Applied Social Psychology,* 18: 229–242.

# INDEX

# ABOUT THE SERIES EDITOR
# AND ADVISORY BOARD

**Chris E. Stout,** Psy.D., MBA, is a licensed clinical psychologist and a Clinical Full Professor at the University of Illinois College of Medicine's Department of Psychiatry. He has served as a NGO Special Representative to the United Nations. He was appointed to the World Economic Forum's Global Leaders of Tomorrow and has served as an Invited Faculty at the Annual Meeting in Davos, Switzerland. He is the Founding Director of the Center for Global Initiatives. Dr. Stout is a Fellow of the American Psychological Association, past-President of the Illinois Psychological Association, and is a Distinguished Practitioner in the National Academies of Practice. Noted as being "one of the most frequently cited psychologists in the scientific literature" in a study by Hartwick College, Dr. Stout has published or presented over 300 papers and 30 books/manuals on various topics in psychology. His works have been translated into six languages. He has lectured across the nation and internationally in 19 countries and has visited 6 continents and almost 70 countries. He is the recipient of the American Psychological Association's International Humanitarian Award.

**Bruce E. Bonecutter,** Ph.D, is Director of Behavioral Services at the Elgin Community Mental Health Center, the Illinois Department of Human Services state hospital serving adults in greater Chicago. He is also a Clinical Assistant Professor of Psychology at the University of Illinois at Chicago. A clinical psychologist specializing in health, consulting and forensic psychology, Dr. Bonecutter is also a longtime member of the American Psychological Association Taskforce on Children & the Family. He is a member of organizations including the Association for the Treatment of Sexual Abusers, International, the Alliance for the Mentally Ill and the Mental Health Association of Illinois.

**Joseph A. Flaherty,** M.D., is Chief of Psychiatry at the University of Illinois Hospital, a Professor of Psychiatry at the University of Illinois College of Medicine and a Professor of Community Health Science at the UIC College of Public Health. He is a Founding Member of the Society for the Study of Culture and Psychiatry. Dr. Flaherty has been a consultant to the World Health Organization, to the National Institutes of Mental Health and also the Falk Institute in Jerusalem. He's been Director of Undergraduate Education and Graduate Education in the Department of Psychiatry at the University of Illinois. Dr. Flaherty has also been Staff Psychiatrist and Chief of Psychiatry at Veterans Administration West Side Hospital in Chicago.

**Michael Horowitz,** Ph.D., is President and Professor of Clinical Psychology at the Chicago School of Professional Psychology, one of the nation's leading not-for-profit graduate schools of psychology. Earlier, he served as Dean and Professor of the Arizona School of Professional Psychology. A clinical psychologist practicing independently since 1987, his work has focused on psychoanalysis, intensive individual therapy and couples therapy. He has provided Disaster Mental Health Services to the American Red Cross. Dr. Horowitz's special interests include the study of fatherhood.

**Sheldon I. Miller,** M.D., is a Professor of Psychiatry at Northwestern University, and Director of the Stone Institute of Psychiatry at Northwestern Memorial Hospital. He is also Director of the American Board of Psychiatry and Neurology, Director of the American Board of Emergency Medicine and Director of the Accreditation Council for Graduate Medical Education. Dr. Miller is also an Examiner for the American Board of Psychiatry and Neurology. He is Founding Editor of the American Journal of Addictions, and Founding Chairman of the American Psychiatric Association's Committee on Alcoholism. Dr. Miller has also been a Lieutenant Commander in the U.S. Army, serving as psychiatric consultant to the Navajo Area Indian Health Service at Window Rock, Arizona. He is a member and past President of the Executive Committee for the American Academy of Psychiatrists in Alcoholism and Addictions.

**Dennis P. Morrison,** Ph.D., is Chief Executive Officer at the Center for Behavioral Health in Indiana, the first behavioral health company ever to win the JCAHO Codman Award for excellence in the use of outcomes management to achieve health care quality improvement. He is President of the Board of Directors for the Community Healthcare Foundation in Bloomington, and has been a member of the Board of Directors for the American College of Sports Psychology. He has served as a consultant to agencies including the